D0742333

A SOCIALIST'S FAITH

Norman Thomas

A
SOCIALIST'S
FAITH

W · W · NORTON & COMPANY · INC · *New York*

COPYRIGHT 1951
BY NORMAN THOMAS

First Edition

PRINTED IN THE UNITED STATES OF AMERICA
FOR THE PUBLISHERS BY THE VAIL-BALLOU PRESS

Contents

Preface

I BEGAN THINKING about this book shortly after V-J Day and worked at it intermittently until the summer of 1950. I thought I had finished my manuscript when the Korean war began. I then revised it and took it to the publisher on September 25. There is in the body of the book no reference to any event after that date—a fact which readers should bear in mind.

This book will appear at a time when the military economy of a warfare state will make most of our discussions of a welfare state seem ironic. We shall have to accept controls such as no democratic socialist would advocate in normal times. Yet we are still confronted by the spectacle of men who maintain that increased federal aid to education or better control of our water resources will lead straight to statism, while at the same time some of them advocate immediate *total* mobilization and *total* conscription of men and women. We shall have to accept selective service—that is, military conscription—on a large scale in view of the military crisis. All the more reason, then, to guard against a hysterical acceptance of the state as the omnipotent and omniscient master of our lives. We accept conscription only for an emergency. Under no circumstances must it be written into peacetime's regular educational processes. There is no single road which leads more directly to the totalitarian society.

All these considerations are subordinate to the problem of averting a third world war without a slavish surrender which at best could only postpone desperate violence. In the long run, Russian imperial communism will perish by the violence which it has invoked. But if first it covers the earth, all the things that we have cherished most will have disappeared. Tolerance, liberty, decent respect for individuals, have been plants of slow growth. If they should be crushed in Western Europe and America, it will be long before they can grow again.

The protection of liberty and peace in America is bound up with their protection in the world. Yet we have learned painfully that the United States is not strong enough to contain communism by military might anywhere and everywhere in the world, not at any price that we can afford to pay. We have also learned that the U.N. has as yet neither the internal structure nor the kind of moral backing among the peoples to make it an adequate guarantor of world law.

I still think that under the circumstances which existed on June 25 we had to find out what might be done by trying. We could not know what would be Stalin's and Mao's tactics in the face of a resolute stand by the U.N. We found out. A great many people here and abroad now think that there would have been no Chinese war if the U.N. had not sent its forces across the Thirty-eighth Parallel. Others believe that General MacArthur's flamboyant final offensive at the Manchurian border provoked war. That offensive unnecessarily worsened our moral and our military position. It was possible only because MacArthur's intelligence was poor and because he persisted in believing, as he once declared in discussing Formosa, that the Asians would respect firmness and back down. Nevertheless, I do not think that Mao prepared such great armies at the last moment simply to deal with this offensive, nor did that offensive account for the Chinese expedition to Tibet or Mao's extraordinary abuse of America. If we had stopped at the Thirty-eighth Parallel, so unnatural was the division that war at best would only have been postponed. If we had not acted at all, sharper tests would have come elsewhere. Imperial communism seeks world power.

Now we shall have to face facts, one of which is that we Americans cannot invest land armies in Asia. If possible, we shall accept negotiation. If the desire of many nations, probably including Great Britain, should prevail, negotiation may lead to seating communist China on the Security Council. The British made a strong case for that before June 25. To accept it now would be a little like negotiating with a stick-up man not only to save what can be saved of one's possessions but to include him, guns and all, in the family circle. I should be willing to pay a price to keep the U.N. in existence, but our European and Asian friends must know that if the end of our effort to enforce law against aggression should be the inclusion of the aggressor among the Big Five, the U.N., while worth maintaining, will have gone the way of the League of Nations as a guarantor of peace.

Stalin has achieved his objective of involving us deeply in Asia, and he presses his advantage in Europe. Western Europe is vital to the life of democracy. We Americans have assumed great responsibility for it by things we did and left undone during and after World War II. Stalin, as master of all Europe, would inevitably use it as a mighty base of operations against the Western Hemisphere.

For these reasons, I cannot go along with Herbert Hoover in writing off everything east of the English Channel at least until our present allies should fully arm themselves. Mr. Hoover's attitude makes that event wholly unlikely. On the other hand, it is true that there is at present little reason to believe that France or Italy would offer determined and effective resistance to communist armies. The rearmament of Western Germany is fraught with immense dangers, and on any terms like those as yet sanctioned by the western allies, it is wholly unacceptable to the majority of the German people, including the most hopeful element in it, the German socialists. The problem is such use of our military strength as will encourage our allies without too deeply committing our forces to the perils of a vaster and more terrible Dunquerque.

We are handicapped not only by division and the war-weariness of Western Europe, but by our own failure to stand forth as intelligent champions of both peace and freedom. We—and that *we* means the western governments, western believers in democracy, western socialists—have left an initiative to Stalin and the communists in posing as friends of peace. Mr. Truman did indeed speak up for foolproof disarmament on October 24. But it was already very late, and his plea was never dramatically pushed. It must still be presented in any negotiations as the one sure road to peace. Never was it so urgent that the American government and people agree on a positive policy of well-being which logically offers a constructive alternative to war.

An immediate foreign policy, important as it is, lies somewhat outside the scope of this book. My socialist faith I should still hold as our one hope in the dark night of war itself.

It remains for me to acknowledge my indebtedness to more thinkers and writers than I have directly quoted. On the practical side, I owe my thanks to Judy Martin and even more extensively to Madeleine Trimmer for the unusual quality of their secretarial help.

I began this book, like my others, with the active help of my wife. Her sudden death in 1947 for a time removed any desire or capacity to get on with my task. I should like here to record the enormous debt I owe her for extraordinary happiness in difficult years and for strength to carry on. Whatever happens in these times of our trouble, I am convinced that there is no substitute for the kind of family life that she made possible for me and for our children.

Norman Thomas

December 26, 1950

A SOCIALIST'S FAITH

Introduction

WITH THE end of World War II, my sense of the necessity of reexamining the nature of socialism and the case for it grew steadily stronger. The emotional climate surrounding socialism in the middle of the twentieth century was greatly different from that of the year 1900, when both the British Labour Party and the American Socialist Party came into being, or from that of the First World War period, when I was drawn to the Party.

The romantic period of socialist enthusiasm has passed. The word *socialism* has been defiled in Germany by Hitler's use of it, preceded by the adjective national. It was not cleansed by Stalin's appropriation of it to describe the character of his totalitarian state. Like other great words—democracy and Christianity, for instance—the terms socialism and socialist have lost clarity and precision of meaning. In the mouths of its enemies—and some of its ill-informed friends—socialism is usually equivalent to any and every form of collectivism. Often it becomes a description of all welfare legislation or the goal to which such legislation might take mankind.

For myself, socialism has always seemed primarily a doctrine and movement consciously concerned with the common good. Therefore, it requires planning. Social ownership seemed a tool, a means, not an end. I have changed somewhat my opinion of the amount of social ownership that is desirable. I have come to recognize that of itself it does not mechanically answer our economic problems and that democratic controls will not come automatically but must be thought out. Yet substantial social ownership in the socialist tradition is basic to a happy solution of problems of production and distribution.

We democratic socialists have been partially responsible for misunderstandings about socialism. We have not made our position clear in relation on the one hand to Marxism and on the other to a purely pragmatic welfare state.

All socialism owes a debt to Marx and has been greatly influenced by him. Yet in practice—and to some extent in theory or lack of it—democratic socialism in Britain and the Scandinavian countries is non-Marxist. The French and Italian socialists who repudiate communism are rather more insistent on their Marxist orthodoxy, which, however, gives them no sure and steady light to guide their course amid the wreckage of the postwar world. Marxism of the communist brand has had its authoritative interpreter in Lenin, and communist Marxism, or rather Leninist Marxism, is under the vigilant guardianship of the political hierarchy of the Soviet Union. Under that guardianship it has become a totalitarian philosophy to be interpreted in theory and practice by the rulers of an absolute police state.

By contrast democratic socialism when avowedly Marxist has suffered from several conflicting tendencies. Often it has defined itself too narrowly in terms of opposition to communism. In that process it has sometimes felt impelled to a sterile orthodoxy concerned to prove that its spokesmen, rather than Lenin, Trotsky, or Stalin, are true interpreters of the Marxist word. On the other hand, their common Marxist origin has often tended to paralyze socialist opposition to communism. Marxism has frequently made socialists apologetic about true democracy. The fairly easy surrender of large sections of former social democratic parties to the communists in Czechoslovakia, Rumania, and Poland cannot be wholly explained in terms of bribes and coercion. Surrender was at least made easier by the consideration, "Are not we Marxists,

however we differ, constrained to stand together against a capitalist or non-Marxist world?"

The situation has been less bad in France and Italy, but I suspect
that there also the necessity felt by socialists to profess a fairly
orthodox Marxism has been a factor—though not the most vital
—in the failure of democratic socialism to constitute that strong
third force which might surely save their countries from communism or a new fascist reaction.

It is by no means my intention to add another book to the Marxist controversy. Yet no book dealing with socialism as it was, is,
or may become, can ignore Marxism. For me the outstanding fact
about it, despite its proven power, is its inadequacy for our time
under any interpretation.

Marx told us how socialism in the inexorable dialectical movement of history would come to power; but he barely suggested
how it would use power. He assumed the humanistic ends generally accepted in the nineteenth century. He claimed to be the
exponent of a science. His followers have tended to treat his writings as inspired scriptures. Precedents for Marxist controversies
are to be found in the realm of theology, not science. Imagine how
science would have been handicapped if Einstein had felt compelled either to prove that he was only interpreting Newton or to
make a frontal attack upon his eminent predecessor, to whom he
and all other scientists owed so much. A sound development of
socialist thinking in the fields of economics and politics has suffered scarcely less from its theological approach to Marxism. Both
the strength and weakness of Marxism find parallels and illustrations in the history of religion rather than of science. The sense of
certainty that Marx gave his followers is immensely valuable in
social conflict. But the quality of that certainty is of the order of
religious faith rather than of proof in a scientific laboratory.

The real greatness of Marx himself has been obscured in the
current controversy. Part of that greatness lay in his capacity for
patient research into the body of historical, political, and economic

knowledge available to him. The sum total of our knowledge, notably in the areas of history and psychology, has been vastly expanded since his time. His own predictions have been put to the test of events, a test which they have met partially but imperfectly. A tremendous mass of literature on Marxism has been developed, but quite obviously no living and vital philosophy has been or can be derived from the conscious effort not to seek truth for its own sake, but to vindicate this or that Marxist doctrine. It was not in this spirit that Marx himself developed the doctrines which gave to the working class of the world so deep a sense of its own revolutionary destiny.

Fortunately for me, socialism and Marxism are not identical, and the American Socialist Party, while heretofore predominantly Marxist, has never insisted that applicants for membership should accept a detailed and infallible Marxist creed.

I had come to socialism, or more accurately to the Socialist Party, slowly and reluctantly. From my college days until World War I my position could have been described, in the vocabulary of the times, as "progressive." In my callow youth I even contemplated writing a book in support of progressivism as against socialism. Life and work in a wretchedly poor district in New York City drove me steadily toward socialism, and the coming of the war completed the process. In it there was a large element of ethical compulsion. Certainly I was no anti-Marxist when I joined the Party, but mine, like much English socialism, was non-Marxist. Later I went through various degrees of belief in Marxism. It was, however, when I was closest to that *ism*—in the early nineteen thirties—that I became most aware of a desire that there should be a synthesis such as Marx did not provide between economics, politics, and the knowledge that had been brought to us by the newer schools of psychology.

That synthesis for which I felt so keen a need then is not even now consciously sought in our great universities, where savants in various fields tend blissfully to go their separate ways in complete indifference to one another's theories or findings of fact. Philosophers, psychologists, physical scientists, economists, and sociologists, by their unrelated theories, exaggerate where they do not create the confusion of our times.

As the years have passed, my belief in the need for developing a more adequate socialist philosophy has increased. Marxism had its great insights, but today not one of its principal dogmas is maintained by Marxists of integrity without elaborate explanation and qualification.

No less an authority than Engels himself contributed to this situation. In a letter he wrote: "Marx and I are partly responsible that at times our disciples have laid more weight upon the economic factor than belongs to it. We were compelled to emphasize that central character in opposition to our opponents who denied it, and there wasn't always time, place, and occasion to do justice to the other factors in reciprocal interaction in the historical process." T. D. Weldon correctly comments: "The whole of this letter, which is dated 1890 . . . is an elaborate attempt to have it both ways, to accept the incompleteness of the Marxist hypothesis and to pass this off as a matter of no great moment." [1]

No serious thinker coming with fresh mind to Marxism one hundred years after the *Communist Manifesto* would find in it a completely scientific explanation of life or even of economics and politics. Marxism's importance lies not in its finality as science or religion, but in its record through a century of extraordinary propaganda power over large masses of men. It did foretell the collapse of the older capitalist system. It did not foretell the specific manner of that collapse which it helped to bring about. It is the state religion of the mighty Soviet Union and the international communist movement. It is reverenced by many democratic socialists, who derive from it at vital points conclusions opposite to the communists.

Clearly the world ought to have some more adequate social

[1] *States and Morals*, p. 156.

philosophy. Any new synthesis of our knowledge and aspirations will owe much to Marx, but it will not be Marxist unless by a very loose use of the word.

I do not approach my own reexamination of socialism in the belief that I can produce for myself, much less for mankind, a philosophic substitute for Marxism. I doubt if any man of my generation can render such service. We have been too much involved in the failures of our time, its loves and hates, its wars and confusions, its dreams and their strange and often ironic endings. But out of our experience and our thinking we may offer something of value to the younger folk who must shape the future. Meanwhile, I can testify that we have found abundant reason for faith in democratic socialism as the best basis for ordering the good society.

To say why to myself or to others has compelled me to look back into the history not only of political and economic developments in the tumultuous years through which I have lived, but also of the evolution of ideas. It has been necessary to try to think about the nature of democracy, the role of the state, and of the church or organized religion in its social aspects.

This book might have become a kind of Education of Norman Thomas, but from the beginning I have sought to make it more impersonal, with the emphasis on socialism. As I have gone along, I have more and more realized that my own experiences and reflections would make my conclusions more of a contribution toward a working program of democratic-socialist action than toward any comprehensive world philosophy. That is not for me to write. But I have thought it a service to face certain questions beyond my present ability to answer in wholly satisfactory style. Others may go on where I have left off in a world in which war or fear of it is no longer the mightiest arbiter of men's thoughts and actions.

Chapter 1

We Believed in Progress

IT WAS MY fortune to be born in an era of hope. No one—certainly no American—who grew to maturity in the years before World War I could in his wildest nightmare have imagined the horrors which have become commonplaces of the daily news since 1914. The science which we trusted has given men mad for power a capacity for the destruction of body, mind, and soul so great that comparisons of a Hitler or a Stalin with barbarian conquerors are grotesquely misleading.

The generation of my youth believed in a fundamental rationality of life and its essential goodness. Most of all it believed in a sure and certain progress of the human race.

When the Korean war emphasized America's second failure to win peace by military victory in total war, I found myself repeatedly recalling Dante's famous lines: "There is no greater sorrow than to remember a happy time in misery." For me, the happy time was the years of my faith in certain progress, the misery my present doubt whether right can ever achieve its own appropriate might so that man and his civilization may endure.

But when I look back on the years of my confident faith I am aware not only that in them were the seeds of destruction but that during them "the mass of men" led "lives of quiet desperation"— which desperation was even then by no means always quiet. The years of my youth were the years of the robber barons, of an aggressive and "soulless" capitalism, of the long day for workers, of an individualism which made miserable provision for the unfortunate. The labor struggle often flared into violence. The spring of the year when World War I began in Europe saw in America the terrible massacre of the tent colony of striking miners and their families in Ludlow, Colorado. There were forty-seven known dead. No punishment was visited on absentee owners, their managers, or public officials responsible for an act without parallel in Hohenzollern Germany.

Culturally, America, especially in the absence of great music and in the quality of its architecture, was, until after the turn of the century, the land of the Philistines. Philistinism was not the cultural expression of unsophisticated virtue. On the contrary, American democracy, while real, was tainted with corruption, especially in the government of its municipalities.

Nevertheless, America was a country of life and hope. The past had been good; the future would be better. Toward the Statue of Liberty immigrants turned with an assurance of asylum and a reasonable expectation of opportunity to which there is in our "liberated" world no parallel. Freedom was limited by color—especially in the South; by bitter poverty; and by the economic exploitation of the acquisitive society. Nevertheless, there was a reality to guarantees of freedom of conscience, speech, the press, assemblage, and association. In the western world men did not live in constant fear of the police state. Cruelty there was, but it was not employed scientifically as a principal technique of government. It never occurred to us that there might be a conflict between liberty and security.

Within the memory of living men chattel slavery had been abolished and the free public school system established. The nineteenth century had been a century of progress. The twentieth would be the century of peace. Democracy admittedly was imperfect but it contained within itself the dynamics of its own reform. As chattel slavery had perished, so would war. I vividly remember my own youthful conviction that all the great victories essential to the onward march of man had already been won; what was left was but to press onward toward that far-off divine event to which the whole creation moves.

This, by and large, was the faith of the churches, even those to whose creeds it was incongruous. To be sure, in and out of the churches there were voices raised in warning, but few paid them heed. Brooks Adams put together his brother Henry's essays in the volume entitled *Degradation of the Democratic Dogma* in 1919, but the principal essays had been written in 1909 and 1910 and attracted little attention. World War I aroused interest in them.

We who shared the prevailing optimism had our occasional moments of doubt but they touched us lightly and passed. I remember when I first read Matthew Arnold's "Dover Beach" my fascinated appreciation of his comparison of our world to:

> ". . . A darkling plain
> Swept with confused alarms of struggle and flight
> Where ignorant armies clash by night."

It was many years before these lines seemed to me a sober description of fact, and my deepest concern became less for the adequacy of socialism or democracy than for the capacity of men to order their affairs under any faith so as to preserve civilization and possibly to save their race from destruction.

Already in my youth, as Matthew Arnold's poem suggests, organized Christianity and the churches had lost something of the hold they once had possessed. But our faith in progress, usually identified with "scientific progress," supplemented when it did not supplant faith in a living God. Whether in the church or in the service of progress, the individual had a sense of vocation and usefulness which today comes hard to us who are caught in the vast web of impersonal forces. Progress, scientific progress, had not yet betrayed itself and us by manifesting its most stupendous power in the atom bomb. The post-Hiroshima man is as skeptical of science as of God as a source of blessing or even security to him. His frame of mind is profoundly negative, at once a reflection of the objective situation and an explanation of his inability to carry on. He doubts his ability to control his own tools for life rather than death.

All this would have been unimaginable to the average American at the end of the century. We could not have held our faith in progress if we had not possessed a sense of security so great that it scarcely rose to the level of consciousness. We accepted it as we accepted the order of nature. Our national security was, we thought, enhanced by the little Spanish war. Individuals might woefully lack economic security but the general social and economic order to all but a handful of radicals seemed to have been built upon a rock. Each depression was followed by greater prosperity. It was not until the nineteen thirties that depression became chronic.

Despite our amoral economics, we had accepted ethical standards for the family and for society. We might suspect a particular helmsman but we never doubted the compass itself. Even an "infidel" like the orator Robert Ingersoll was using the ethical standards of Christianity when he criticized Jehovah.

Socialism and radicalism in the English-speaking countries accepted these ethical standards and wanted to apply them in economics. Some socialists criticized the family as a selfish institution. These critics did not dream that the dissolution of family ties so obvious by the middle of the twentieth century would leave us with no satisfactory substitute, dangerously adrift, dependent for the atmosphere in which the next generation must grow up on nothing better than the Hollywood version of a cheap but irresistible romantic love between a man and a woman or a succession of them.

Modern fiction bears witness to a terrible preoccupation of the victors in two world wars with sex and alcohol. In such concerns, ignoble as once they would have been judged, is at least escape from the jungle men call civilization. An editorial in *Life* brings out this attitude in discussing a popular novel: "But the more devastating point made by *The Naked and the Dead* is that life back home in America which shaped Mailer's G.I.'s is just as ugly, arid, boring and uncomfortable as a jungle campaign to mop up a particularly nasty little island in the tropics." [1]

In literature and the arts there has been a striking growth of the cult of the unintelligible. This is not progress, nor does the scientific discovery of the role of the unconscious justify the modern worship of it. The twentieth-century Dionysus of our machine age is an unlovely god whose victories over Apollo are in no sense triumphs of the spirit of man at its greatest.

In general, with the single and important exception of the growth of a better conscience on race relations, the years through which I have lived have been years of moral retrogression.[2] In my youth humanitarian appeals based on sympathy for individual suffering and respect for individual rights had close hearing and respect. When I was a boy the gross injustice done to one man, the Jewish Frenchman, Captain Dreyfus, stirred the conscience of the world. Even after World War I millions of men and women, Americans and foreigners, were profoundly moved by the fate of "a good shoemaker and a poor fish peddler," Sacco and Vanzetti. Today, although rather paradoxically there have been in America some gains in civil liberties and racial fraternity, we listen calmly

---

[1] *Life* editorial, August 16, 1948, "Life a Freudian Nightmare."

[2] I say this despite improvements in the status of workers and the advance of social legislation which elsewhere I applaud. This progress had moral values but is primarily due to our immense advance in technology and the efforts of the workers in their own behalf rather than moral conscience. Our colored fellow citizens have also fought their own battles but the element of conscience among the whites has played a larger role than among capitalists.

to dozens of individual tragedies even less excusable than the execution of Sacco and Vanzetti.

Our modern respect is for power, not pity. Sympathy is for our own kind. Not *cruelty*, but the *enemy's* cruelty moves us. And even for the enemy we have grudging respect if by cruelty he "gets things done." In long years of experience, I never found audiences so unmoved by tales of suffering, slavery, and the plight of displaced persons as in the years 1945–48. Men argued, openly or in effect: it is expedient that one innocent man—or many—should die rather than that our nation—or our cause—should perish. They comforted themselves that "you can't make an omelet without breaking eggs"—so long as their eggs were unbroken. And a member of a pacifist circle pleaded that Stalin couldn't be so bad because he had heard a well-known Russian apologist say that "there were *only* two million human beings in Stalin's slave labor camps."

Even the generous relief from America which lightens the picture was too largely a weapon in conflict, *against* communism, *for* our kinsmen of various national groups represented in our population.

When Mussolini invaded Ethiopia, Elizabeth Daryush wrote:

"Mildness is no more, Tolerance is done to death,
Pity is buried deep, even Pardon is shut down
Among the shadows, starved of all but ghostly breath." [3]

The succeeding years piled up evidence mountain high to the bitter truth of her words. To socialists before 1914 the present emotional climate would have seemed incredible. For them in the early years of the century the whole historic movement of men and forces was directed toward a universal socialism, a federation of cooperative commonwealths. The typical socialist never dreamed of doubting the capacity of men freed from ancient tyrannies to triumph easily once and for all over poverty and injustice. Crime was the child of capitalism and would die with it.

[3] Elizabeth Daryush, *Selected Poems* (Swallow-Morrow).

Progress might be marked by some violence of revolution but, in the familiar Marxist metaphor, that violence would be merely the birth pangs of the new order already developed in the womb of the old. And there was strong hope that in the democratic countries the revolution would be peacefully achieved by the power of the ballot backed by the power of organized labor. Thousands of American supporters of Eugene Debs in his successive Presidential campaigns confidently expected to live to walk behind his carriage in his inaugural parade.

Perhaps if it had not been for war we Americans might have found our faith in social progress largely justified. More than once I have reminded myself—and occasionally audiences—that if I had been told that within a little over a generation so many of the social reforms in which I, a young and ardent church and social worker, believed had been achieved or begun, I should have thought the millennium definitely attainable. Instead I write as one concerned for human survival.

The principal objective fact which we believers in progress had overlooked was the imminence and gravity of large-scale war. We did not believe that peace was absolutely assured. Hence peace societies flourished. Most Americans deplored the fact that military conscription and the race in armaments made Europe an armed camp. Nevertheless, we could not imagine total war. And we agreed with H. G. Wells's hope that if war should begin, sheer horror of it would bring wisdom.

This false confidence had a degree of rationality in the light of history. The post-Napoleonic settlements reached by the Congress of Vienna, and the uneasy balance of power politics had placed definite limits on Europe's frequent wars. Together with the growing power of the United States they had prevented a military imperialism from invading the Western Hemisphere. Asia and Africa had afforded room for European expansion at the expense of peoples too weak to resist modern weapons. Great Britain had a head start and was the only world power of the nineteenth century. Circumstances plus a certain British genius for rule gave her an empire at the price of relatively small violence. The *pax Britannica* had some of the quality of the earlier *pax Romana*—a point which I have heard convinced anti-imperialists admit in our troubled times. The Boer War damaged British prestige both for liberalism and military prowess, but the excellence of the settlement which established the Union of South Africa did much to restore it. Few there were to worry about the fate of the native majority when their quarreling white masters combined to share their rule.

So time marched on; the world grew more crowded. Russia, Japan, and Germany became major contestants in smaller imperialist conflicts destined to produce the world war which nobody wanted and few believed possible. It is now a commonplace to say that these conflicts were implicit in the two basic economic and political concepts which dominated world organization: capitalism and nationalism. Capitalism demanded expanding markets, new sources of supply of raw materials, new opportunities to gamble for higher profits on investments than could easily be found in industrialized countries. Since the world was organized into national states, each claiming absolute sovereignty, since tariffs and trade restrictions became more and more the order of the day, capitalism was obliged to function along national lines. This was a severe restriction on its original *laissez-faire* philosophy, but it gained for capitalist interests the powerful support of national states and a curious emotional identification of national patriotism with their profits. Since the economy of none of the nations on the European continent had conquered poverty or banished unemployment, militarism and imperialism served as forms of boondoggling to provide jobs, a boondoggling hallowed by nationalist emotion.

The real religion of 1914 was this patriotism. For it Christians proved that they were willing to kill Christians, and workers to murder their comrades. Before the coming of that evil day, Christianity might make feeble protest. An enlightened humanist like

Andrew White might proclaim that "above all nations is humanity." Socialist internationalism might offer a rival faith. But on the eve of the first of two world wars, as at their end, nationalism was the supreme and divisive lay religion of the common man of every land.

As I remember it at the outbreak of the First World War, I, who was a progressive—not yet a socialist—interested in peace and opposed to imperialism, never thought of war in these basic terms. All of us discussed particular issues and particular wars or threats of war. Our thinking was in terms of reactions to slogans like "manifest destiny," the "white man's burden," the Monroe Doctrine, the "Open Door in China," the "Yellow Peril." And we silenced such fears as we had by assuring ourselves that the world was too civilized for large-scale war which might be prevented by such simple devices as arbitration treaties. The autocrat of Russia, in the time he could spare from fighting Japanese and his own revolutionists, promoted peace conferences at the Hague. An inventor like Alfred Nobel, a Swede, did his bit for peace by adding dynamite to the forces of destruction which would make men turn in horror from war, while to make assurance doubly sure, from his profits he established an annual prize to be awarded the person who best served the cause of peace. A captain of industry like Andrew Carnegie endowed peace societies, and Norman Angell, in *The Great Illusion*, brilliantly proved that war didn't pay. Socialists inconclusively discussed a general strike against war or mobilization. Surely such a world, we thought, was safe from great wars. Such was the common opinion in the nations which, never wanting large-scale war, stumbled and blundered into it under the pressures of imperialism and militarism which they had wanted. "Progress" had put us squarely on the road that led through two world wars to the atom bomb.

At the end of the second, it was the bomb which made most articulate our fear for the future and cast its black shadow over any hope of progress except to destruction. Our apprehensions were intensified by the rapid development of cold war between the two great powers left by World War II and the ideological forces which they represented.

But there was to my mind an even deeper and more fundamental cause for profound anxiety which was clearly apparent by mid-century. It was doubt of men's capacity under any politico-economic creed and practice to satisfy the insistent demands of restless multitudes for a more generous supply of daily bread without drastic rearrangement of populations or extensive birth control or both.

I had shared the optimism common among socialists which led us to declare: "The problem of production has been solved; poverty need be no more; abundance requires only the application under proper social arrangements of knowledge and skills already ours." It was a conclusion amply warranted by the resources and achievements of the United States.[4] Even in terms of the world, that conviction is by no means completely false, but to give it realistic truth in practical affairs it must be rigidly qualified. Certainly we collectively possess, or are on the threshold of acquiring, the knowledge and skill to utilize the riches of earth for the destruction of poverty. But the application of that knowledge requires a profound change in some of our dearest institutions and in the loyalties associated with them. We think and act almost wholly under the spell of nationalism. Only the United States of America and the Union of Soviet Socialist Republics have within their borders the resources for solving the problem of poverty on anything like a purely national basis. Other nations, even the most intelligent and fortunate of them, live under continuing threat of the ruin that may overtake them from the actions of stronger powers.

The Neo-Malthusians like William Vogt question the possibility

---

[4] See, for instance, *U.S.A., Measure of a Nation* by Carscaden and Modley (Macmillan), or still better, *America's Needs and Resources* by Dewhurst and Associates (Twentieth Century Fund).

that the earth with its steadily dwindling cover of topsoil can support a population which in many areas is increasing "as if by explosion." Their critics have refuted these fears by pointing out practicable methods of increasing food supplies by war against insect pests and rodents, soil conservation and restoration, genetic improvement in seeds, water farming, including the development of algae, better development of fishing, and in general by more scientific techniques and better tools. These plans of the experts are reassuring, even exciting. But they cannot be carried out haphazardly by "free enterprise." They demand close coordination of skills and techniques and social controls only possible under governmental planning and in many cases planning on a worldwide scale. At best they require time, and that the present increase of population seems to deny to many lands. That fact makes voluntary birth control and a knowledge of its methods (of which a utilization of "rhythm" may be one) more important. Even if one accepts the belief that increased industrialism is for obscure reasons followed "in the long run" by a reduction in the birth rate, there is a dangerous time lag in the process. Men, women, and children do not eat "in the long run" but now.

No nation ever checked its rate of growth in the early stages of industrialization. Even an elementary application of modern health measures greatly decreases infant mortality. Yet, while their populations increase, Indians and Chinese and men of many other nations are becoming more and more aware that other human beings in more fortunate regions have escaped the ever-present fear of starvation. Under the shadow of that fear half of the world's present population lives. The hungry in lands of scarcity cannot afford to buy surplus food from more fortunate regions where surpluses exist and go to waste. These masses will not forever fatalistically accept their old hunger. Yet ignorance, racial and nationalist pride, and the dogmas of certain religions stand in the way of birth control in the very places where it is most important. In like fashion nationalist sentiment and the nationalist organization of our economy stand in the way of extensive migrations which in any event would bring but temporary relief to countries with very high birth rates.

These fears for the future are anything but speculative. In Italy, for example, the population is increasing at the rate of almost half a million a year. Italy is already fairly well industrialized. Much could be done for agriculture and industry that the De Gasperi government has not done; but no program, communist or non-communist, offers ground for confidence in a solution of the basic problem without great emigration or birth control or both.

The population problem is even more serious in Japan, Korea, India, and other Asiatic countries. It exists on a massive scale in a predominantly agricultural China now fallen into communist—and hence potentially aggressive—hands.

In his valuable book, *China: The Land and the People*, that expert authority, Gerald F. Winfield, after developing a bold but practicable program for raising more food, controlling floods, and conquering certain diseases in China, feels compelled to add this warning:

"China can raise her standards of living only as she applies modern knowledge to the productive processes on the farm and in the factory to the advantage of a population that stays within quite definite limits. If, in modernizing, she also increases her population at a rate similar to that of Japan, ending up with as many people on the land as there are now, then there is little hope of raising the standard of living. Farm sizes would then remain the same, in spite of the fact that a number equal to half the present population is shifted to other employment. If production per man in the rural districts does not increase sharply there will be no domestic market large enough to support an extensive industrial development. If China is to improve her standard of living she cannot afford to double her population in the process of shifting from an agricultural to an industrial economy, but if death rates are lowered as much as they have been in India, China could have a population of 800 million by the end of this century. The natural resources of China cannot possibly produce a decent standard of living for that many people. These resources will have to be worked to the limit in order to provide a standard of living that is equal to only one-sixth of the American standard in 1929 if a population increase of no more than 33 per cent takes place. The crux of the problem is the necessity of bringing about a drop in the birth rate at least as great as the drop in the death rate." [5]

It is facts like these that we must face in working for human progress, and it is against the background they provide that I, born in the generation of hope, must reexamine my socialist faith in terms of what may be if we try, rather than of certain and predestined progress.

[5] *China: The Land and the People*, Gerald F. Winfield (William Sloane Associates), pp. 338–339. Copyright, 1948, by Gerald Winfield.

Chapter 2

Socialism in 1914

SOCIALISM, by 1914, had not come to power in any country, but it was a world-wide force. Its objects were the end of exploitation, the establishment of justice, and the conquest of poverty. These required, socialists believed, the public ownership and management for the common good of the means of production and distribution—at least of the basic instrumentalities of the economy.

The roots of socialism were very old but in its modern form it was a product of the coming of the machine age, not to be understood except in relation to it.

The social order in which socialism had its rise and against which it struggled was dominated by the twin—and by no means completely harmonious—ideologies of capitalism and nationalism. Such international order as there was rested on a precarious balance of power. In theory *laissez-faire* capitalism was international and was controlled by completely amoral economic laws. These were the laws of the market and its self-maintained equilibrium. In the golden age of capitalism before World War I, despite nationalism, militarism, high tariffs, and some restrictions on immigration, there was relatively a free flow of men, materials, and money under the devoutly accepted fiction of an international gold standard. There was also a great exploitation of the workers everywhere and of the natural resources, including topsoil, on which life depends. Capitalist development was primarily for the benefit of the European imperial powers and more particularly the dominant owning class in them. The system psychologically as well as economically carried in it the seeds of revolution against it. Socialism was the principal expression of a conscious opposition.

There was socialism before Karl Marx. There would have been socialism without Marx, but the dominant form of socialism on the eve of World War I was avowedly Marxist. He and his friend and collaborator, Friedrich Engels, had made socialism appear no longer as merely a beautiful social and ethical hope but a predestined goal in the development of human society. They had given to the workers of the world a religious faith curiously parallel to the Christian faith which they had rejected. In the achievement of an earthly paradise, the working class was the Messiah, and the revolution the Apocalypse. However mighty seemed the strength of the exploiters, their system was doomed by its own internal contradictions.

There was in Marxism, moreover, a profound and stirring moral revolt against "the self-estrangement of man in modern capitalism," his role as a tool to be bought and sold on the market like the machines with which he worked.

It was these aspects of Marxism which gave it its strength, but by no means was this the whole of the elaborate body of Marxist doctrine. Marx and Engels lived and worked through many years while events marched rapidly. They wrote much and not always like men consciously constructing a system. Marx himself gave thanks that he did not have to be a Marxist. There were differences of interpretation and development of Marxism even while the master lived. Later Marxism was almost to rival Christianity in the variety of its sects. By 1914 Lenin and others had fore-shadowed the developments which were so profoundly to divide socialists after World War I. Nevertheless, there was a body of Marxist doctrine on which there was widespread agreement.

Theoretical Marxism was an ambitious attempt to derive from life, or to impose on it, a unitary philosophy. Marxism had its own metaphysics, its own doctrine of the state, its own economics, its own theory of the dynamics of change. By no means all these aspects seemed equally important to the various socialist parties and groups which acknowledged their debt to Marx in 1914.

In metaphysics Marx, the pupil of Hegel, inverted the Hegelian dialectic and gave to matter or to material forces the place Hegel gave to the Idea. He kept the Hegelian triad of thesis, antithesis, and synthesis and applied it to history in terms of economic development. The existing historical situation at a given time could be expressed in terms of a *thesis* against which contrary forces (*antithesis*) were struggling, forces destined to emerge in a new *synthesis*. This process of change or of becoming as the law of life was rather inconsistently to end with the final synthesis of world-wide socialism. Marx's main illustrations were derived from the development of capitalism out of feudalism. The explanation seemed to fit so well that it was easy for Marxists to apply it un-critically to the whole course of human history.

After the Russian Revolution, the Bolsheviks made a great effort to impose dialectical materialism upon all art and science. It became an official philosophy of the universe interpreted by the high priests of a totalitarian state. But in 1914, to the average socialist in the western world, dialectical materialism had been reduced to an economic interpretation of history.

Marx himself never formally defined economic determinism but, in his *Critique of Political Economy*, he used language which fairly well explains his theory. He wrote:

"In the social production which men carry on they enter into definite relations that are indispensable and independent of their will; these relations of production correspond to a definite stage of development of their material powers of production. The sum total of these relations of production constitutes the economic structure of society—the real foundation on which rise legal and political superstructures and to which correspond definite forms of social consciousness. The mode of production in material life determines the general character of the so- cial, political and spiritual processes of life."

Marx himself once qualified absolute determinism by declaring that man makes his own history.

On the European continent, socialism with few exceptions was not only antichurch but anti-revealed-religion. This I think was due less to Marxist metaphysics than to the Marxist contention that "religion is the opiate of the masses." The irreligious or non- religious aspect of Marxist socialism was in line with the rational- ism of the times, but it was chiefly the consequence of the general identification of the churches with the interests of the ruling classes and its own character in many lands as the greatest of land- lords. In countries where there was not so complete an identification socialism avoided a definitely irreligious stand. The American So- cialist Party early declared religion to be a matter of the private conscience and entitled to the protection given to freedom of conscience. In the English-speaking countries, Christian Socialists played an important role. Many of the older leaders of the British Labour Party were recruited among active workers in Church and Chapel. In the United States Walter Rauschenbusch powerfully argued that socialism was necessary for a modern application of the teachings of Jesus.

In the Marxist doctrine, the agent of progress—rather, the Messiah—was the working class. The internal contradictions of capitalism might inevitably doom it but it was the business of the workers, conscious of the complete division of interest between themselves and the owning class, to make certain that doom by activity in the class struggle. This conflict was inevitable as long as the economic order divided men in classes. Socialism was con- cerned that workers should organize in order to wage it intelli- gently and effectively. There was in Marxist socialism a strong tendency to define the working class or the proletariat narrowly in terms of wageworkers in factories rather than in terms of all active producers of wealth. It was class conflict as a necessary condition of the ultimate formation of a classless society which was and is the emotional heart of Marxism. But in reality class conflict never sprang from a simple principle of division of owners and workers, much less provided an automatic guarantee of constructive revolutionary action.

Marx took over from the earlier *laissez-faire* economists the doctrine, sometimes called the "iron law of wages," that wages could never rise above the cost of the subsistence and reproduction of the working class.[1] Since the progress of capitalism, as Marx believed, meant the growth of more and more powerful corporations and the squeezing of small producers and the middle class generally into the proletariat, he argued that the outstanding fact of capitalist production would be an increasing misery which in itself would bring the hour of revolution to a class into which had been pressed the most vital elements of the community. "Workers of the World, Unite—You have nothing to lose but your Chains—You have a World to Gain" had by 1914 proved a stirring slogan rather than an exact description of facts. There was a very considerable difference in the weight of chains the workers wore even within each national state, still more between them. Socialism had been compelled to act within the limits of national states and to take account of patriotism as a strong emotional accompaniment of that nationalism which, along with capitalism, was the organizing factor in nineteenth-century civilization.

There was another doctrine of great importance to Marx and to the early Marxists which by 1914 was in practice ignored by most socialist parties. That was the Marxist theory of value and surplus value, the basis of which was inherent in the iron law of wages Marx had taken over from the early and orthodox *laissez-faire* economists. As Marx developed this doctrine, however, especially

[1] Late in his life, he attacked Lasalle's version of the "iron law of wages" in his *Criticism of the Gotha Program*.

in the third volume of *Capital*, it was far more than a generalized statement that all wealth was created by some kind of labor. It was an attempt to treat with algebraic precision such matters as the composition of capital, the rate of profit, and of the decline in it,[2] which would mathematically determine the time of revolution.

Rank-and-file socialists found strength in the notion that labor created wealth and was entitled to the surplus value of which it was deprived under the profit system. But comparatively few of them read and fewer of them understood the detailed formulas of Marxist economics which at some points were seriously in error. Marx's theory of price and profit, in the nineteenth century and early twentieth, was the subject of bitter controversy between Marxist intellectuals and their critics. But as the twentieth century wore on practical interest in the subject waned. After the war, Lenin's interpretation of Marxism put little stress on the matter. The development of Russian economy has had nothing to do with Marx's theory of price and profit. In a society which Stalin says has already achieved socialism there is no evidence that wages are fixed on any other principle than the judgment of a police state concerning the relative requirements of the state apparatus and the necessary concessions to the various economic groups in the population. The Soviet political state imposed an economic system on a predominantly peasant population without much regard for Marxist or non-Marxist "laws" of economy.

I remember a socialist discussion shortly after World War I at which the Marxist theory of value and surplus value was raised in its detailed form. One of the ablest American Marxists prefaced his informal contribution to the discussion by saying that he had not thought about the matter "for ten years." Most Marxists, even before World War I, contented themselves with sociological generalities about the workers as creators of wealth and they admitted

---

[2] Capital, Marx held, was divided into *variable*, which went to hire labor, and *constant*, which was invested in machinery. Profit was derived from variable capital.

that Marx was wrong, at least in his time schedule for the economic collapse of capitalism.

In 1914 the chief matter of active controversy among Marxists, as in the whole radical movement, had to do with the attitude that should be taken toward the state. Left-wing socialists were socialists with syndicalist leanings. Pure syndicalists were anarchists in their dislike and distrust of the state. They disagreed with socialists that it must be captured for use in a transitional period by the workers. Their slogan was all power to the producers, that is, to the unions. They believed in direct action by unions rather than in the ballot. The First International of the workers while Marx still lived had included anarchists, and the bitter controversies between Marx and Bakunin had contributed to its death. The Second International, formed after Marx's death, excluded anarchists, but socialism was not free from syndicalist tendencies.

In America, the Socialist Labor Party, oldest of socialist parties, in the nineties had fallen under the vigorous leadership of Daniel De Leon, later to be praised by Lenin. For him the road to power demanded the organization of one big Marxist union—rather a federation of unions—of workers. Participation in elections was useful chiefly from an educational point of view. Once the workers were properly organized, they could demand and would receive a delivery of power into their hands. The threat of a general strike would be enough.

Gene Debs never belonged to the Socialist Labor Party but was a leader in the Midwestern social-democratic group which in 1900 merged with the socialists, who, under Morris Hillquit, split off from the Socialist Labor Party to form the present Socialist Party. Debs later helped to form the Industrial Workers of the World which he left when that organization repudiated all electoral action. The sharpest controversy in the Socialist Party prior to World War I was between the syndicalists or near syndicalists and the believers in the value of electoral action. The latter, led by Morris Hillquit and Victor Berger, won in the 1912 convention.

In western Europe where political democracy was fairly well

established, labor, under varying degrees of socialist influence, had gone into politics in Germany under the Social Democratic name, in France as Socialists, in Great Britain as the Labour Party. The last named was a comparative newcomer into the field. Socialists had been active in forming it but the party was not Marxist or in the beginning even socialist. It was born at a meeting in Memorial Hall in London on February 27, 1900. But it acquired strength, first shown in the election of 1906, largely as the result of the Taff-Vale decision, which permitted a levy upon trade-union budgets for damages caused by strikers during trade disputes. Not until 1918 did the Party adopt an avowedly socialist program, of which the principal draftsmen were the Fabians, Sidney and Beatrice Webb. But the most dynamic group in the Party was from the beginning the older Independent Labour Party under the leadership of Keir Hardy, an ardent socialist.

All these European parties, whatever their name or the kind and degree of their Marxism, were unquestioning believers in democracy and had reformist planks in their programs, none more so than the German Social Democrats, the most powerful of socialist parties, in which, however, Eduard Bernstein's effort for a revision of Marxism had been defeated.

Not only had no socialist party come to power by 1914, but there had been what in retrospect seems extraordinarily little discussion of what they would do in power. The difficulties of a transition period were little considered. Comparatively few socialists in the western world were aware that Marx—in his *Criticism of the Gotha Program*—had once spoken of a "dictatorship of the proletariat," a phrase which he never explained. Much later, in 1891, Engels wrote that "the Paris Commune . . . was the dictatorship of the proletariat." The Commune in its brief life never got far in socialist construction. It was concerned to destroy the bureaucratic military machine. It was never a one-party government with stringent controls over working-class freedom of speech and association such as the Bolsheviks later imposed.

On the eve of the great war, socialist or working-class parties were more or less numerously represented in the parliaments of the belligerents. They even had representation in the Russian Duma with its very limited power, and both the Social Democrats, already divided into majority and minority groups, and the Social Revolutionaries had proved their strength with the masses in the continuing struggle against the tyranny of the Tsars.

This summary statement of socialist beliefs and socialist strength before "the lights went out all over the world" is completely inadequate to an understanding of the emotional appeal of socialism in the springtime of its hope. I cannot adequately describe it. I only came to the socialist movement during World War I. But, at least until the communist split, enough of the old spirit lingered, and there was a sufficiently vivid testimony of my comrades to it, to give me a keen sense of the joy, the hope, and the sense of brotherhood which socialism brought to its true believers. It gave them something to live and work for even when work meant sacrifice. Poor men and women gave time and money to the Party with amazing generosity. Racial and national prejudices persisted among socialists but they were more nearly wiped out in the fraternity of the workers of the world than in any of the churches.

One of the pioneer members of the Independent Labour Party in Britain wrote words concerning its meetings and its members that with few changes could be applied to socialism everywhere, Marxist and non-Marxist, in the morning of its hope:

"The fervor of the great audiences that assembled in centers like Glasgow, Bradford, Leeds, Huddersfield, Birmingham and Bristol was quite without precedent in British political history. Men who had grown old in years had their youthful enthusiasms renewed under the glow and warmth of a new spiritual fellowship. They were born again; they joyfully walked many miles to listen to a favorite speaker; they sang Labour hymns; and they gave to the new social faith an intensity of devotion which lifted it far above the older political organizations of the day. The women members of the movement were self-sacrificing beyond all experience. . . ." [3]

[3] Quoted in *Fifty Years March* (Odhams) by Francis Williams.

I do not want to exaggerate socialist virtue. Many men and women in socialist parties and more on their fringes were moved by hatred of the rich and fortunate, rather than by love of one another. Socialism never banished all jealousy or cupidity. Conflicts over points of doctrine within the socialist movement were fought with a full measure of the theological bitterness which always characterized similar controversies in the churches. And, as in the churches, personal aspirations for leadership and power were deeply involved in theoretical discussions. Marx had set an unfortunate pattern in his contest with the anarchist Bakunin. (Marx was by no means wholly the "Red Prussian" a recent author, seeking a sensational success, tries to make him. But with all his dogged and self-sacrificing devotion to his cause, he was scarcely a lovable character, and communists can justly claim that he fixed a pattern for smear tactics in controversy in his disputes with Bakunin. Certainly he was no Abraham Lincoln or Gene Debs in his human relationships.)

It was not, however, until the rise of the Communist Party that controversies within the radical or revolutionary movement destroyed all sense of solidarity or of ethical standards. The general rule was that quarreling socialist, syndicalist, or anarchist groups would come to each other's aid against attacks from the capitalist class or the state. All these groups had a great integrity about announcing their position and proclaiming their loyalty to their cause. It remained for communists to make concealment of their real allegiance a major tactic. It remained for communists, in the words of that wise socialist, Charney Vladeck, "to make virtues out of practices which we regarded as sins even when we indulged in them." Machiavellianism may or may not have been implicit in Marxism. It remained for the Bolsheviks to make it a standard practice.

The chief glory of socialism was its internationalism. That had gone so far that there had been considerable discussion of socialist resort to a general strike against mobilization in the event of war. The Socialist International, however, was never more than a debating society. It strengthened socialist comradeship and gave a measure of direction to socialist thinking and programs, but it never got around to drawing up a plan for implementing international socialist resistance to the beginning of war. Neither had socialists been much quicker or more imperative than nonsocialists in sounding the alarm before or after the nations began their blind and breath-taking plunge into war. They believed theoretically that the capitalist-nationalist social order bred war; some of them talked about the inevitability of war under capitalism, but in general they did not really expect large-scale war keenly enough to plan specifically to prevent it or rapidly to end it by turning it into social revolution.

For this there were several reasons. Socialists, even in countries where they had representatives in Parliament, had no inside information whatsoever about the plans of government or any of those developments of foreign policy which had not already been published in the press. Optimists who before World War I or after World War II talked glibly about the power of "the workers" or "the people" to prevent the wars which they do not want overlook the fact that in every case, even in the democracies, governments confront their people with accomplished facts and often with no effective choice except between evils. Nowhere has democracy been so much of a failure as in its control of the foreign policies of governments.

In the last analysis, that failure is due to the religion of nationalism from which not even socialism has freed modern man. Effective political action is within the confines of political states and when national interests impinge upon each other cool judgment is always sacrificed to the tremendous emotion of patriotism or negatively to fear of an enemy worse than the most unpopular domestic ruler. So it was conspicuously in 1914 when cool second thought might have averted a war which was not to the true interest of any class or any government.

An important factor in preventing sober second thought was the speed with which the long practice of peacetime military conscription enabled Germany, Austria-Hungary, Russia, and France to mobilize for war. World War I was outstanding proof that peacetime military conscription, which never prevented any war or guaranteed victory in it, might hasten its coming. European socialists had not liked this conscription but they had not effectively opposed it. And some socialists even thought it good preparation for possible fighters on the barricades. All their young men at an impressionable age had been subjected to the kind of training which teaches men to accept militarism and war even if they do not love them. Mass warfare on nationalist lines had been carefully planned. Internationalist opposition to it had only been talked about. When the test came, it was no wonder that the voice of the drill sergeant speaking in the name of patriotism proved stronger than the voice of international solidarity. The one socialist who might have made a difference, the great French orator and statesman, Jean Jaurès, was assassinated by a French "patriot" before he could speak. Socialists soon were killing socialists, even as Christians were killing fellow believers.

For this tragic failure internationalist socialism could offer the excuses we have discussed. It could make the melancholy boast that when it was caught in war it tried sooner and more earnestly both to bring peace and to knit up its own severed ranks than did ecumenical Christianity. There was also a higher percentage of European socialists who stood out from World War I than of Christians.

Nevertheless, in the retrospect, it has long seemed to me clear that the first great failure of international socialism, a failure which was the betrayal of its greatest idealism, lay in its relation to World War I. It was the kind of failure which, by blunting the idealistic and humanistic elements in democratic socialism and denying its claim as a living witness to world-wide fraternity, enormously handicapped its recovery and progress. This failure gravely injured those attitudes and convictions upon which democratic socialism depends. It gave weight to those factors in Marxism which emphasized social conflict in terms of an amoral struggle for power. Democratic socialism suffered more than the churches from the war, although its guilt was less, partly because the churches had a supernatural salvation to offer and partly because they had long since come to terms which permitted Christians, in the event of war, to render unto Caesar their consciences, which by Christian definition were God's.

What made the situation worse was the fact that it was usually the more democratic and moderate socialists who supported the war, while the left-wing minority in the European countries opposed it as "imperialist" and furnished the nucleus for Lenin's Communist International. Social-democratic opposition to dictatorship and violence was compromised in the stormy postwar period by the war record of the majority socialists. In Great Britain there was greater right-wing opposition to the war, some of it on the basis of religious or philosophical pacifism. In America the Socialist Party regarded the war as imperialist and opposed America's entrance into it. Defections of convinced socialists were few and chiefly among the intellectuals. The periphery fell away rapidly under war conditions.

It was not merely democratic socialism but democracy in general which was injured by the war. When Woodrow Wilson took America into the war it was, he said, to make the world safe for democracy. Victory in it had no such result. The method of war was itself a factor in setting in motion the forces of totalitarianism. Mr. Wilson's great opportunity was to use his country's moral and economic power to bring about a negotiated peace. In the retrospect it is fairly clear that that might have been possible at almost any time after the first battle of the Marne on terms better in themselves, or less bad, than the peace at Versailles and far better adapted to an orderly progress. For Woodrow Wilson as for the socialists there is the excuse that to have risen to the opportunity would have required an heroic capacity for vision, decision, and leadership unprecedented in history. Nevertheless, it was thus that democracy might have been given not only a degree of external security but an inner confidence in the power of rational action which was denied by the long-drawn-out war of mud and trenches, terminating in the bad and stupid peace of Versailles.

It is now popular to judge World War I as if the Germans were as guilty as were the Nazis in World War II. As a matter of fact, no competent historian writing between the two wars ever assessed the whole war guilt on the Germans. War itself is the mother of atrocities but the stories of peculiar German atrocities in World War I, unlike World War II, were almost wholly false. Civil liberties fared about as well in Germany as in England, France, or America.

These facts came to be recognized by the people in the years between the two wars. Americans rather generally accepted the view stated very clearly by the conservative Walter Millis (among others) in *The Road to War* that economic forces brought us into the conflict. The Nye committee in the Senate reached somewhat similar conclusions. The result in the victor countries was a powerful antiwar feeling. Some of the bravest English and American soldiers in World War II had earlier taken or sympathized with the so-called Oxford Pledge not to fight for their country. Alas, this antiwar attitude had never been powerful enough or wise enough to persuade the nations to take those steps which might more easily have been taken before either Hitler or Stalin came to power for the prevention of war and the establishment of limited world government. The socialist failure to prevent World War I or to end it on reasonable terms was part of the general democratic failure by which democracy itself as a vital force was incalculably weakened. Never since the end of World War I or the Versailles Conference has there been so easy or so clear-cut and dramatic an opportunity to save mankind by the right choice of logical alternatives as both the socialists and Woodrow Wilson missed. Their failure paved the way for fascism and communism.

Chapter 3

The Communist Revolution

BEFORE the Peace of Versailles was signed, two socialist revolutions had taken place, one in Russia and the other in Germany. Under war's reverses, two military empires had collapsed. To socialist enthusiasts the day of the workers had dawned. The Marxist hope was realized.

Socialist development of the revolutionary situations, first in Russia and then in Germany, took radically different lines with radically different results. Yet, from the standpoint of man's millennial desire, both were failures. The failure in Germany was obvious even before Hitler came to power. It was devastating in its effect upon socialist morale in Europe and America. It was one reason why many young idealists turned to communism rather than to socialism in the thirties. To them the Bolshevik revolution seemed an outstanding success, and in their eyes its methods were sanctioned by the results.

Even democratic socialists like myself, despite fears of dictatorship, viewed the Russian revolution optimistically until the time of Stalin's purges or, in some cases, until his pact with Hitler. The disillusionment was bitter and painful. It drove some of its victims far to the right. Later on, Russian resistance to Hitler's attack brought Stalin widespread confidence and support in the United States even from conservatives. The single speech most uncritically eulogistic of Stalin which I ever heard from a noncommunist was given by Wendell Willkie, titular leader of the Republican Party, after the trip on which he discovered "one world."

At the end of the war, so tolerant was American opinion of Stalin, with whom we had been allied in the fighting, that I felt obliged to spend much energy in speech and writing to elaborate the facts about Stalin's betrayal of the ideals of true socialism. So rapidly did this situation change, however, and so deeply were the American people stirred by the development of the cold war, that it became no longer necessary for me to work out in detail a criticism of communist totalitarianism. Therefore, I rewrote this chapter. Indeed, the change in the American attitude is so extreme that it is hard for me to remember how coldly my warnings about the essential nature of communism inside and out of the Soviet Union were received in the years 1944–46.

Its enemies must admit that the rise of communism and its success in organizing its power first in the U.S.S.R., then in the satellite states, and now in China, is an enormously impressive achievement. It represents a tremendous triumph of collectivism, a terrifying example of the ease with which multitudes, having first fallen under the spell of a mass movement, can be put and kept under a ruthless dictatorship. Even those of us who were convinced of the implacability of the communist drive for power thought in the summer of victory (1945) that war weariness and the need to improve his economic position would restrain Stalin in aggression. The speed of communism's progress was in considerable part made possible by mistakes in American and British policy during and after the war. However one may explain it, its victories were at the expense of true socialism and all real freedom.

In terms of human dignity and the withering away of coercive power under a steady growth of fellowship which had been vital in the socialist program, communism has been worse than a socialist failure. It has been a socialist betrayal. It has substituted for the socialist commonwealth the most absolute state in history, a state which seeks total authority over every realm of life, a state whose political hierarchy, through complete control of the means of communication, supplemented by torture and concentration camps, has imposed its philosophy, its standards of art and science, its political and economic theories and their day-by-day application, upon a vast part of the world's population.

True, the communist state has wiped out the exploitation of the workers by a class of private owners; but it has substituted for this an exploitation of them by the state, which has added unrestricted police powers to the powers of an owning class. It has reestablished chattel slavery for millions of persons sent to its terrible work camps without any semblance of fair trial. And it has done all this under ingenious slogans and with a propagandistic skill in exploiting the real and alleged crimes and blunders of its opponents which have won it a great deal of mass support both inside and outside of the territories which it controls.

That fact is profoundly significant for any study of social theory and practice. In action communism has earned Ignazio Silone's characterization of it as "Red Fascism." The dictatorship in the Kremlin pioneered in every crime except racism which fascism and Nazism practiced. Yet communism's professions of regard for the working masses, its activity in popular drives in their behalf in countries under noncommunist control, and its militant anti-racism, continue to gain for it supporters who are blind to its performances where it has power.

In its chief aspects, the history of the Russian revolution and the rise of communism is well known. It had been generally believed by Marxists that the triumph of socialism would require the existence of an industrial working class educated and organized to take advantage of a capitalist collapse brought about by capitalism's own internal contradictions. War was recognized as one form of collapse. Yet the first avowedly socialist revolution took place in a country still semifeudal, in which peasants rather than industrial workers were the most numerous and apparently the most powerful group among the masses.

Lenin did not so much interpret as modify Marxism by his development of the theory of the dictatorship of the proletariat. Many socialists, Rosa Luxemburg, for instance, interpreted the phrase to mean a temporary dominance of workers over a dispossessed master class during a period of reconstruction. Among the workers themselves who, together with the peasants, constituted the vast majority of the population of every country, democratic processes would prevail even in the transitional period. It was Lenin who recognized that any effective dictatorship must be exercised by an elite, by a chosen few under rigid discipline, which in turn they would impose upon the masses. Only so, he thought, could the debris of the broken capitalist state be cleared away and the transition achieved to a world-wide socialist society in which the state would wither to nothingness. His problem was to gain enough popular acceptance of his elite or of his tightly disciplined party so that it would be considered by large numbers of the workers in particular, and by the masses in general, as their tool, or better, as their leader and shepherd. Government for an indefinite transitional period must be by the Communist Party. Its elite, possessors of naked political power, set out to be masters rather than servants of economic forces.

In Lenin's theory the Party was to be a dedicated group bent on serving the interests of the workers and the peasants, interests which it understood better than the masses themselves. Its loyalty to the working class would justify any means of deceit or violence which might advance its ends. To the triumph of the working class the interests of the individual could always be sacrificed. Lenin, in his sincere belief that with the disappearance of a capitalist class and the abolition of exploitation of workers and peasants by private owners not only the dictatorship but the state itself would wither away, overlooked the fact to which all human experience bears testimony: men covet power at least as much as they covet property, and few men and no organized groups of men have ever voluntarily laid down power. The time has never seemed to them ripe to give over the guardianship of the people. It never will.

The current rationalization of dictatorship is the purported necessity to protect mighty Russia against capitalist encirclement —a doctrine which stands squarely in the way of any honest co-operation of communist leaders for world peace. It is the business of the United States, through its foreign policy, to make that rationalization appear as implausible as possible to the Russian people. But we can be sure that if by great good fortune that convenient rationalization should be discredited, the dictatorship would still find reasons for hanging on to power.

That Lenin had a chance to establish his proletarian revolution under the dictatorship of the elite was largely due to the very backwardness which to most socialists had made a socialist revolution in Russia seem impossible. The Russian army and the Russian government collapsed under the strains of World War I because of their own internal weakness and inefficiency. The first revolution was a negative affair against Tsarism rather than for anything precise and definite. A great many socialists of the Menshevik group believed that Russia must go through a period of capitalist development before it would be ready for real socialism. Socialists might guide, control, modify, and hasten that process, but not abolish it.

Even Lenin was sufficiently impressed with this view of Marxism to believe in the early days of his own regime that the Russian revolution would fail unless it could be extended rapidly to western European countries in which industrial development was far more advanced. It was the business of his dictatorship to hang on to Russia while by every possible means it hastened the process of world, or, at any rate, European revolution.

It was only under Stalin that it finally became clear that the very backwardness of Russia, added to its size and potential resources, made possible a successful revolution in one nation under rigid control by a determined and ruthless party. The Russians had been trained to an acceptance of authority. They were accustomed to a lower standard of living than the peoples of western Europe. They were relatively immune to foreign attack or to those pressures which a smaller country less strategically located could not resist. Indeed, foreign attack and foreign pressures played into Lenin's and later into Stalin's hands. Lenin, the internationalist, in the twenties could capitalize on Russian nationalism and patriotic resentment against the bungling, halfhearted intervention of western powers. At the same time, he could count on widespread working-class, socialist, and liberal opposition to that intervention in Great Britain, France, and America. And Stalin in the forties could successfully exploit Russian patriotism against Hitler.

It was, however, a capital mistake of western observers to conclude that Stalin, either in his struggle for power against Trotsky or later as the ally of the western nations against Hitler, ever abandoned the thought of world revolution. The difference between him and Trotsky was one of timing and tactics, of judgment concerning the rate at which world revolution must develop. Stalin remained a believer in the necessity of eventual world-wide triumph of communism in order that anywhere it might be absolutely secure. He emphasized Lenin's use of any tactics, including unbounded deceit and violence, to achieve that result. He advertised his belief in his writings to the world influential sections of which persisted in not believing him.

Marxist interpretation of history leaves no room for the role of the hero, yet it is exceedingly doubtful whether the communist revolution could have succeeded except for the qualities of leadership which Lenin displayed. Trotsky, but not Stalin, played an almost equally significant role in the critical years of the revolution. Later, in his defeat of Trotsky and his long supremacy, Stalin proved himself a great organizer of power, an enormously successful manipulator of mass movement, made more rather than less potent by his apparent immunity to ordinary considerations of comradeship or of kindness.

It would be a mistake to infer from the success of the communist elite that its triumph was purely a matter of power politics and its pitiless use of violence, wholly unrelated to great political and economic forces and to the dominant interests of the masses. The communist rulers of Russia in the beginning carefully exploited the popular demand for land, bread, and peace. In the Second World War they exploited very successfully the ancient Russian patriotism and pride as against the brutal German invaders. Today they give the masses security for their nation and a certain low degree of economic security against unemployment. They are making them literate and giving them some public facilities for health and culture. They pay homage to the working class even when they reduce heretical workers to bitter slavery and impose upon free workers a status of subordination such as western capitalism could not exact. To a real extent they compensate in the minds of many of their subjects for the economic hardships which they impose by the visions of plenty to be achieved when at last the Soviet Union is fully industrialized.

But it would be a mistake to imagine that the whole population of Russia, to say nothing of the satellite states, is content in slavery. The far-flung extent of the Soviet secret police organization, the recurring purges, and the immense number in the Russian concentration camps, are evidence to the contrary. Once it was said that as a result of Stalin's purges there were no Quislings in the U.S.S.R. during the recent war. But we now know that the Germans were fairly well received in the Ukraine until they instituted their own terror, and that General Vasilov took a whole army over to his country's foes. Terrorism and the fear which it engenders are major elements in maintaining communist power.

Yet terrorism does not altogether explain communism's success, especially on its road to power among peoples who have had some opportunity to learn the truth. In this whole situation lie problems of paramount importance to socialism, democracy, and the tactics of the present cold war, problems much discussed among socialists. Some of them call for more explicit statement and examination which I shall put in the form of answers to questions frequently presented to me:

1. Will communism continue to be the principal beneficiary of the Marxist tradition?

I think the answer is *yes*, despite the fact that Leninism contains elements not derived from Marx which Marx, who feared Russia, would have rejected. As we have already said, the extravagant homage paid to the dead Lenin and the living Stalin is completely opposed to Marx's teaching. Neither personal nor party dictatorship is a Marxist doctrine. Moreover, communism, whenever it wins power, stands Marxism on its head by using its political might to determine the speed and nature of economic change. This is to reverse the Marxian doctrine that politics must be the expression of economic development. According to Marx, an awakened, organized, and self-conscious proletariat must be the active agent of a revolution essentially determined by an inexorable economic process. By no Marxist judgment, not even Lenin's in the first months of his revolution, had Russia reached the stage of development necessary for the success in one country alone of that revolutionary economic change which a resolute political dictatorship succeeded in forcing upon her.

Despite all this, the communists, as avowed heirs of Marx, have the advantage of conspicuous success in gaining power, and of a secular church in interpreting and applying the true doctrine. Moreover, there are elements in Marxism which either suggest or readily lend themselves to the communist interpretation: for example, the uncompromising doctrine of class conflict and the amoral theory of the materialist dialectic. Socialists have a right, indeed a duty, to challenge the communist expropriation of Marx and Engels. It is particularly important to do this since in Asia among the intellectuals more than in the western world socialism was Marxism. Stalin should not be allowed without contradiction to pose as Marx's sole heir.

Nevertheless, in the light of events there is small ground for hope that a democratic version of Marxist socialism will prevail over communism in the minds of the majority of Marxists. Marx cannot be made the prophet of democratic socialism in the middle of the twentieth century, however one may estimate his role in the years before World War I.

2. To what extent is communism peculiarly "Russian," "Asian," or "eastern," and therefore subject to important modification in the western world? And is it true, as at least one recent writer has claimed, that the nature of communist development would have been different if it had won out in Germany in the years following the First World War?

That Lenin was influenced by the Russian environment in which he was born and by older non-Marxist Russian theorists and practitioners of revolution is generally admitted. Stalin, in his outlook, was an Easterner as against the Westerner, Trotsky. The Russian people, like the mass of Asians, never knew such a degree of democracy as was achieved by the West, and their standard of living was far lower. All these things were and are important to the development of communism.

It is, however, an error to overemphasize the "eastern" quality of communism. It owes too much to Marxist theory and to psychological attributes common to mankind. Germany did not become communist, but it developed its own mass movement, a fascism imitative of communism in ruthlessness and in some respects even crueler. Hitler, its hero, was a psychopath to a degree that Stalin is not, and his appeal was even more to the irrational in man and to mob emotionalism.

Whatever the origins of communism, it impresses its pattern on its slavish adherents in all countries east and west. The manners and morals of American communists are the manners and morals of Molotov and Malik. One who has been involved in controversies with them can appreciate what American Secretaries of State have suffered in their dealings with Molotov, Gromyko, and Vishinsky.

3. Is it reasonable, in any near time, to expect such a modification of communism that it will live in amity with democracy, or noncommunism, in our world?

Perhaps in time. But not in any near time. The oft-cited facts that Russia is not a have-not nation in respect to resources and that the Russian people undoubtedly want peace, are important for an American policy directed as far as possible toward the Russian people as distinct from their dictators. It is wholly desirable to refrain from giving Stalin propaganda material to play on the people's fear of attack by capitalist or "fascist" nations.

This fear may in some degree be felt by the rulers themselves. But the main drive of communism for world-wide power is based on a sense of destiny stronger than fear. Communism is still universal in outlook and appeal, although communist internationalism under Stalin has been subordinated to a Russian imperialism which has provoked such a nationalist revolt as Tito's in Yugoslavia. Herein may be found the Achilles heel in Stalinism, compounded as it is of Leninist internationalism and a revival of the imperialism of the Tsars—a fact which Americans should remember in their relations with China.

4. There remains the exceedingly important question of the nature of the communist strength. Why has it so wide an appeal even at a time and in places where its actual performances in oppression are or can be known?

The answer is not to be found in any mere set of economic facts. It lies largely in the Party's offer of a road to power to men and groups who now feel themselves disinherited. Some of them begin as idealists but soon become drunk with ambition for power. At the same time communist dictatorship is accepted by millions because in our bewildering world they fear life and freedom, because consciously or subconsciously they want over them a strong shepherd and the discipline he imposes. Much of communism's strength lies in the darker places in men's souls.

By no means is it born wholly of the failures of democracy. But these failures contribute enormously to it, especially in the field of race relations. In practice, as opposed to propaganda, communist equality of races or individuals has been grossly exaggerated. Russia has not even given equality of slavery to its peoples. The dictatorship is still practicing genocide in the little Baltic states as it practiced it against the peoples of the five autonomous areas dissolved during and immediately after World War II. Responsible Jewish spokesmen are even indicting it for some degree of anti-Semitism.

Nevertheless, communist freedom from any dogma of white supremacy among the Mongolian tribesmen of Siberia and in China recommends it to great multitudes of the colored peoples whose imperial masters have been the western "democracies." And the standard of living in the U.S.S.R. represents progress to Chinese coolies.

Hence, as wisdom to guide us Westerners in the cold war, the complete—and increasingly popular—repudiation of poverty as an outstanding cause of communism is seriously in error. Dorothy Thompson contributes to that error when she writes: "Communism has not advanced by spontaneous revolts of impoverished masses, but by force springing into breaches opened by betrayal. And its greatest ally is fear."

This judgment, which Miss Thompson applies to China, contains some elements of truth, but is far from a sound appraisal of the tremendous appeal of Mao and his communists. As compared with the corrupt Nationalists, they offered immediately some land and more hope, and with them both an end of war and, temporarily, a relative honesty in government. Communists are the obvious enemies of the local tyrants and exploiters: landlords, usurers, and grafting officials.

The evidence of the essential evil of communism is strong. So is the evidence of its debt to the advantages of position given it gratuitously by the western leaders in the years 1943–46. But we shall misjudge the situation if we fail to understand communism's appeal to the masses in noncommunist lands as a force for new life and hope. It grows strong on the crimes and blunders of democracy. Despite its own worse crimes—which are still widely disbelieved—it has the towering advantage of being in a position to say to millions of resentful colonials and to the disinherited masses generally: "Our enemies are your enemies. Let us make common cause!" Any successful opposition to communism requires the propaganda of the truth about its performance. Even more does it require us to change the bitter truth about race discrimination and economic exploitation in our imperfect democracies.

Chapter 4

The Social Democratic Failure
in Germany

ALTHOUGH collapse had
made possible both the Russian and the German revolutions, the
Russian was more truly won by revolutionary forces. The German
social democrats took over because they were the logical party to
inherit power from a defeated government. It was a legacy for
which, at the end of 1918, there was comparatively little competition.

It was also a legacy for which the German socialists were ill
prepared. Their theory of Marxism had taught them little about
what to do were power even temporarily to be dropped in their
laps. Their German sense of order and respect for regularity of
administration led them uncritically to take over a large part of
the apparatus of the imperialist state: schoolteachers, civil servants,
and judges. They, along with the rest of the German people, were
mentally as well as physically exhausted by the war and by a

hunger light only in comparison with the desperate misery of Europe following World War II. They had no plan, no outstanding leaders comparable to Lenin, Trotsky, or Stalin, and they were sorely beset, on the one hand, by fear of what the antisocialist governments of the Allies might do if they should press socialization and, on the other, by the bitter and violent opposition springing up from left-wing elements which rapidly fell under communist leadership. Some of the military tactics used in putting down Spartacide revolts, and the murder of Liebknecht and Luxemburg, alienated or deeply antagonized large sections of the people and constituted a stain on social democracy which the far more violent and ruthless communists never tired of exploiting.

Meanwhile, by an act of folly for which the world paid dear, the Allies had finally compelled representatives of a German social-democratic government to sign the treaty containing an acknowledgment of the *sole* guilt of Germany for the war. It is evidence of the inadequacy of a narrow economic interpretation of history that this act of social democrats, under pressure, became one of Hitler's most useful resources. It contributed to the rise of Nazism almost as much as the reparations section of the Peace of Versailles and the French occupation of the Ruhr.

In theory and practice, German social democracy, despite its claims to a rigid Marxist orthodoxy, proved more democratic than socialist. It put its emphasis upon the setting up of a democratic constitution, apparently in the belief that under the right sort of democratic political government the workers and their allies would be bound to establish socialism. Were they not a majority of the population and was not socialism a natural expression of their interests? The tendency to explain Nazism in terms of German psychology and history has obscured the fact that the Weimar Constitution was generally hailed as a democratic and progressive document embellished with many of the latest gadgets of political science. Under it, workers' rights and civil liberties were nominally well protected. Elections were by a form of proportional representation which could be justified in pure democratic theory, but which in practice tended to paralyze democratic action by encouraging innumerable small parties or groups and necessitating government by coalition.

It has been the fate of the Weimar Republic and the democratic parties which supported it to be criticised by communists and some noncommunists for giving too much civil liberty to the reactionary and fascist groups which ultimately destroyed it, while it achieved no credit among anti-German extremists for any regard for individual freedom. The experience of Germany is still cited by Americans who argue that civil liberty should never be extended to those who in power would destroy it. This, I think, is a misreading of German history. It was far less what reactionary groups, and later and more effectively the Nazis, said, but what they prevented others from saying by violent interference with meetings, by street brawls and assassinations, which helped to undo German democracy. These crimes were all overt acts with which even Jefferson acknowledged that it was the business of government to deal. Not too much civil liberty, but too great weakness before conspiratorial groups, demagogues, and the mobs they incited was the offense of the various coalition governments which ruled Germany in rapid succession under the Weimar Constitution.

Even so, the final failure of German democracy, socialist and nonsocialist, lay in the field of economics. Of the many factors which contributed to Hitler's rise to power, the greatest was the world-wide depression which came at the end of the twenties, a few months earlier on the European continent than in the United States. In Germany it came under a government which already had a well-developed system of social security and in which the bargaining rights of workers were well established. Further resort to these measures in a country which had been defeated in a great war and lacked the resources of America could not possibly do for Germany what Roosevelt did for the United States.

The very perfection of practices adopted in the interests of the workers tended to their defeat. The public as consumers felt with some reason that the bargaining between organized employers and organized workers too often simply meant that the employers conceded wage increases in the assurance that they could more than compensate themselves by price increases unopposed by labor. When unemployment became extensive and chronic, it was the rising crop of young men who were its especial victims because, under union rules of seniority, older workers kept all the jobs there were. An increasingly large army of young men who were kept by joblessness from paying dues or even joining the unions was a principal source from which Hitler recruited his party.

German social democracy, however, was pretty well discredited among eager workers and the younger socialists of all countries for its failure before Hitler came to power. Its hope that the workers and hence socialism would win in a country as industrially advanced as Germany, once a democratic constitution was established, was frustrated. It received power which it had not known how to use as the result of defeat of capitalism and nationalism under the Kaiser. That defeat after World War I was by no means so complete but that both capitalism and nationalism were revived in a defeated Germany which managed to stage before the great depression and the triumph of fascism a considerable degree of economic recovery. When world depression made Germany its especial victim it was not Marxism either of the democratic or the communist sort which proved able to exploit the situation but rather its deadly enemy, Hitler's National Socialism.

History, in short, played strange tricks with Marxist tradition. Belatedly and after its own fashion it fulfilled his prophecy of the collapse of private capitalism, but it refuted any notion that, as a result of that collapse, socialism in any desirable form was destined, through the automatic wisdom of a working class freed from its chains, to conquer poverty, abolish the class division of society, and turn a society of mutually suspicious nationalist states into a federation of cooperative commonwealths. Fascism became the heir of the German revolution. Marxists had never predicted its triumph. Yet the defeat of German socialism was not so absolute but that it revived after World War II as Germany's best hope of democracy.

The nature of fascism and the manner of its rise are exceedingly important in any revaluation of socialism. The communists have fitted fascism into the Marxist scheme of things by explaining that it was the last stage of capitalism or "capitalism with its mask off"; that it was a counterrevolution engineered and financed by big business with popular demagogues as its agents. This theory of fascism, this denial to it of any revolutionary character, is not borne out by the facts. Fascism was not an orderly development of capitalism but, in an important sense, a revolution against it toward an evil type of state-dominated economy. Individual Italian and German capitalists, in the blindness of their complete opposition to all forms of socialism, gave valuable financial assistance to Mussolini and Hitler. Foreign capitalists, banking and munition interests in the earlier days, and partners in international cartels in the later days, helped to build up fascist power. Salvemini makes a strong case that Italian fascism, at the time of Matteotti's murder, would not have survived except for the active help of Wall Street as well as the British Foreign Office. International munition interests subsidized Hitler's rise to power. French, British, and American corporations found profit in cartels under the control of the Nazi state.

Nevertheless, fascism's basic appeal was to the little man as a little man, a man resentful of the power both of the great corporations and the great unions. It was an appeal to restless veterans of World War I and, in its later stages, to the unemployed. The Nazi economic program was originally an unintelligible but emotionally attractive piece of demagoguery which the Nazis ignored when they got power. The driving power of Nazism lay largely in its exploitation of a narrow racist and revengeful nationalism. Mussolini's fascism originally was less racist. Everywhere fascism, although not proletarian, was plebeian rather than patrician in its essential nature—even when aristocrats and industrial tycoons supported it. Its leaders developed and exploited a mass movement psychologically equivalent to Lenin's and Stalin's movement.

Italian fascism came to power against the background of postwar confusion in Italy, division of working-class forces and popular discontent with the results of the war. Its romantic imperialism gave it favor with the Army and the King, who yielded to what might have been little more than an *opera-bouffe* march on Rome.

The Nazis and their political allies after a longer struggle finally won power against the background of the great depression, the division and blundering of their enemies, and the senility of President von Hindenburg. It was a power confirmed by popular election in which, after gross intimidation and the infamous Reichstag fire, the Hitler alliance (but not the Nazi party) got a bare majority of the popular vote.

The Nazis then lost little time in reducing their political allies to abject submission. They suppressed all free labor unions and substituted for them a labor front under government control. For the most part, they kept the corporate machinery of German industry, allowed it to operate for profit and, by a combination of rewards and punishments, easily held the loyalty of the managerial class. At the same time, the Nazi government established a rigor of control over the whole economic system and a degree of planning completely inconsistent with the economics of private capitalism or anything remotely like "free enterprise." The government could remove the heads of the great corporations. It kept the machinery of social security for the workers and provided approximately full employment under an arms economy.

For a considerable time after the Nazi government came to power, communists, socialists, and the more orthodox economists vied with one another in predicting for different reasons the collapse of the fascist type of collectivism or state capitalism. No such collapse occurred. The social and economic consequences of fascist triumph under the German form were revolutionary, unless one insists on reserving the word *revolutionary* for a triumph of the working class. In no way was Hitler the tool of big business. He was its lenient master. So was Mussolini except that he was weaker.

Fascism may have been one form of logical evolution out of a capitalism which had long since outgrown genuine *laissez faire*, but it is a denial of facts and a dangerous distortion of reason to see in it merely a last stage of capitalism consciously desired by capitalists as capitalists.

It was a mistake that cost the European masses dear because it was a large element in the communist misjudgment of the Nazi revolution. In Germany, under Moscow's orders, the communists regarded the social democrats as their real enemies and dubbed them "social fascists." On occasions, they actually united with the Nazis to embarrass social democrats. From Hitler's triumph in 1933 until the end of 1934, communist bosses in Moscow continued to believe that the Hitler regime, as a last stage in capitalism, would somehow be a prelude to a true communist revolution. It took almost two years before Stalin was convinced that Hitler was his most dangerous enemy and that he must begin to build up some sort of united front with democratic movements and countries which he hated or despised. So little was his heart in this tactical union that he was able cold-bloodedly to make a virtual alliance with Hitler in the summer of 1939. Neither dictator loved the other, each sought to use the other under exactly the same amoral type of power politics. Stalin did not love Hitler when he made the quasi alliance with him any more than later he loved Great Britain and America in the war alliance which Hitler's attack forced on him. From the beginning, his tactics were to advance world revolution and Russian power by letting his enemies, fascist and democratic alike, smash themselves. It is equally true that Hitler's hatred of all Marxism never prevented his appropriation of communist tactics or blocked an alliance with Stalin when it was convenient to his purposes. The struggle for power imposes its own tactics and tends to subordinate all ideology to the winning of victory.

Looking back on the years, I find it hard to put in words the strain upon the thinking and emotional feeling of western socialists as they contemplated in succession the failure of German social democracy, the seeming success of Bolshevism, the rise of fascism to power in Italy and Germany, the proof which the purges brought of communist degradation, and, finally, the temporary alliance of two forms of dictatorship. To explain all this, leaders of the various Marxist factions or parties had to torture their scriptures in support of their actions as arbitrarily as Christian sects had interpreted the Bible.

On any plain reading of the facts, the interval between the two world wars saw the growth of the Bolshevik revolution into enormous power at the price of a deterioration of socialist ideals amounting to betrayal—a betrayal, however, which grew out of Lenin's own doctrine of the road to power. It saw an ineffective social-democratic revolution in Germany which was eventually followed by fascist revolution and the suppression of all avowed international or Marxist socialism of every form by torture, the axe, and the concentration camp.

Nevertheless, both the communist and fascist revolutions definitely abolished *laissez-faire* capitalism in favor of one or another kind and degree of state capitalism. In neither form, fascist or communist, did the masses, through any sort of democratic process, either as workers or citizens, control the basic means of production and distribution. In varying degree, these basic enterprises were collectivized under the undemocratic control of an elite, which had at its disposal all the powers of a police state. This presented to democratic socialists a situation very different than anything they had seriously contemplated before or even during World War I. Before 1939 it cannot be said that in practice democratic socialists were much more successful than nonsocialist believers in democracy in grappling with the situation.

In a very real sense, World War II continued World War I. The second war was the unfinished business of the first. And yet to a greater degree than I, for one, realized in 1939, the situation was made different by the rise of totalitarian states in which capitalism largely had become state capitalism. Thus economics and politics were even more closely tied together than before World War I.

Chapter 5

Socialism in Western Europe
Between the Wars

ALTHOUGH the rise of communism and fascism overshadowed history between the two world wars, it by no means monopolized it. There was a genuine vigor of democracy not only in the United States but in Great Britain and the English-speaking dominions of the British Empire, in the Scandinavian countries, in western Europe generally, including France and Spain. In France the triumph of a reaction which would have led to an avowed fascism was held off only by a popular front in which socialists and progressives had to include the Communist Party. The coalition, under that fine humanitarian socialist, Léon Blum, as premier, was unable conspicuously to revitalize or revolutionize France and Blum was not in power either at the time of the Munich crisis in 1938 or at the outbreak of war in 1939. There was a good deal of doubt about or opposition to the war among some of the French socialists, and the communists withheld any active support of it or even sabotaged it so long as it was an "imperialist" war; that is, until Hitler attacked Stalin, after which the well-organized communists became a very important element in the resistance movement.

In Spain, the monarchy fell without resistance by reason of the internal weakness of the forces behind it. In its final crisis, Alfonso was unable or unwilling to play the part of strong dictator and none of his supporters assumed the role under the shadow of the legitimate monarchy. Spain developed its own popular front government, which in action had many of the weaknesses inherent in coalitions and was slow in carrying out political and economic changes which were imperatively necessary. Nevertheless, Spanish fascism, intensely clerical, came to blood-stained power only by grace of the active intervention of the Italian and German fascist governments with the scarcely less damaging passive interference of the western democracies, including the United States, under a hypocritical guise of neutrality or nonintervention. So afraid were the labor movements in France and England of war or internal troubles that, until it was too late, they gave a more or less reluctant support to the nonintervention program of their governments. The French popular front government, when it was in office, permitted a considerable supply of arms to Spanish Loyalists through leakage across the border, but the holes weren't big enough to admit tanks and airplanes to counter those with which Hitler finally won the war for Franco. President Roosevelt enforced American neutrality laws rigidly against the Loyalist government but he refused to apply the same laws to the shipment of military supplies which, if small, were nevertheless important to Italy and Germany, whose governments were clearly engaged in undeclared warfare against a friendly nation.

By and large, the performance of popular front governments in both France and Italy contributed little to socialist theory except for the proof they gave of the obvious weaknesses of coalition. At best, in time of crisis, coalition governments are only better than the available alternatives to them.

There was, however, one feature of the economic situation under the Loyalist government in Spain during the civil war which deserves thoughtful attention. A great deal of the economic activity of the nation, from the running of hotels to factories and stores, was taken over by the unions. Spanish labor was divided into two major groupings, the Confederación Nacional del Trabajo under anarcho-syndicalist inspiration, and the Unión General de Trabajadores, predominantly socialist. Both bodies appear to have done a competent emergency job in a very difficult situation. I do not know of any parallel achievement of unions as such in the control of economic activity. The defeat of the Loyalists put an abrupt end to the experiment and prevented any proper appraisal of it or its probable evolution.

In world politics it was the success of the Spanish counterrevolution which gave fascism its arrogant confidence. The Spaniards were the guinea pigs on whom the techniques of the new blitz warfare were worked out to the edification of the German High Command, with no corresponding enlightenment of the French or British. It was also in Spain that Stalin experimented in the techniques of combining Russian military force with native communist political organization and propaganda. He was not in a position to put in enough military aid to win and he exacted a high price both in gold and in political subservience from the Loyalist government for the small aid he gave. Nevertheless, he learned tactical lessons which he has been able to use very successfully in eastern and central Europe once the Nazi power was destroyed.

The greatest nation or, rather, group of nations, in which democratic socialism made striking progress between the two world wars was the British Commonwealth. The years saw the rise of labor governments to power in New Zealand and Australia and the organization of a strong mass party, democratic socialist in ideals and organization, in Canada under the name of the Canadian

Commonwealth Federation. It was not, however, until World War II was well advanced that that party won its first significant electoral victories.

In Great Britain itself the history of the Labour Party was checkered. Whereas in most of the countries in Continental Europe labor unions and socialist parties had grown up together, and the predominant unions were avowedly Marxist, in Great Britain the labor movement was powerful long before there was a strong Labour Party of a socialist sort. Of necessity it began to develop a rather radical working-class program but it was slow in becoming avowedly socialist.

British socialism had had a long and interesting history before Marx, and later, independently of Marx. Its fires were banked by the electoral reforms and factory legislation of the nineteenth century. They were never extinguished. Of Britain, more certainly than of any other country, it can be said there would have been a strong socialist movement if Marx had never lived. Moreover, British socialism and ultimately the British Labour Party, while unquestionably opportunistic and reformist by rigid revolutionary standards, were no more so than the orthodox German social democrats and, favored by the historic situation, they not only survived but grew to power while the German movement was crushed.

The story of the rise of British labor to the power which it now holds is by no means a story of even and uniform progress. It includes an experiment with the general strike as well as with electoral machinery. The general strike of 1926 was not avowedly revolutionary. It was not proclaimed by communists, who have learned to use it on their road to power, or by disciples of Sorel, who had preached it as a revolutionary tactic, or of the American, Daniel De Leon, who held that once the workers had organized one big and inclusive union along sound Marxist lines, they could compel the capitalist class to surrender to them, probably by the mere threat of a general strike. The British strike grew out of sympathy with the desperate position of the coal miners. It evoked impressive solidarity of the workers against a vigor of middle-class opposition which Marxist prophets of its decay hardly expected. It was on the whole free from violence. It is doubtful whether in any other country a strike of similar magnitude would have been so peaceful—remember the violence in far less extensive American strikes. Even in England it would not have remained nonviolent. It was called off by labor leaders who did not want violence and who had no revolutionary program or organization to put in operation should the government collapse.

In socialist and labor ranks there was much controversy about the lessons of the strike but on the whole it was agreed, openly or tacitly, that such a strike was a dubious weapon for labor unless (1) it was intended merely as a demonstrative affair, limited in time; or (2) directed against a particular act of aggression by the government or reactionary forces—in Germany it had been successfully used against the Kapp Putsch; or (3) it was part of a definitely planned revolutionary movement. Since the workers themselves are most dependent upon regular supplies of food and have least in reserve, a general strike must be won very quickly or not at all. A prolonged general strike would almost of necessity shift into a violent attempt to seize key positions of economic and political power.

At any rate, by tacit consent, British labor, after the general strike, once more turned its energies to parliamentary political action. Previously, in the election of 1924, it had emerged as the largest single party in the House of Commons, although it had far from a majority. Rather than arrange a coalition, the Liberal Party allowed Labour to take the government, well knowing that it could block any genuine socialist legislation which it might oppose. On these terms Ramsay MacDonald and an able cabinet took office. Their tenure was short. The Liberal Party deserted them. In the general election which followed the Conservatives won a sweeping victory with the aid of a forged letter purportedly from the Russian Zinoviev. By 1929 MacDonald came back but once more only by Liberal Party consent. He did little for labor or socialism. He did not even outline to Parliament a socialist program. The Labour Party was gravely compromised.

Then a piece of good fortune befell it. Ramsay MacDonald suddenly deserted it to form, unexpectedly, a national coalition government which he thought would make his power more secure. He carried little support with him from the ranks of his party. On the face of it, his desertion was a calamity. Actually, it absolved the Labour Party from having to vindicate to itself and to the country a policy of inaction.

The experience proved the necessity of a positive socialist program and the undesirability of taking office without power. A few years later, as an exception to their rule, the Labourites, in the very great emergency of the war and in the face of invasion, joined Churchill's war coalition cabinet with a definite understanding that, with the winning of peace, they would go their own way and seek by political methods genuine victory for a socialist program.

The British Labour Party is not merely a party of the workers. Indeed, it won postwar victory with much middle-class support. But the Party is still strictly a labor party in the sense that predominant control is vested in the unions affiliated to it and that controversial issues are decided by bloc voting; that is, the officers of the union who are delegates to the Labour Party convention can vote the entire union membership. The British genius for compromise has tended to increase the power and influence of the active members of the Party who participate directly in its local organizations rather than merely through their unions. Nevertheless, sympathetic British observers have criticized it on the ground that its dependence on the unions for funds, together with the weight of unions in final decisions, has sometimes prevented the nomination of the best man for a particular office and has resulted in a disproportionate expenditure for certain favorite union candidates. It has even been said that "the Conservative Party kicks its superannuated leaders into the House of Lords; the Labour Party kicks them into the House of Commons"—an exaggeration not without some truth.

Between the two wars the happiest evidence of men's capacity progressively and cooperatively to improve their condition without violence was to be found in the little Scandinavian countries. By a combination of good fortune and good sense they had kept out of World War I and escaped most of its bitter heritage. In 1905 Sweden and Norway had arranged an amicable separation. Norway achieved complete independence under circumstances which made her a willing cooperator with the neighbors with whom she was tied so closely by blood and history. The strong pressure of labor unions and socialists was a very important factor in this happy result. Folk schools, especially in Denmark, and the cooperative movements both of producers and consumers, have been unusually successful in training the peoples of the Scandinavian nations in working together as free men.

So strong was the cooperative movement that there was a tendency in America in the thirties to acclaim Scandinavian well-being simply in terms of nonpolitical cooperatives. This completely overlooked the importance of the organized labor movement and the fact that in Sweden, Norway, and Denmark, Socialists formed the strongest political party. Socialist Prime Ministers headed cabinets which rested on a coalition with agrarians more harmonious and constructive than coalitions usually are. Even Finland, which had not escaped World War I or a brutal aftermath of conflict between Red and White terrorists, had regained in the thirties a democratic government with the Social Democratic Party a strong political factor.

In none of these Scandinavian countries had either socialism or the millennium been achieved. In none of them did any party work out a comprehensive social theory to justify its pragmatic program. They still professed Marxism. Perhaps their chief contribution to social and political philosophy was the evidence they gave of the value of diversity of instrumentalities in the advancement of the common good. The state did not try to be monolithic or totalitarian. Collectivism took different forms. There was a wholesome competition between state-controlled and cooperative enterprises. What I saw of housing in Stockholm in 1937 deeply impressed me with the value of this type of diversity and competition.

But over all, at least as early as 1937, hung the shadow of approaching war. No one was more keenly aware than responsible socialists in Sweden and Denmark of the dependence of the small countries upon the peace and decency of their powerful neighbors. Absolute sovereignty or absolute independence was clearly for them a fiction even in time of peace. The guarantee of prosperity of the Danish agricultural economy and for Swedish mines and timberlands and factories lay primarily outside the countries themselves. As a Danish official said to me, "We have to adapt ourselves to the economic policies which Hitler imposes roughly, and the English more politely."

I have cited only so much history as has been significant in my own thinking for a revaluation of socialism. That requires brief reference to the Socialist International.

The Second or Socialist International—as distinct from the Communist—was revived after World War I. Before many years had passed it included almost all noncommunist socialist parties. It was a debating society which seldom met. Circumstances and the political and economic organization of the nations in which socialist parties were growing to power compelled them, whatever their devotion to internationalism, to act along national lines and to reject any international controls. In time that became a natural reaction to the rigid control exerted from Moscow over the Third or Communist International.

The Second International defined its policy or, rather, its poli-

cies, since there were wide areas of disagreement, in terms of the
degree of its theoretical opposition to Leninism and its views on
the practicability of cooperation with communism. It developed
no vigorous and powerful interpretation or revision of Marxism.
It gave little leadership to the socialist fight against the march of
fascism. Its physical death, when its offices in Brussels were hastily
abandoned before the Nazi blitzkrieg, had been preceded by a
general debility.

Between the two world wars the workers found it harder to
unite even emotionally across national lines than in the springtime
of socialist hopes before World War I. Not only was the Second
International weak but there was never a vital socialist grouping
of delegates in the League of Nations or even in the International
Labor Office. There were socialists who were prominent in Geneva
but more or less of necessity they acted primarily as delegates of
their nations or of their labor unions. As such they felt that they
had more than their chains to lose even if theoretically they realized that they had a world to gain.

Whatever were the limitations on the progress of socialism in
Europe between the two world wars, collectivism grew apace,
and that not merely in communist and fascist nations. Our memories are short and Americans are inclined to think of the enormous
growth of state control over economic processes in Europe and
even in their own country as largely a legacy of World War II.
But several years earlier I remember that I repeatedly challenged
the eulogists of free enterprise to dispute my contention that, in
a world which had not developed according to the Marxian formula, the ghost of Karl Marx would nevertheless feel more at
home than the spirit of Adam Smith—and that not merely in continental Europe, but in Great Britain under a Conservative government, and in America under a New Deal government which vied
with Republicans in devotion to something which both called free
enterprise. No one ever took up my challenge. World War II
simply emphasized the end of any real approach to *laissez faire.*
Controversy raged over the degree and kind of collectivism.

Chapter 6

Socialism, World War II, and Its Aftermath

Iᴛ ɪꜱ ᴇᴀꜱʏ enough for a socialist, Marxist or non-Marxist, to point to the economic roots of World War II. It was provoked by fascism, and fascism itself had economic as well as noneconomic roots. Fascism intensified the imperialist rivalries of great powers, some of which (Germany, Italy, and Japan) were, comparatively speaking, have-not nations. World War II, like World War I, was born out of the capitalist-nationalist system. The differences were that between the two wars the moral contrasts between the fascist nations and the imperfect western democracies were much greater than those which existed between the combatants in 1914; that capitalism, even in the western democracies, had become more collectivist and more subject in each nation to the direct control of the political state; and that fascism was possessed of a more aggressive popular ideology than the earlier capitalism.

Under these circumstances, the statement so common among socialists during and after World War I that "capitalism is the cause of war" obviously needed explanation and qualification. Its indirect contribution was great. Individual capitalists were not the cause of World War II. The capitalist class had been wiped out in Russia and reduced in Germany to a position subservient to Nazi political leaders. No appreciable number of capitalists in England or later in the United States wanted war for their own advantage. British labor was convinced of the necessity of war against Nazism a little sooner and more completely than Chamberlain's Conservative Party. In the United States, Thurman Arnold and others after this country was in the war argued that the cartels, many of them formed under German leadership, were responsible for the war. Perhaps this was true to some extent indirectly, but never to any such degree as Arnold insisted. At this point he made his own peculiar contribution to what he had earlier described as the "Folklore of Capitalism."

This extreme denunciation of cartels as warmakers stirred in me certain wry memories. Over and over in the twenties when I was preaching the necessity of socialist internationalism, I was told, "You don't have to have socialism. All that is necessary is that the great industrial interests in various countries should come to some sort of agreement and not try by their commercial rivalries to drag their countries into war for trade." Well, they came to some sort of agreement. Big industrialists were not conspicuous leaders in getting America into war. Some of their corporations, for example, the Aluminum Company and Standard Oil of New Jersey, were roundly denounced because by their cartel agreements they delayed and hindered American preparation for war. Yet some socialists, like Mr. Arnold, who is no socialist, were later to blame these cartels for the war. Such blame was due only as cartels under private monopolist or state capitalist control contributed to an unhealthy economy which furnishes a fertile soil for seeds of war.

In so far as there were personal devils responsible for World

War II, they were politicians and militarists rather than business men. European socialists, who had generally deplored a war which they could not or did not effectively resist in 1914, became the most passionate supporters of the Allied cause in the Second World War. Two years after its end, the American Socialist Party was regarded a little coolly by most other socialist parties, not only because of its numerical weakness but because of its opposition to American intervention in the war. (This opposition was emphatically not shared by the American Social Democratic Federation, which boasts that it was the first political group to declare plainly that America must enter the war.) Few, however, of the European socialists who were somewhat critical of the American Party had let their opposition to fascism lead them to support the entry of their country into war until war itself came to their doors. Only the Swedish socialists in responsible positions in government were able to keep out. If the others in the little democracies of western Europe were less successful, it was not for lack of trying. The majority of the French socialists and a bigger majority of the British supported war before their countries were attacked, but scarcely before their nations' interests were terribly jeopardized by Nazi aggression.

The fact that socialist opposition to fascism had been purer and more ardent than, let us say, Churchill's—he had once praised it in Italy—did not lead the British Labour Party to work effectively for a better program for peace than his. The Party's notable electoral victory after V-E Day preceded the final formulation of the Potsdam declaration but Attlee felt constrained to sign the document, which represented a triumph of vengeance and stupidity and in its inevitable application by the triumphant Kremlin turned eastern and central Europe over to the communists.

The Potsdam declaration was the climax of the failure of all nations to act before World War II for economic and political federation, followed by the failure of Churchill and Roosevelt to seek rational conditions for war's settlement.

This failure in a revolutionary situation gave the Kremlin its

chance. The western powers followed a policy of virtual appeasement until the summer of 1946. Then the cold war began. By 1950
Europe was divided through the heart of Germany into the Communist East and a West given a second chance (not yet fully realized) largely by American aid under the Marshall Plan.

These same postwar years have seen an increasing sharpness of
division between socialists and communists on the continent.
Neither had been completely exterminated under Fascist terror.
In most countries the Marxist groups had cooperated in the underground resistance during the war and, after V-E Day, circumstances forced them to continue an uneasy cooperation. As time
went on, socialist parties in eastern Europe, if they survived at all,
felt compelled to accept a subordinate position, not too critical of
communism. Those socialists who refused were, as in Poland,
driven underground. For the time being, even in the nations at
the mercy of the Soviet Union, it suited communist tactics to go
slowly in forcing an absolute one-party system, and docile socialist parties were useful to them for their effect upon internal
and external public opinion. In the Russian zones in Germany, the
submission of the socialist parties was brought about only by direct
coercion through controls of food, newsprint, etc. These tactics
were extended to the satellite states.

In continental Europe immediately after the war Christian popular parties emerged. They were obliged to insert economic planks
in their platforms which by all former standards could only be
described as socialistic. At first there was hope that these parties
might have a genuine vitality derived from a Christian social ethic.
But as time went on, this hope, notably in France and Italy, diminished. The parties too largely became catchalls for the enemies of
communism and, to the degree that the Roman Catholic Church
was strong, ecclesiastical interest was too much concentrated on
organizational rights and privileges dear to the hierarchies. In
France the Mouvement Républicain Populaire (M.R.P.) lost heavily to De Gaulle's personal following.

In that country 1947 saw the final end of socialist collaboration with communism, and in Italy the formation of a new Socialist Party under Saragat, in opposition to Nenni's collaborationist Socialists, who are effectively controlled by the communists. In 1949 an effort toward a larger unity of anticommunist socialists in Italy led to a further split and the organization of yet another Socialist Party.

Apparently the difficulties had more to do with personalities than with principles. But behind all this, as behind the weakening hold of French socialists on the masses of workers, lay the fact that socialists, as part of a third force opposed to communism on the one hand and reaction or neofascism on the other, had not succeeded in evolving a successful program for dealing with the land problem in Italy or the shocking unbalance of wages and prices in both France and Italy. As members of coalition governments they had held communism, extreme reaction in Italy, and De Gaullism in France at bay—with the potent help of American economic aid. They had not developed any stirring appeal to supplant or supplement their rather sterile Marxism.

It is an historical irony that socialist parties in office, despite their theoretical internationalism, are peculiarly subject to short-run considerations of a nationalist sort. Granting the long-run benefits of integration in Europe—indeed its necessity for a truly viable economy—it is the workers to whom socialists particularly appeal who will feel most quickly short-run effects of the abolition of tariffs and other protections of their position within their own countries. Any democratic-socialist movement in Europe could be shipwrecked on the rocks of unemployment even though, as a result of progress in political and economic integration, Europe and European workers generally would be far more secure a few years hence.

Here is a problem not to be solved by appeal to a Marxist text. In a somewhat different form nationalism and the nationalistic shape of existing institutions also bedevil communism despite its monolithic organization. Original Leninist theory allowed neither for the revival of Russian imperialism within communism nor the nationalism of Tito's revolt.

The whole problem of continental Europe would logically have been far more easily solved if the United States had from the beginning consciously aided the forces of democratic socialism and consciously worked toward the establishment of a United States of Europe as a peace objective. But that would have been too much to hope from an America shouting its own belief in free enterprise, uneducated in any slogan of victory save the unconditional surrender of fascist powers, compelled to operate amid Europe's nationalist fears, hates, and interests.

In consequence, we had in critical years a dangerous and confused American policy which, however, had some good features. Perhaps the wonder is that our intentions remained so good. Nevertheless, good intentions plus the Marshall Plan cannot undo the damage which has been done. Marshall Plan aid greatly stimulated economic recovery in France and Italy without seeing that it was sufficiently shared by workers and peasants.

The passing years seem to increase the probability that Germany, broken as she was by utter defeat and unconditional surrender will, nevertheless, be a decisive factor in Europe's fate. The cold war demands that the Russian and the western blocs bid for German support. French and Polish fears on their respective sides may check but will not stop this process.

Concerning the success of democratization in that part of Germany under the western powers, there were by midcentury varying opinions, most of them not too optimistic. Yet in North Rhine–Westphalia, wherein lies the Ruhr, the election of June, 1950, showed surprisingly small percentages for communism or neofascism. A majority favored socialization of Ruhr industries.

Russian tactics had made hatred of communism widespread, but Russia was in a position more easily than the West to assure a reunion of a divided Germany, a fact of immeasurable value to German communism.

Unquestionably Nazism is not spiritually dead in Germany, and fascism is not spiritually dead in Europe. Most Americans had expected too much from military occupation. They forgot the obvious facts. Here are some of them. To masses of Germans their defeat seemed the outcome of overwhelming physical force, not of moral might. Military occupation preceded by indiscriminate bombing of cities, and followed by equally indiscriminate destruction of German industrial potentials through the dismantling of factories and other procedures, does not teach democracy or respect for its nominal exponents. Still less did Allied acquiescence in the communist displacement of more millions of refugees, this time of Germanic blood, than Hitler had had time to displace teach enlightened humanity and regard for the dignity of the individual.

As time went on American policy toward Germany improved. We kept the Germans alive; provisioned and fed West Berlin despite the Russian blockade by a remarkable airlift; extended Marshall Plan aid and gave great power to the duly elected German government of the Western Zones. We gave freedom to German democratic socialists to organize and agitate. But our general economic policies, notably in the Ruhr, gave aid and comfort to a return of the very capitalism which had gladly supported Nazism and probably would again if circumstances should favor it.

The Germans still constitute the largest and most industrially proficient national bloc on the European continent outside Russia. Their intelligent and cooperative support is invaluable to the western nations.

In Western Germany today the one force most definitely anti-totalitarian and pro-democratic is the revived German Social Democratic Party, which, however, is passionately devoted to a reunited Germany. It proved its quality in leading Berlin's opposition to Russian intimidation. Its integration into a unified movement for democracy and socialism is imperative for European health and, therefore, of vast importance to the United States.

To this truth democratic socialists in the rest of Europe generally agree, but the progress toward the reestablishment of a democratic, nondictatorial, Socialist International, like progress toward a United States of Europe, continues to be painfully slow.

In many respects the physical recovery of western Europe in the five years following the war has been remarkable. There is no equivalent moral recovery. European capitalism, perforce, has accepted immense controls from national states even under more or less conservative governments. Its conduct in Italy, France, and Western Germany shows how stubbornly it clings to profit and power and how real a fact a confused class conflict remains. By no means is communism permanently defeated in western Europe.

In Asia its victories have been amazing. Democracy, having defeated Japanese autocracy, is generally on the defensive. China is taken over by the communists. They wage aggressive war in Korea. Communism is everywhere a threat, although in India, Japan, and perhaps Indonesia there are signs of real strength in a democratic-socialist movement among the people. That movement is handicapped by hunger, overpopulation, and the lack of experience with democracy. It is even more handicapped by the failure of the western powers from the Cairo conference onward to prepare in time a positive program to supplant the old colonial imperialism and forestall Stalin's new communist imperialism. In a later chapter we shall discuss the bearing of these facts on peace.

Chapter 7

Socialism in the British Commonwealth

WHEN Great Britain immediately after the war, to the immense surprise of the American public, gave a decisive majority to the Labour Party over Winston Churchill and his Conservative cohorts, it was an event of extraordinary significance for democratic socialism everywhere and something of a shock to conventional opinion in America.

To be sure, socialist parties had long constituted the governments in New Zealand and Australia. In Canada, a democratic-socialist party, the Cooperative Commonwealth Federation, had successfully administered the affairs of the predominantly agrarian province of Saskatchewan for a year. These facts were important but they did not greatly disturb the peace of mind of the most fearful lovers of "free enterprise" as "the American way of life." Not even the National Association of Manufacturers believed that these British Commonwealths were going communist or cru-

cifying freedom. In practice they were using a democratic state
in the interest of predominantly agricultural society. When in
1948 labor or socialist governments, first in New Zealand and then
in Australia, were defeated, the victors were committed to change
nothing important that their predecessors had done. In both cases
they promised to increase old-age pensions. Australian socialism
has been hampered by the nature of the Australian constitution
and, to be frank, by the racism of Australian socialists. But the
Labour Party after the election was still stronger than any party
in the coalition which defeated it. The very fact that these socialist
parties could be defeated after holding office in New Zealand for
fourteen and in Australia for eight years, was clear proof of
socialist respect for freedom and the multiparty system. In these
countries, as in Sweden, Denmark, and Norway, the facts of history made the poor jest, "the difference between communism and
socialism is five years," obviously and ridiculously false.

But socialism in Great Britain, mother of capitalists, long banker
and workshop for the world, the great imperial power of the nineteenth century, was another matter. The excitement which it
stirred up still continues and the confusion of judgment of the
English performance which persists in America would be funny
if it was not essentially so serious.

Thus, in March, 1949, so able a journal as *Fortune* in a leading
article, "Socialism by Default," written by one of its editors,
John Davenport, discovered a virtual identity between Truman's
program in America and the British Labour version of socialism.
Both were "soft socialism" and both led necessarily to the totalitarian state. By May, 1950, another editor, John Jessup, was writing in the same magazine that Britain was recovering but not by
socialism. All the credit belonged to the capitalist segment of the
economy. This despite the facts: (1) that the Labour government
was still in power although by a reduced majority; and (2) that
the Conservative Party was thoroughly committed to a welfare
program of the sort that the Luce publications vehemently op-

posed in America. *Fortune* has never condescended to harmonize its gospels.

If these things were done by *Fortune*, it is easy to understand the confusion of the ordinary press and politicians. America needed Britain increasingly as an ally in the cold war, yet these brethren could not afford to admit any virtue in socialism. When the dollar crisis became acute in 1949, the reasons had little to do with the socialist government as that able nonsocialist journal, the *Economist*, pointed out. But some American editors saw a great chance to use the British stick to beat the American dog. Thus, the Scripps-Howard press prefaced a long series of articles which did it no journalistic credit with a statement that for all the billions America allegedly lost in trying to help Britain, "we still can get value received. England can provide us priceless lessons of experience, if we will only study them. She has been carrying out on a vast scale social and political and economic schemes on which we also either have started or with which we are flirting."

Generally speaking the American press rejoiced when the Conservatives under Mr. Churchill reduced the Labour Party majority to a very narrow margin in the election of 1950. Few of our papers bothered to tell their readers that the Conservative Party program went much farther in the service of the welfare state than Truman's program, which they had denounced as socialistic. In fact, too many editors, congressmen, and others bothered very little about facts in Britain. In discussions I've heard them make them up as they went along. But some editors and other defenders of "free enterprise" were uneasily aware of the Conservative position in England and its significance. In radio discussions with me, John T. Flynn, literary hero of the National Association of Manufacturers, and Herman Steinkraus, then president of the National Chamber of Commerce, contended in effect that England had long ago abolished true capitalism of the American sort, a "competitive capitalism"—illustrated, I suppose, by the strength of our private monopolies. Indeed I was at times driven to conclude that no

Britishers but only their American critics could save Britain, the mother of capitalism.

This confusion of thought, or what passes for thought, in America did not arise from confusion of action in Britain. On the contrary, the Labour Party had the unique distinction of carrying out in its first five years the program which it had presented to the electorate in 1945. The Conservative Party by 1950 was equally precise in promising to keep everything the Labour Party had done except that it would stop the process of nationalizing steel. In brief, it promised to do more for the people and tax them less.

This general acceptance of the welfare state in Britain by no means meant that between 1945 and 1950 all Britain's urgent economic and social problems had been solved. Definitely it remains to be seen whether under any government, or any political system, a nation of forty-nine million people can live well on an island a little larger than the State of New York which is compelled to import four-fifths of its raw materials and half its food. England lived relatively well even after it was no longer the chief workshop of the modern world because of its immense holdings in foreign countries, holdings cut about in half by the Second World War. It is now compelled to pay for its necessary imports almost entirely by exports. It must do this against competition in a world still in the grip of nationalist psychology and nationalist economics.

Nevertheless, since the war, with American aid, Britain has maintained practically full employment; it has increased its production over 1938 by some 30 per cent, the best record in western Europe. American aid, the British might well argue, was due them not only for standing alone so long in World War II at such cost to themselves, but also for constituting the front line in the cold war against the Soviet Union and its satellites. Britain is a rampart far stronger than any country on the European continent.

To say that Britain's principal economic problems are inherent in its geographical and historic position is not to assert that the application of the socialist platform has completely fulfilled socialist dreams and has raised no problems for socialists to examine. The contrary is the case. In the British laboratory one may with care distinguish between problems peculiar to Britain and those inherent in the working out of democratic socialism. Some of the latter problems we shall list before this chapter is ended.

But first let us take a longer look at history. In retrospect it is clear that the Labour victory in 1945 was an enormous boon to mankind. A Conservative victory at the war's end might well have been a body blow to the democratic cause in western Europe.

Consider, for instance, how unlikely it is that Winston Churchill, that old lion of empire, could have done what Clement Attlee did: grant India her independence on terms and in a spirit which led Nehru to keep India in some sort of shadowy relation to the British Commonwealth of Nations. Under Churchill's continued rule India, and probably Burma and Ceylon, would have been added to the sore spots which actively threaten the health of the world.[1]

In Western Europe the effect of the socialist victory was enormous. It suggested to masses of workers that there was an alternative on the one hand to communist tyranny and on the other to reaction or to a neofascist despotism. It was a visible sign that democracy could be used in orderly fashion to effectuate profound and important changes in a social system. The very fact that in England itself the triumphant workers were compelled by conditions to endure austerity and that they accepted those conditions in so orderly a fashion gave mankind a practical ground for faith in democracy on a scale nowhere else to be found. If between 1945 and 1948 a British social order had been as turbulent and insecure as it was in France and Italy, it is a moral certainty that communism would have taken over Europe to the English Channel.

Meanwhile at home the Labour government did the most Chris-

---

[1] Bevin and the Labour government did far less well in handling the difficult problem of Palestine, but in the end they assented to the establishment of independent Israel.

tian job in recorded history in making goods in short supply available to those who needed them most. It obtained a high degree of trade-union approval of its so-called austerity program and an agreement not to press for general wage increases. On the other hand, in the much derided but very popular public-health program, its housing and educational programs, it added substantially to the real income of the masses.

Its most questionable acts were the controls it set up over the "direction" of workers to jobs. Frankly these were emergency measures, approved by the Trade Union Council and abandoned early in 1950.

Still later in the same year the Labour cabinet found it possible to drop a great deal of the rationing of goods by which it had enforced austerity. The American press saw in this just a political move in anticipation of a new general election, a "stealing of Churchill's thunder," an "appeal to the middle class." Perhaps these considerations entered in but it is fair to remember that even the most leftist of British socialists had agreed with the austere Sir Stafford Cripps that these controls were born of emergency needs, not of socialist philosophy.

Its first program of social ownership was carried out by Labour's nationalizing the Bank of England, the badly managed coal mines, and the railroads, with generally satisfactory but not miraculous results. It also set in motion the nationalization of steel.

In socializing these industries and services British socialism suffered acutely from the paradoxical fact that, to work well, socialism like any economic system needs generally healthy conditions, while it is only unhealthy conditions which lead people belatedly to call in the socialist doctor. Thus the government had to get increased production of coal before it could modernize the machinery of the mines, which had been allowed to deteriorate shockingly under private ownership.

Making allowances for these facts, it is true that socialist experience in Britain brought out clearly problems which, with greater or less intensity, will face all democratic socialism.

The most obvious of these problems is sometimes expressed in the cynical conviction that since "there will always be bosses," *i.e.*, managers, social ownership will never appeal to the workers. It is true that there have been unrest and occasional wildcat strikes in nationalized industries in Britain and that the acceptance of responsibility for production by the workers has been less than optimistic socialists had hoped. But it is also true that conditions have improved in nationalized industries and that in general under the Labour government the man days lost in strikes have been far fewer than after World War I or than would have been the case if the Conservatives had won.

To American socialists the British provisions for consumer and worker representatives on public authorities seem inadequate. The explanation which the British socialists offer is that the workers have to be first educated to the desire and capacity for administrative responsibility and hence the government was constrained to begin with advisory councils.

Unquestionably there has been some feeling in the unions that life was simpler and maybe better when their job was to fight the boss without worrying about production and the effect of strikes upon the whole economy. But that feeling has not prevailed, and on the whole the wonder is that the change from the climate of conflict into which trade unionism was born into the climate of responsibility has gone as well as it has.

Nevertheless, the fate of democratic socialism depends largely on farther development both of a sense of responsibility among the workers and of machinery of control for its exercise.

British experience has brought to light two problems not automatically solved by any text of socialist scriptures. First, what constitutes fair compensation for owners of industries which are socialized? How avoid the danger that owners of a sick industry will be pensioned off at a higher cost to society than if they were compelled to accept the risk of failure under private enterprise? These questions are often broadened out to the general inquiry:

will not a dynamic economy be dangerously burdened by the political necessity of keeping big industries going despite economic considerations?

We shall be better able to suggest answers to these questions after further inquiry into problems of capitalism and socialism. Certainly we socialists may rightfully insist that compensation to owners should as a rule be related to the prosperity of the industry rather than of the whole country and that all bonds should be amortized within a reasonable time.

Second, what constitutes a fair wage, particularly in a socialized industry, and how can it be determined?

Obviously not mechanically by any formula yet discovered. In Britain, as in America, collective bargaining represents a way of arriving at wage settlements. It never achieves absolute fairness in ethical terms, and as the be-all and end-all of union procedure it tends to narrow workers' loyalties to a syndicalist concern for their own industry. Under private ownership it encourages manager and worker alliance to soak the consumer in the interest of higher prices and higher wages. Nevertheless, collective bargaining today, as reinforced by minimum-wage provisions under law, presents the nearest practicable approach to giving workers some control over the conditions and rewards of their work. If it cannot be absolute, it should not be completely abandoned in socialized industries. Indeed it cannot be abandoned if socialism is to keep the workers' support. Since strikes, the ultimate recourse of workers, raise fewer problems in private than in socialized industry and since in some essential industries and services (which in Britain are pretty well socialized), where even temporary discontinuance of service imposes inconvenience and peril on the public, strikes will not be lightly countenanced by any responsible government, there is a strong case for keeping a segment of industry under private ownership in which collective bargaining may more easily set standards for all general wage agreements.

This is not a rejection of socialism as modern socialists conceive it. If Britain has not found a final answer to this wage problem, the claim of her government that even in years of necessary austerity it has been able to match increases in production by increases in social and individual income for the workers seems well-grounded. Indeed, it was confirmed by the findings of Findley Weaver, an American economist attached to the Embassy, summarized in the *New York Times*, August 23, 1950, that British workers enjoyed a 22 per cent increase in consumers' goods over the prewar standard and that this increase was mostly due to increased production and full employment. High taxes had heavily cut the real income of the wealthy and to a less extent the middle class, but taxes and the redistribution of the national income had not destroyed incentives, as was proved by the overall increase in production.

I am less puzzled by British socialist difficulties with wage problems than by Labour's neglect in promise and performance of that nationalization of land long dear to the heart of British socialists. For a good many years, British socialists and laborites were inclined to accept the Henry George principle of the expropriation of the rental value of land by a tax as the primary element in asserting social claim to land. But almost nothing has been heard of it under the Labour government.

Yet from all sorts of angles the land problem is pressing in Britain. For centuries it was preeminently true in that country, as Lloyd George used to say, that to prove one's legal title to land one must trace it back to the man who stole it. Highhanded land enclosures in the eighteenth century were a major factor in driving landless men into the factories. Land ownership is still highly concentrated.

At the same time in that crowded island land is scarce and precious. It is needed for conflicting purposes. Much good agricultural land must be sacrificed to the growth of urban areas and the desire of the people for well-ordered suburbs. More is necessary to supply parks and recreation for a growing population. At the same time, an increase of the domestic supply of food is vital. These problems are interrelated yet the tendency has been to treat agriculture and town and country planning as separate matters.

In both fields something good has been done. The theory and practice of town and country planning are far more advanced than in the United States, and theoretically at least the government has asserted the right of the nation to the unearned increment arising from the *future* development of land.

In agriculture much power was given to the Minister of Agriculture in the interests of a program of "stability and efficiency." All parties in Britain have agreed to controls to achieve these ends which have been bitterly and often unfairly attacked by American critics in the name of "free enterprise." There has been genuine improvement in agricultural production, despite some irritation at "bureaucratic control." There has not been the correlation one would expect between the Ministry of Food and the Ministry of Agriculture. By and large a final socialist answer to Britain's land problem is yet to be found.[2]

Underlying many of the Labour government's difficulties are the differences in interest between workers and middle-class folk. These differences are not by any means wholly a matter of pounds and shillings. It is true that the process of socialization and high taxation, largely a result of the cost of wars past and prospective, have brought the virile British middle class some economic loss less compensated by social income than in the case of the workers. The middle class in considerable numbers supported the Labour Party in 1945 and must continue to support it if democratic socialism is to succeed on its own terms. That class also has much to gain from peace, security, and a well-ordered society. But class divisions have produced differences in loyalties and ideals between the workers and the middle class. The former have painfully learned solidarity in their unions through struggle. Their loyalties

[2] On this complicated subject I refer readers to Robert Brady: *Crisis in Britain, Plans and Achievements of the Labour Government* (University of California), a mine of information apparently fairly presented. I do not, however, wholly agree with the author's standards of judgment or his application of them.

are less individualistic than those of the middle class. On the other hand, the middle class, especially in Britain, has felt a high sense of responsibility to the country and its interests—even if too often it has seen them through the spectacles of class interest. It has developed more critical judgment and probably a somewhat keener concern for individual liberty than the workers.

There is bound, therefore, to be a difference in the approach of these two classes to social problems. Thus, middle-class indignation at what seemed unjustified strikes of working dockers in two successive years had much justification. Yet the dockers' strikes bore testimony to a capacity for loyalty. One year it was because the workers believed that they were being asked to unload a Canadian "black leg" ship, that is, a ship whose union men had struck and been replaced with others. (Actually some questions of union jurisdiction in Canada were involved.) The next year they struck because some of their number were disciplined. Communists doubtless ably exploited grievances and, to a certain extent, led the strikes. With both of them the government finally coped without resort to such extreme measures as capitalist America has on occasion used or as communist Russia would have used. But back of these disquieting strikes was a fine although inadequate and ill-informed loyalty of workers to their fellows, a loyalty which long experience in struggle had exalted to the first principle of their ethical code. Clearly what is needed here is education in loyalties.

The nature of these loyalties and the political and economic machinery appropriate to them we shall be better able to determine when we have examined more carefully the general conditions of democracy, the failures of capitalism, and the strength of the socialist answer in terms of wider application than to British problems. In that examination, no thinker can afford to ignore an honest facing of British achievements between 1945 and 1950.

On the eve of the Korean war, those achievements had brought a relief from austerities and economic tensions rather beyond the earlier expectations of foreign friends and critics. In July, 1946,

Professor Joseph Schumpeter had written: "In the United States alone there need not lurk, behind modern programs of social betterment, that fundamental dilemma that everywhere else paralyzes the will of every responsible man, the dilemma between economic progress and immediate increase of the real income of the masses." [3]

That judgment holds true, I think, in Britain and everywhere else, but in the United Kingdom the possibility that the dilemma would be manageable looked bright at the end of June, 1950. Then came the Korean war and the necessity of a degree of armament that would once more strain British economy and make probable a return to austerity. This is a prospect that a Labour government could better make endurable than could the Conservatives. But should the latter return to power in the shadow of war, it would be even more certain than in happier circumstances that their government would not and could not return to anything like the old capitalism or repudiate the welfare state.

The increased international tension which threatens further progress in British social welfare emphasizes comparative failure of the British in one important field. They have contributed little to a powerful socialist internationalism or to a possible United States of Europe. The socialist leaders have displayed no genius in overcoming the very real obstacles which would confront any British government, and especially a socialist government, in working toward economic and political unity with western Europe. In judging this matter, we Americans should remember that historically and geographically Britain's position is different from the French. Her obligations to the British Commonwealth are real. When Count Coudenhove-Kalergi first aroused interest in a United States of Europe back in the twenties, he contemplated a United States of Europe which should lie between the Russian boundary and the English Channel. He thought of it as a kind of balance in a world family of nations to the other great groups, the Union of Socialist Soviet Republics, the United States of America and its

[3] Third edition of Joseph A. Schumpeter's now classic *Capitalism, Socialism, and Democracy* (Harper), p. 384.

hemispheric allies, and the British Commonwealth of Nations. In his mind the conditions did not then exist which now make it necessary for Britain to be integrated in the United States of Europe. Today the situation is greatly changed partly because of communist division of Europe.

Integration is not made easier when there is a sharp difference of economic standards and ideas between the nations concerned. A more or less democratic capitalism and democratic socialism can coexist in the world but it is very hard to unify for the first time nations with different economies. I realized that with new force when I heard M. Paul Reynaud at a dinner of supporters of a United States of Europe in New York cleverly tie up federation with an attack on the British socialist control of prices as against free enterprise which should dominate an economic union worth having. His conservative audience loved it. But his attitude made me better understand British caution on such a proposal as the Schuman plan for a coal and iron pool under a supranational authority.

Yet here again it is likely that grim realization of defense requirements will prod Britain, like other western European nations, to greater progress toward an integration upon which the ultimate hope of escape from communist conquest may depend.

Chapter 8

Socialism in America

IN THE EVENTS I have been describing, I have often referred to the role of the United States of America. But I have not discussed social developments in it. The story is important and doesn't follow the Marxist rules.

By any simple interpretation of the Marxist formula the United States, by all odds the greatest of industrial nations and that in which capitalism is most advanced, should have had long ere this a very strong socialist movement, if not a socialist revolution. Actually, in no advanced western nation is organized socialism so weak. Its indirect influence has been greater and is increasing, but it is not what the Marxist formula would lead one to expect.

This weakness of socialism is not due to the fact that fascist or communist collectivism has fallen heir to capitalist collapse. Between the two world wars, there were fascist elements in America which, however, neither then nor since have coalesced into a strong fascist movement. American communism achieved considerable power through indirect influence rather than through numerical strength. But rumor has it that Stalin is scornful of the weakness of his American party. The richest nation in the world and the most industrialized proclaims its faith in "free enterprise," which it rejects in practice. Its actual economy would puzzle Alexander Hamilton, but it is still avowedly capitalist.

Three major factors explain this phenomenon. They may be properly described as economic, sociological, and political.

The economic factor is the relative success of American capitalism until our own day. That success is failure measured by what we have a right to expect in view of richness of the American endowment and man's mastery over natural forces and machines. American capitalism has not conquered poverty; still less has it averted depressions which on the average have been sharper and more extreme than in European countries prior to World War II. Nevertheless, the American economic system, predominantly capitalist, has been able to provide the highest standard of living in the world and to open far more doors of opportunity to the ambitious, enterprising, and fortunate than any other nation.

In this it was powerfully aided by historic circumstance as well as by the extent of its resources. Capitalism in Europe developed out of feudal restraints. Capitalism in Europe antedated the coming of the age of power-driven machinery and was somewhat backward in applying the newest inventions and discoveries of science. Capitalism in America grew up with the machine age. It was American capitalism which developed mass production on a scale of which earlier economists, *laissez-faire* or collectivist, could not dream. Mass production, as Henry Ford was perhaps the first great industrialist dimly to understand, requires mass consumption, which in turn requires high wages. The productivity of capitalism and the successful pressures of organized workers refuted the iron law of wages even in Europe, but it took mass production to make it partially plain to the American managerial if not the owning class that goods produced on an assembly line, from soft drinks to automobiles, not only make possible a high standard of living for the masses but demand it if factories are to keep going. No small owning class, however wildly luxurious might be its standards of living, could possibly purchase or use what American machines can produce.

Recognition that continuance of production requires high purchasing power never went far enough to make the managers of private monopolies and oligopolies understand the kind of planning necessary for steady prosperity. The worship of profits stood in the way. So we had the curious phenomenon that the world-wide depression of the thirties, in terms of unemployment, was most marked and most chronic in the United States. But such was the productivity of the American system that the unemployed, through made work and home relief, received a better living than regularly employed workers enjoyed in the "socialist" paradise of the U.S.S.R.

A second reason for the strength of the American economy was its continental scope. The United States had within its own borders the richest free-trade area in the world in respect both to resources and markets. It knew what it could count on without reference to the manipulations of tariff makers or the restraints of fortified boundaries. The European continent had no such good fortune and it was the wisdom of the Founding Fathers, statesmen rather than business men, which gave American economy this blessing. For its rapid growth American industry owed far more to free trade at home in a demilitarized federal union than to protection by high tariffs against foreign competition.

An even more important difference between European and American capitalism was the American tradition which gave the healthy, ambitious, and reasonably lucky young men of the farming and working classes a better chance to rise out of their class than with it.

It is the restless minority which always takes the initiative in social and economic change. Europe was a settled continent without "frontiers" in the American sense. The aristocratic and feudal tradition was carried over into capitalism so that it was very hard for the sons of workers to get the education they needed for the professions, including engineering, or to rise into the managerial class. By comparison the road was easier in America. There was a rags-to-riches, log-cabin-to-White House, poor-boys-who-became-famous tradition in America which, however exaggerated, emphasized a substantial kernel of truth. Until late in the nineteenth century the westward-moving frontier spelled opportunity. Both before and after the geographic frontier was no more, American industry kept a sharper eye out for talent among its workers than its British or Continental counterpart. A large proportion of its generals, colonels, and captains, as well as its sergeants, was drawn from boys who made their way up from farm, office, and factory. Of course, there were many failures but, by the time the ambitious man had sensed that failure, he was usually too old and dispirited to become an active leader in the radical or labor movement.

American labor has had some exceptional leaders, but it has only been in very recent times that either the labor or the farm movement seemed to offer to young men a satisfactory form of lifework with tolerable economic security and a chance to fulfill an honorable ambition. Able young men were neither driven by desperation nor enticed by opportunity into the American labor and radical movements. Here lay, I think, the greatest single explanation of the comparative weakness both of organized labor and of the radical movement in the United States. It is a weakness that, in respect to the labor movement, has ended with the rapid rise of powerful unions in the last fifteen years.

The second or sociological factor in the slow growth of socialism is closely related to the economic. It is that in the United States, even more than in western Europe, there was the rise of what has been called the sociological middle class, which early Marxists did not anticipate. Capitalism has been able to pay very satisfactory wages to a managerial class. Strictly speaking, managers are workers for hire; certainly they are not self-employers, but the size of their incomes and the nature of their work have tended to identify them in interest with owners rather than workers. Thanks to the extension of shareholding in that remarkable economic invention, the impersonal stock corporation, managers are also to a certain extent owners—by no means necessarily in the enterprises in which they are employed.

Marx was mistaken in his estimate of the rapidity and completeness of the disappearance of an economic middle class. He was even more mistaken in his failure to anticipate the strength of the sociological middle class. Sometimes that class has lined up with big owners in a curious disregard of its own long-run economic interest. There never was an economic man who instinctively saw where his profit lay and acted solely to advance it. There always have been men who wanted profit and material gain but who saw their interest through the distorting spectacles of faulty education, prejudice, and all sorts of emotions.

The third factor in the slow development of *organized* socialism in the United States was and is political. Not only our framework of government but our rules concerning political parties make it extremely difficult for a new party to grow to major dimensions. Since the rise of the Republican Party under conditions which have not recurred, there has been no successful development of a third party in terms of continuing numerical strength. Many so-called third parties, Populist, Prohibition, Progressive, and Socialist, have appeared. Some of them have elected local officials and even congressmen. Collectively, they have had a disproportionate influence upon state and national legislation, but none of them has come near to power in a Presidential campaign. Most of them have been absorbed again into the amorphous Democratic and Republican parties, whose power to absorb contradictory elements often has seemed proportional to their lack of principle. This is a situation which I have found that few foreign observers understand.

It arises primarily from the fact that we do not have a parliamentary but a presidential government. In parliamentary democracies, it was only necessary for a socialist or labor party to elect a few representatives and make a good record. Their representation could rapidly snowball. In the United States, every four years the election of all members of Congress is subordinate to the election of the President. It is only the exceptional man in an exceptional situation who can command much individual attention for his own campaign for Congress or even the United States Senate in a Presidential year. Often the average congressional candidate can scarcely get audiences at his own meetings and the money he and his party spend on broadcasts for him is largely wasted.

From time to time liberal, progressive, and radical blocs have risen in the House of Representatives and the Senate, but they never have yet preserved a continuing momentum, much less grown into a political party, because every four years they have had to subordinate their principles and program to the question: which of the two major party contenders for the Presidency would they support? Presidential candidates, able men or mediocrities for whom all the people have a chance to vote, absorb the popular interest in elections. More and more that interest has boiled down into a choice between major candidates because anything else was "throwing away your vote." One could argue stridently or eloquently that there is no worse way to throw away your vote than to vote for what you don't want and get it; that minority parties and protest votes have had an influence on American politics so great that their supporters were, in a sense, far more important figures on the political scene than an equal number of the mob who voted Republican or Democratic. It made small impression. Even Gene Debs, a romantic and beloved figure among workers, never got more than a million votes—that were counted—and that in a year when he was unjustly confined to prison and his major opponents were those complete mediocrities, Harding and Cox. My vote in 1932 and Henry Wallace's in 1948 can only be explained (as over against the popular interest in our campaigns) by this obsession of the voters with the two-party system.

If Americans could vote for a President on a preferential ballot in which their second choices would count toward a majority once their first choices were eliminated, the results might have been very different. But actually Americans who concentrate almost all their political interest on the Presidential campaign cannot vote directly for President at all. They vote, state by state, for members of the Electoral College who, in the plan of the framers of the Constitution—a plan which was a dead letter from the beginning—would then, in their wisdom, choose the best man for President. Each state has as many electors as it has senators and congressmen. To make matters worse, so far as the democracy of the Presidential election is concerned, the winning party in each state takes all the electors. A plurality of one vote in New York State is as good as a million. It delivers all forty-seven electors to the victor.

Moreover, disproportionate representation of sparsely populated states and Southern discrimination against Negroes result in grave violations of the principle "one man, one vote" when it comes to the election of the President. Thus, in 1948, one voter in South Carolina had almost the weight of eight voters in New York in the Presidential election.

As a result of these things, the United States can have and has had Presidents duly elected by a majority of the Electoral College who were in the minority in the popular vote. The last example was Benjamin Harrison. It is quite the usual thing for defeated candidates or their supporters to calculate with what a relatively small shift of votes in certain states they might have been elected without having achieved a popular majority. This sort of thing is fraught with danger in the American system and a fear of it operates emotionally against a third-party candidate.[1]

This fear is given additional support by the further fact that under the Constitution, if no candidate should get a majority of the Electoral College, the election is thrown into the House of Representatives where each state, New York with its 13,000,000 inhab-

[1] For developments in the campaign of 1948 and afterwards which bear on this problem, see Chapter 17.

itants, and Nevada with 110,000 (census of 1940), would be entitled
to one vote. In the campaign of 1924, the cry, "a vote for La Follette [the Progressive and Socialist candidate that year] is a vote to
send the election into the House of Representatives," lost that vigorous campaigner hundreds of thousands of votes, thereby greatly
discouraging what had looked like a strong movement toward a
mass farmer-labor party in America.

To these Constitutional handicaps to the rise of a third party
must be added the historic situation which, at least until 1948, gave
us that political anomaly, a Democratic Party based on a solid
South predominantly Protestant, conservative, and fearful for
white supremacy and, in a far less solid North, on municipal machines usually rather corrupt, predominantly Catholic in religion,
fairly radical or progressive in politics, and relatively free of racial
or nationalistic prejudice. (That is to say, the party organization
in urban areas must achieve a kind of balance of various prejudices
or loyalties of different hyphenated American and racial groups
which makes for some tolerance at the same time that it diverts
attention from sound programs for progress.)

Each political party, moreover, is in reality less of a national
organization than a federation of forty-eight state parties with a
common name and a common interest in winning office at Washington—scarcely more. Each state has its own rules and from 1912
on, when the big Bull Moose scared the politicians (and especially
after 1932), the tendency in many states has been to make and
interpret election laws so as to monopolize the ballot for the two
old parties. It is exceedingly difficult and expensive in such important states as Ohio, Illinois, and California for minority parties
to stay on the ballot or to get on by petition.

Indeed, in those states and many others the law has so many
tricky provisions that a rigid enforcement of it by hostile administrators can be used completely to deny effective choice to
voters, except as between the major candidates. This, for example,
happened in New York, whose law is not one of the worst, in the
campaign of 1946. It was not "reactionary" Republicans, but

"liberal" Democrats, with the full knowledge and consent of such professedly ardent liberals as Herbert Lehman,[2] formerly governor and then candidate for the United States Senate, and James Mead, candidate for governor, who were so desperately anxious to win an election that they managed to have all those minor parties thrown off the state ballot which had nominated independent candidates for governor and United States Senator. This, they were able to do because a divided Court of Appeals upheld a rigid interpretation of the law. Thus, in certain counties nominating petitions, honestly signed but collected by a canvasser whose own election district was inadvertently misstated on the papers, were held invalid. Since the law required a minimum of fifty valid signatures in each county to nominate for state-wide offices, the Socialist Party was barred from the ballot. Other minor parties on similar technicalities were kept off. But no technicalities were seriously invoked against the Liberal and Communist parties. The first had endorsed Mead and Lehman; the second had withdrawn its candidates against them.

The final political factor which militates against the rise of a third party is our American system of nomination by popular vote through primaries—a system which has no parallel in other western democracies. Here again one must deal not with a uniform law but with forty-eight state laws, some of which are deliberately framed to encourage the hope that a popular rising of voters, not necessarily registered as Republicans or Democrats, may capture one or another of the old parties for a favored candidate. It is this primary system which from time to time has made possible the election of progressive officials, even congressmen, and the rise, for longer or shorter periods, of relatively progressive groups to the control of the state political machine of one or another of the major parties. It was the very clever manipulation of this primary system in both old parties by the Anti-Saloon League which

---

[2] The former governor redeemed himself by his courageous rebuke to Cardinal Spellman for the latter's attack on Mrs. Eleanor Roosevelt and by his vote against the McCarran bill.

made possible the passage of the Prohibition Amendment. All of this gives color of political realism to the argument of those radicals who say, "It is easier to capture an old party than to build a new one"—an opinion greatly strengthened by the circumstances of Truman's victory in 1948. We shall return to this when we are ready to discuss what ought to be the new tactics of the Socialist Party. Here I emphasize it as one of the major reasons for the failure of any social or radical party to grow to strength in America.

For the slow growth of organized socialism there have been other causes than the major economic, sociological, and political factors which we have discussed. The rise of a socialist or even a militant labor movement has been handicapped in the United States by chattel slavery and the gross racial discrimination which was by no means ended by the Civil War. Thousands of very poor white farmers and workers thought of themselves as members of a dominant race, even when they were sharing an economic exploitation almost as bitter as that to which their colored fellow citizens were subject. I shall never forget the gloom of an old-time socialist in Birmingham, Alabama, when the depression of the thirties was near its lowest depth. He told me that he had asked some of the unemployed white men whether they would rather the government should offer all the unemployed, white and black alike, jobs at $4.00 a day, or a differential scale under which the white would get $3.50 and the colored $3.00. The majority preferred the latter arrangement.

I always found it difficult to believe that that would be the reaction to a real test and fortunately the growth of better racial feeling among workers in recent years has been marked. The C.I.O. especially has contributed much to it. Nevertheless, the exploitation of racial feeling is still an important resource to an owning class.

Immigration prior to its drastic limitation had a double effect on American socialism. It brought ardent socialists to our shores but it checked the growth of a homogeneous working class. Linguistic and nationalistic differences loomed large among workers and were systematically exploited by many bosses.

Another reason for slow growth of socialism in America between the two wars was the conviction that countries where socialists or communists held office were worse rather than better off than America. Roosevelt, we socialists often were told, was making a better job of it than did Ramsay MacDonald. Our explanations might have been sound; they commanded little attention from the workers.

None of this acquits American socialism of responsibility for its own failures and shortcomings, especially in the field of organization. Gene Debs's death in 1926 deprived the Party of a leader with an extraordinary appeal to the masses. After his release from the Atlanta Penitentiary, where he had spent some time for his Canton speech criticizing the war, he was the object of widespread affection, but the state of his health and other factors prevented his recovering in the postwar period the leadership which he had formerly exerted. He had no successor in popular affection.

The Party which suffered from his loss had previously suffered severely under the extraordinary persecution which, during and after World War I, did so much to mar the record of the Wilson Administration as the champion of freedom or democracy. It suffered even more from the communist split.

In the thirties the Party went through a period of internal strife, of which the principal but not the sole cause was the vexing question of the theoretical and practical relations of socialism and communism. The failure of German social democracy, the great depression, and too great faith in Russian progress, supplied fertile soil for controversy. By one of history's jests the right wing which left the Party in 1936, alleging that it was too favorably inclined to communism, soon found itself working in New York State, however unhappily, with communists in support of Roosevelt, through the medium of the American Labor Party, while the main body of the Party, finally disillusioned by the purge trials, went its way in complete opposition to the communists.

I am, of course, an interested witness since so much of my life was bound up with the Party and I have been six times its candidate for President. Nevertheless, I am seriously of the opinion that neither our mistakes nor our internal misfortunes were much greater than those of socialist parties in other lands in the same period. The numerical decline in membership and in votes had, I think, little direct connection with our internal trouble. Thus, in 1934, when factional feeling was at its height in the Socialist Party in New York State, I got the highest vote the Party ever received for United States Senator, and the Party ticket as a whole did well in terms of the low standard of its past performances. The reason was simply that the swing to Roosevelt had not yet got fully under way.

His personality, his immense courage in managing his physical handicap, and his brilliant political achievements were unquestionably major factors in the arrest of the growth of socialism on the one hand or communism and fascism on the other. He was able to do what he did on a pragmatic program never philosophically critical of the capitalist system because capitalism, under the impact of a depression, accepted reforms for which the development of mass production made it able to pay. Although "the American system" could not end unemployment under the Roosevelt reforms, it could take relatively good care of the unemployed. First and last Roosevelt's role was that of the expert politician—in the better sense of the term—rather than of the constructive thinker.

It would be interesting to know what Marx would have made of the Roosevelt record. In the terrible depression year of 1932 neither his party's platform nor his own elaborations of it differed very greatly from the Republican philosophy as expounded by Herbert Hoover. Some of his strongest points were his condemnation of deficit financing and of Hoover's increase of the size of bureaucracy, especially in the appointment of various committees to which he referred problems.

The people were in an angry mood. Their failure consciously to adopt a socialist philosophy did not prevent some of the most conservative groups like the farmers from using violence to prevent foreclosures. In the main the masses voted for Roosevelt as the one sure way to dispose of Hoover. There was no such affection for the winner as in 1936 or subsequent years. I shall never forget the sweet-faced little old lady, dressed like Whistler's mother, who waited to speak to me after a late overflow meeting in San Francisco. "Mr. Thomas," she said, "yours is the first socialist speech I ever heard and I like it. But I can't vote for you. Not this year." And the whole expression of her face changed. "Because this year we've got to *get* Hoover." Literally hundreds of people wrote or told me that they had intended to vote socialist until the last minute and then were afraid that that would give the election to Hoover.

In office, as the Republicans loudly asserted, Roosevelt came nearer to carrying out the socialist platform than his own in respect to immediate demands but not in respect to fundamental socialization. It is probable that he sincerely thought that he was reforming capitalism. His New Deal had various phases by no means always consistent with one another, still less with socialism. His National Recovery Administration (the blue eagle) at first helped labor to organize but later, as a visiting Italian journalist enthusiastically told me, it was developing a "corporative" pattern such as Mussolini preached. When the Supreme Court declared it unconstitutional, it gave Roosevelt an issue but also relieved him of an embarrassing setup. He swung over to emphasis on trustbusting, not very successfully carried out. We socialists were very critical of certain features of his fiscal policies and of parts of his agricultural program.

Nevertheless, looking back on the results of his work under pressure of crisis, I think that, after first overcoming a sense of panic in America, he rendered three services of great value. First, he brought America in line with a world-wide trend toward social-security legislation. Second, he gave status and bargaining rights to labor unions. In their gratitude to him, they overlooked things which they would not easily have forgiven another President, like his advocacy of a labor draft in the war. Their instinct was sound in realizing that Roosevelt, under a peculiar set of historical conditions, had given them that which they had not won for themselves. To be sure, he could not and would not have done it without their previous struggle and without their capacity to take advantage of the opportunities that his policies afforded. That able and ruthless organizer and leader of labor, John L. Lewis, essentially Republican in his usual politics, was later to turn from Roosevelt in bitter hatred; yet it was Roosevelt's policy which gave him his chance to rebuild his broken union. In 1936, when Lewis and the union contributed heavily in money and activity to Roosevelt's triumphant reelection, I said to some miners in the anthracite region (where Lewis' popularity was not great for reasons internal to the union), "I suppose Lewis' support means a lot to Roosevelt." To which the answer was, "Hell, no! Roosevelt's support means a lot to John L." After his death, in labor circles Roosevelt's name became a convenient and powerful symbol for "liberalism."

Finally, Mr. Roosevelt performed a great service in restoring popular faith in the possibilities of effective democratic action through the ballot box. Even during the comparative prosperity of the Coolidge epoch there was a widespread and growing disbelief among workers that much could be achieved by political action. The masses had a cynical contempt for the men for whom most of them voted. It was taken for granted that "the interests" or "big business" owned both old parties.

That feeling had much to do with the La Follette movement in 1924, but in general, and especially after the collapse of that movement, the tendency was toward indifference to political action. By no means had the failure of American voters to produce a powerful socialist or communist movement evidenced complete satisfaction with the scheme of things; still less had it meant that Americans were simply content to work through two parties which most of them agreed stood for nothing in particular except desire for office. The direct action tradition of the Boston Tea Party has been strong in American history. One has only to remember such a partial list as this: Shay's Rebellion, the Whiskey Rebellion, Dorr's Rebellion, the "Tin Horn and Calico War" of New York State farmers against the old landholding patroons, the Underground Railroad, John Brown at Harpers Ferry, the Ku Klux Klan both in its earlier and its later form, the I.W.W. with its repudiation of any faith at all in the ballot, and, to bring the story up to date, the militant resistance of the farmers to sheriff's sales and foreclosures between 1930 and 1933.

In my considerable experience with audiences and forums, nothing was more marked than the difference in popular attitude toward the possibility of effective action through a democratically elected government between the time of Roosevelt's first and second election. To have produced that change was a real service to democracy and this service Franklin Roosevelt rendered. It survived his death and helped the people in the interest of liberalism to elect Harry Truman, no Messiah, in the face of a well-organized Republican opposition, backed by wealth and the principal newspapers.

Unfortunately, by the time of Mr. Roosevelt's death he had to a high degree counterbalanced great service to democracy by grave disservice, this by the way he got us into the war and the measures he took and did not take to win a just and lasting peace. It is by now fairly well agreed that Roosevelt deliberately created a situation which made our involvement in war a virtual certainty by measures which he assured the people would keep them out of it. There was a strong case (which I did not accept) that the United States should enter the war openly as a holy crusade in which its own ultimate safety was bound up. The case for the Roosevelt approach to the war, which Pearl Harbor made inescapable, a case which his supporters frequently use, was simply that the people had to be manipulated into the conflict.[3] This sort of case implies a profound distrust in democracy and a willingness to use means

[3] This argument has been stated with unusual candor by Professor Thomas A. Bailey in his book, *The Man in the Street*.

completely inconsistent with the education of the people in reaching straightforward and honest decisions.

Even more hurtful to democracy was the President's approach to the peace. He dropped the inadequate idealism of the Atlantic Charter for the emotional ideal of unconditional surrender, a negative method of capitalizing on war's hates. There is no evidence that he sought to achieve European unity. He certainly sought peace by indiscriminate appeasement of the Soviet dictatorship.

Perhaps the whole task of winning a decent peace settlement was beyond anyone's competence. The point is that in Europe and Asia in the closing years of the war and the first years of post-war confusion, American policy, inspired by Roosevelt, did not even try the roads that might have led to a far better peace than is now possible. Whether by reason of the nature of war itself or his own incapacity, Roosevelt, like Churchill, was a far greater leader for war than for peace. Democracy in the English-speaking nations under their leadership won the war without the imagination or the power to win the peace.

By his domestic policies in the United States, Roosevelt advanced his country toward a pragmatic socialism; he left a weakened socialist organization in a powerful and bewildered country. By his peace policies or lack of them he made the going for democratic socialism or any constructive substitute unnecessarily difficult throughout the world. Still worse, he greatly aided Stalin's drive for power. It is an insufficient defense of his record to say that some other leader might have done worse.

Chapter 9

A Century's Development in
Theories about Mankind

BEFORE considering a program for the future we must turn from external history to a more careful inquiry into man's possibilities.

It is a commonplace long accepted among us mortals that man is at once the hero and villain of his own history. The years which we have been so rapidly reviewing have piled up evidence of the contradictory nature and performance of human beings under the strains of living. Not a single fact would need to be exaggerated in drawing pictures of man but little lower than the angels or no higher than the devils. In the last analysis all theories of social organization, all plans for progress, must reckon with an uncertain human capacity for sustained decency and intelligence. And on this, despite recent gains in our knowledge of ourselves, the wisest philosopher cannot safely dogmatize.

Certainly the hundred years since the promulgation of the *Com-*

munist Manifesto have seen a genuine increase in man's knowledge about himself and his universe. They have created an intellectual climate in which old controversies about the nature of reality, of idea versus matter, have taken very different shape. Not idealist philosophers, but physicists have led us to look for the ultimate explanation of matter in terms of energy best expressed in mathematical formulas. Various pragmatic philosophies have become popular. On man himself and the complex society of which he is a part, biology, psychology, and sociology have shed much light.

But these sciences have by no means united to produce any single comprehensive philosophy, and many of the explanations they offer or suggest are still controversial and contradictory. Scientists are, however, pretty well agreed in discrediting popular generalizations about human nature, and what it will or will not permit us to do or to hope. These generalizations have ranged from affirmations—today seldom heard—of man's infinite perfectibility or educability to sweeping denials of his capacity to achieve any truly good society; from emphasis on freedom to new insistence on various types of determinism in human conduct.

If there is a human nature which determines man's conduct and destiny, the process is far more subtle and obscure than in the case of other animals: ants, bees, wolves, beavers, whose social conduct is instinctively determined. Man is man, separated from the rest of animal creatures by his capacity to use tools, and by his ability to talk and to reflect about the world and himself. Within wide limits set by man's physical and mental equipment, human nature is an amazing variable. It is an attribute of St. Francis of Assisi and Adolf Hitler; Albert Schweitzer and Joseph Stalin; Gandhi and his assassin. It is by definition common to the primitive human beings who lived under the amazingly different cultural patterns so well described and discussed by modern anthropologists. They scarcely attempt to explain why in a given case a particular pattern should have emerged out of the vast variety of possibilities.

The response of different men or often of the same man at different times to a given stimulus, *e.g.*, fear, varies greatly and is not precisely predictable. Toynbee discusses at some length two civilizations, the ancient Spartan and the more recent Ottoman, in which the habits of the ruling class and their techniques of government ran directly counter to the usual reactions of men, that is, to human nature. Witness the extraordinary discipline of pain to which the Spartiates subjected their children through centuries, and the astonishing practice of the dominant Turks in governing their empire through slaves trained from childhood for the task to the exclusion of their own sons.

Such divergencies in cultural pattern or civilization among men, all possessing human nature, cannot be explained altogether satisfactorily by economic determinism or any current psychological doctrine of normal or abnormal conduct as exemplified by the individual in our own society.

It seems safe, however, to make this generalization: mutual aid, in Peter Kropotkin's phrase, has always been a dominant factor in human evolution. Even class exploitation, *e.g.*, under feudalism, did not strip the subordinate classes of all rights to a place in an integrated society. Slaves in human history were originally strangers, foreigners, enemies, victims of war and conquest, and, therefore, outside the reciprocity of rights which existed within the tribe. It was only from war and conquest that such a monstrous institution as the existence of outcastes in India, multitudes excluded from the hierarchy of the dominant society, could originate. And the institution was perpetuated only under a religious dogma that made these outcastes the victims of their own sins in a previous incarnation which they had utterly forgotten. Its abolition is the chief glory of the new India.

In comparison with primitive cultures and older civilizations, *laissez-faire* capitalism was unique in its contempt for a theory and practice of reciprocal rights and responsibilities of men and groups to one another and to society. Its economy was held together by a cash nexus. It did indeed break yokes of chattel slavery and serfdom, but the acquisitive society which it created to an appalling degree sacrificed mutual aid to worship of individual success measured in money. (Think of the significance of our common phrase, "Mr. Jones is *worth* a million dollars.")

Most nineteenth-century socialist and radical thinkers were preoccupied by the injustice of institutions and class relations and, by a natural reaction against them, were optimists about human nature. Criminals were the product of a bad environment, one of the many evil consequences of an unjust social order the quality of which was determined by the nature of private capitalism.

Socialists, as I have said, took over the economic man from the early *laissez-faire* economists. I have heard men who should know better talk as if this automatic calculating machine in human form was a Marxist invention. On the contrary, Marx and Engels proclaimed a far less naïve economic determination. Class interest rather than personal was dominant, and the individual could transcend both personal and class interest in the acceptance of socialist truth. Neither Marx nor Engels was himself a proletarian or found any personal economic advantage in socialism.

If no student nowadays believes in that strange unlovely economic man who always knew his own interest and acted on it, it is not because his successor, the *mass mensch* or the Freudian man, is a more promising character as the architect of the good society. If men really knew their true economic interests they would scarcely have been guilty of the particular follies which twice in a generation have drenched the earth in blood, and they would have found a way ere this more adequately to harness their marvelous tools to the production of abundance.

The vast extension of slavery in "socialist" Russia, the outbreak of mass slaughter by opposing religions in free India, are but the most striking bits of evidence that neither an economic creed nor a political and religious ideal, however passionately embraced, will of itself bring the good society. In the last analysis that depends upon the human material as well as upon plans for its organized activities. Indeed, the planners themselves are human.

The general trend of scientific thinking runs counter to the optimism of most nineteenth-century liberalism or radicalism. The revival of the theological doctrine of original sin is significant of the widespread sense of guilt, deeper than the psychoanalytic concepts of repression and frustration, among men whose conquests of natural forces have no parallel in social achievement.

Biology tends to strengthen its emphasis on heredity. Mendel is as significant a figure for our thinking as Darwin or Freud or Einstein. The Mendelian laws are not changed by environment or education. But this scientific truth has been twisted into an ugly and dangerous lie by pseudoscientists with their doctrines of racial superiority and inferiority.

Early men presumably had common ancestors at some remote evolutionary period. But group differences in physical characteristics and culture appear as far back as anthropological study goes. No completely satisfactory correlation of physical traits with cultural development has been established. There has been a steady mingling of "races" defined by color, shape of skull, and other physical characteristics. Correlation of national cultures in our day with racial traits physically determined has been less and less scientifically possible. Indeed, the scientific use of the word *race* has become more and more doubtful. Popularly race is usually determined by color. But not even that characteristic is present to explain the usual but unscientific application of the word *race* to the Jews. Nevertheless, despite our inability even to define race with scientific accuracy or to agree on the psychological characteristics which are racially determined, most of us persist in discussing racial superiority or inferiority.

The techniques by which pseudoscientists have established the superiority of a given "race" have involved a very selective use of history and have not eliminated environmental factors. Even when two races live side by side in the same geographic setting (like the blacks and whites of Jamaica studied by Davenport and Stegerda) they are divided by social conditions which are in part the heritage of the long slavery of the blacks. This fact shows itself in the average behavior and achievement of individuals.

To the somewhat dubious degree that the Army Alpha Test of intelligence given to soldiers in World War I indicated true differences, they were regional rather than racial. "For example, northern soldiers averaged higher than southern soldiers in this order: Northern White, Northern Negro, Southern White, Southern Negro. . . . The differences were the result of unequal educational opportunities in the two sections of the country." [1]

In any case, it is clear that the differences in mental ability are much greater within each race than between races. To ascribe mental inferiority to a colored race in America which has produced not only athletes and musicians but scientists of the stature of George Washington Carver is a very unscientific performance. Franz Boas has well said: "If we were to select the most intelligent, imaginative, energetic, and emotionally stable third of mankind, all races would be represented."

Another abuse of the truth about heredity springs from the efforts of men who seek short cuts in eugenics. There is, for example, the unproved assumption that superior economic and social status of itself evidences superior heredity. Since in America college men and women have not been reproducing their numbers, some amateurs in eugenics leap to the conclusion that the level of intelligence or ability will fall. "The best," *i.e.*, the college-bred, "the intelligentsia," "the managers," are not passing on their superior hereditary qualities.

Now, it is one thing to preach to the better-educated sections of our community that if they prize their own biological inheritance, they should pass it on; it is another thing to assume that hereditary qualifications are the sole or even the chief explanation of class division. Opportunity and education play an enormous part in determining whether a man is a rank-and-file worker or a member of a managerial or professional group.

We all have a great many ancestors, most of them unknown to us. Nobody knows in how many Europeans the blood of Charlemagne may flow. Men breed vegetables or animals for definite and

---

[1] Alpenfels: *Sense and Nonsense about Race.*

specific purposes desired by the breeders and not by the bred. They set the objective standards. And they can control the breeding through enough generations to establish the hereditary characteristics they desire. There is no one to play a similar role in human breeding. Except on the undesirability of certain extremes like the feeble-minded, we are not fully agreed concerning what we do want of our breed. Think of the horror if Hitler and the Nazis could have manipulated breeding as well as education to establish their type of master race. Even concerning the definition of undesirable feeble-mindedness, still more on the process of controlling it, there is disagreement. Eugenic progress requires far more study and thought. According to Hebrew legend, God's own experiment in improving the quality of Adam's descendants failed. His chosen, Noah and his sons, perpetuated all the vices which God had hoped to wash from the earth by the waters of the flood.

It is in any case extraordinarily difficult to separate biological inheritance as a factor in shaping civilizations from environmental influences. One of the ablest seekers into the mainsprings of human conduct and hence of human civilization, Ellsworth Huntington, expressly stated that his objective was to analyze the role of biological inheritance *and physical environment* (italics mine) in influencing the course of history. He never precisely separated them. He is probably better known for his theory of the effects of climate on civilization than for his theory of "kiths," groups determined more directly by language and culture than by strict and demonstrable biological inheritances.

We have this to comfort us: genius, talent, exceptional abilities spring up in unexpected places. It is doubtful if country church yards give rest to many "mute, inglorious Miltons" (genius is rare); but unquestionably they harbor many a man or woman who with different education, opportunity, and external stimuli might have made a great mark in this world.

In our present society, college degrees are poor evidence of biological superiority. The G.I. Bill of Rights was our first large-scale attempt to open college doors to those who desired higher education and were capable of it regardless of the economic status of their parents. The results are encouraging. Heretofore colleges, despite scholarships and opportunities for the ambitious to work their way through, have been largely recruited from a somewhat restricted economic class. Moreover, many fathers have sent sons and daughters who went willingly or unwillingly for all sorts of extraneous reasons having little to do with any ability except the modicum required to "get by" and even in that they often required much extra assistance. Ideally, higher education should be for those who want it and can take it whatever the economic status of their fathers. Education for those of other tastes and capacities should also be better developed.

The crusaders for a better society can reasonably accept this minimum assurance: most men of every race have more brains and latent abilities than they use. No man is infinitely perfectible, but most men of all races and classes are well enough endowed to be capable of a better education than they have received and of a higher level of social conduct than they habitually practice.

This statement is not refuted by slurring references to the low average intellectual age revealed by the Army intelligence tests in World War I. It is decidedly useful to develop tests which may reveal and discover the innate intelligence and the specific biological aptitudes and capacities of individuals. It has been, however, a serious mistake to assume (1) that perfect tests have been found to determine hereditary equipment apart from environmental conditioning, and (2) to correlate intelligence quotients with age groupings. A man with an intelligence quotient indicating mental capacities such as psychologists expect from a normal boy of thirteen is in reality very different from a thirteen-year-old boy, especially a nonexistent "normal" boy. For better and worse, his outlook and capacity have been determined by experiences and development peculiar to an adult and they are not adequately determined as measured by intelligence tests. Psychologists are increasingly aware of these facts. Modern intelligence tests do not deprive us of hope in man's capacity to establish and maintain the good society.

More serious doubts are suggested by the revelations of crowd psychologists and psychoanalysts concerning the irrationality and cruelty of which all of us, including the most intelligent, are capable, especially when we act together in the awful unity of the crowd, the herd, or the mob. Every demagogue, every popular orator, revivalist, or politician in recorded history to some degree has been a practitioner of the arts that make men act like a crowd or a herd. Every student of history has known the story of such extreme manifestations of crowd psychology as the Children's Crusade, the Tulip Mania, and the Mississippi Bubble. Men could not and would not fight large-scale wars except under the influence of crowd psychology. Yet the attempt to examine these phenomena scientifically and formulate a theory of crowd conduct is very modern. Such writers on it as Gustave Le Bon, Wilfred Trotter and Everett Dean Martin appeared many years after Marx had tried to explain human conduct in terms of economic determinism. Unquestionably economic forces were at work in the Children's Crusade. For one thing, it took care of the hordes of children made homeless by the ruthless slaughter of the Albigensian heretics at the behest of the Roman Church. The economic motivation of the Tulip Mania was obvious. But the results cannot be explained in terms of economic rationality but of the crowd psychology of men who at one and the same time lose their individuality, their frustrations and responsibilities, and yet find a dreadful sort of self-fulfillment as members of the herd.

There is a fellowship of men which escapes the terrible unity of the herd. It is not hypnotized by its own emotion or completely at the mercy of the leader who best manipulates its primitive loves and hates and prejudices. The hope of society lies in our human desire and capacity to live and work together on terms that put a premium on fellowship and discourage mob action.

Study of the behavior of men in crowds is only one phase of the modern interest in psychology in which lies much hope of men's understanding themselves and managing their affairs better in the light of that knowledge. Carefully conducted surveys have established the fact that the problem of labor relations and the calling and settlement of strikes often involve other than economic considerations concerning wages and working conditions, fundamental as these are. The monotony of some jobs, the attitude of management, including foremen; the desire for group power and authority; the tendency of men under certain pressures to go to extremes from apathy to obstinate rage and sometimes back again: all these enter into the picture.

In the course of a life which has involved me in various attempts to mediate disputes ranging from family quarrels to strike situations, I have seen settlements delayed or defeated by personal pride, anger, or plain hurt feelings when every dictate of common sense and economic interest would favor their acceptance.

Understanding the psychology of the individual as well as the crowd may be very helpful in preventing the rise of situations of conflict from strikes to wars, or in settling them after they have arisen. It cannot be said that our increased knowledge as yet has found adequate expression in action, least of all in international relations where the strain is greatest. But it helps in understanding the powerful appeal of communism to reflect that bitterness and hate are in its theory rationalized and given a kind of nobility as means to ideal ends. Thus is it psychologically possible for a communist to enjoy hate and destruction as do many noncommunists [2] and yet get the idealistic satisfactions that come to the seeker after a distant Utopia.

The particular aspect of modern psychology which is perhaps most important and certainly dominant in its hold over public attention is the process of psychoanalysis. This we owe to Sigmund Freud. He himself made three valuable discoveries of great importance to the effort of man to fulfill the injunction, "Know thy-

[2] Even in the Magnificat, Mary thanks God that "the rich He hath sent empty away."

self." A British authority, Ernest Jones, thus summarizes them: "(1) The existence of the unconscious and the dynamic influence of this unconsciousness; (2) the fact that the splitting of the mind into layers is due to an intro-psychical conflict between various sets of forces, to one of which Freud gave the name 'repression'; (3) the existence and influence of infantile sexuality." Freud, his disciples, and his critics like Jung and Adler, have let loose a flood of words which, more or less correctly used, have entered our speech: thus, superiority and inferiority complexes, inhibitions and repressions, compulsions and obsessions, the id, the ego, and the superego. Like every original thinker Freud started a process rather than laid down a final truth and his work is being continually subjected to development and criticism, particularly in respect to the dominant role he gives to direct and indirect sex motivation of human conduct.

Belatedly there is something of an organized effort to reconcile religion not merely with psychiatric methods but with Freudianism as a philosophy. Of that I am highly skeptical, though not because Freudianism is "scientific" as religion is not. Freudianism, despite its insights, meets no true scientific tests as an adequate explanation of human history, including the rise of religion, in terms of sex and "the original Oedipian revolt." [3] Religion surely cannot accept this theory, but neither, I think, can science.

Many intellectuals are repeating today the sort of mistake they made in the thirties. Now they are turning uncritically to Freud as then they turned to Marx—in both cases after the infallibility of their hero had been discredited. It's a safe guess that soon they will be giving the boys who believe that man is determined by his endocrine glands a whirl. Or they may turn their attention to Dr. William H. Sheldon's interesting and genuinely important effort to establish a correlation between individual physique and temperament, both properly measured. (Dr. Sheldon distinguishes between

[3] For an important discussion of this subject, see "God and the Psychoanalysts," by Irving Kristol, in that valuable magazine *Commentary*, November, 1949.

a man's character and temperament; the former is what he makes of his temperament.) Any thorough consideration of psychology and psychiatry must, it seems to this layman, take account of Dr. Sheldon's work.

Meanwhile, of the strength of the sexual urge—although from a different angle than psychoanalysis—the statistical inquiry of the Kinsey group of scientists gives significant evidence. It reveals to us a pattern of sexual behavior very different from the sexual standards generally professed in the western world. Dr. Kinsey points out interesting and important correlations between sexual behavior and economic and educational status, but he scarcely reduces sexual behavior to a function of economic determinism.[4]

The comparatively modern science of psychiatry, greatly influenced by the Freudian school, is undoubtedly making real progress in dealing with problems of individuals and offers promise under proper conditions of reducing the increasing burden of the mentally sick upon society. Nevertheless, so far as I, an interested layman, can judge, neither psychoanalysis nor as yet psychiatry as a whole has been an unmixed benefit to mankind. In too many cases understanding on psychoanalytic lines is far from producing any cure. The proper practice of psychiatry requires a quality of character, as well as knowledge, by no means possessed by all its practitioners. The extent to which in popular psychiatry guilt is ex-

[4] Some statisticians have questioned Dr. Kinsey's statistical method. Some psychiatrists have challenged its results on the grounds of the unreliability of human memory and the subconscious urge which makes men report their wishes as fulfilled in deed.

Whatever may be the result of further research and discussion on these subjects, it is well to point out that, valuable as the Kinsey inquiry may be as a realistic appraisal of what is normal or abnormal sexual conduct, any valid ethics of sex or of the family must go beyond anything yet revealed by this inquiry. For instance, the inquiry has applied only quantitative tests to sexual satisfaction. There are also qualitative values, and the greatest satisfactions may be denied by promiscuity. Man in his evolution has acquired habits and institutions which depend on something far removed from mere gratification of primitive impulses. It may be true that our ethical and legal assumptions of what ought to be normal in sex relations are contrary to statistical fact, but it still remains important to inquire how these standards arose and what real values they may embody.

plained away and any sort of categorical imperative reduced to a matter of repressions or inhibitions does not promise well for society which, for its own health, requires a concept of right and wrong and self-discipline in living up to it. Some versions or perversions of modern psychology minister to the growth of a cult of irresponsibility in moral and social relationships which is one of the perils of our time. In a modern parable of the prodigal son, he would return to his father and say, "Father, I suppose I have sinned against heaven and you, but, after all, it was Mom's fault —I am a victim of Momism."

So far attempts to interpret social conduct almost exclusively in psychiatric rather than economic terms have been very unsuccessful. They break down at least as completely as an explanation of the varieties of cultural patterns among primitive peoples. Useful suggestions have been made by psychiatrists, for instance in the explanation of anti-Semitism, but the wartime books which sought to explain what was wrong in Germany as primarily a problem in psychiatry were neither scientific in method nor illuminating in result.

Wars may possibly be explained by "the frequency of neurotic ills traceable to the immaturity of the masses." But that is not their soundest explanation. Social and psychological maladjustments interact, but the sickness of our times is predominantly social and an amazing number of individual neuroses are the product of the economic and social strains.[5] There is always the deep problem, which the best psychologists of all schools recognize, of the degree to which it is valuable to help men to be normal in their adjustments to an immoral society—for example, to the practice of mass homicide, and the pursuit of success regardless of human costs.

In this field of social conduct, it seems to me, more valuable work has been done by creative writers influenced by the modern psychologists than by the psychologists or the psychiatrists directly. No technical psychological discussion of the Russian communist

[5] See "Psychiatry for Everything and Everybody" by Siegfried Kracauer in *Commentary*, March, 1948.

mentality is so illuminating as Arthur Koestler's *Darkness at Noon*, or Victor Serge's *The Case of Comrade Tulayev*. No psychological speculation on the German traits which made Nazism possible is as valuable in the effort to prevent new manifestations of it as David Davidson's *The Steeper Cliff*, which makes vivid a fear beyond the power of almost any man to withstand. The reeducation of Germans or any social group will be more successful if the teachers will occasionally remind themselves that "there, but for the grace of God—or the favor of fortune—go I."

One outstanding contribution of the newer psychology to the study of human conduct was Erich Fromm's thought-provoking *Escape from Freedom*. It would have been even more valuable if his examination had covered a wider range of historical observation; it deals mostly with Germany. There is also merit in the criticism that what men fear is not freedom itself but the anxieties and the responsibilities that its exercise entails. Nevertheless, we owe much to Dr. Fromm for emphasizing the fact that by no means is freedom (which under the most favorable conception is not a whimsical individualist absolute) a constant, self-consistent, and compelling ideal for men. We are more likely to seek specific freedoms than freedom. Minorities want "freedom" in order to serve their own interest or their own concept of what is right, but when those minorities gain power their concern is no longer for "freedom" but for "truth" which must be enforced for the salvation of men or the well-being of society.

Since men do fear freedom as well as love it, there is always the danger that the achievements of psychology in understanding and methodology may be harnessed to the service of a government in the management of men for its own amoral ends. Some sense of that danger came to my mind when I read that admirable book, Stuart Leighton's *The Government of Men*. This is an enlightened and sympathetic account by a trained psychiatrist of problems and solutions for them in the great concentration camp for Japanese-Americans at Posten, Arizona, during the war. The problems in these concentration camps were unnecessarily created by a morally

and politically indefensible evacuation of West-Coast Japanese and
Japanese-Americans under the impact of a curious mixture of un-
warranted fear, prejudice, and greed. The skillful management of
men in such a situation cannot justify by its excellence the tyranny
by which the situation was created. Nevertheless, we can count as
assets the insights into human behavior offered by the new psychology and its techniques for judging and achieving "attainable
goals."

As yet comparatively little has been done by scholars or scientists
to bring together in synthesis the theories of psychology, biology,
and economics. In *Touchstone for Ethics*, the distinguished biolo-
gist, Julian Huxley, makes a notable effort in this direction. To my
mind he is more successful in suggesting that ethical standards may
be derived from the whole evolutionary process, biological and
social, without intervention of revealed religion, than in the particular synthesis of Darwin, Mendel, Freud, and Marx which he
has constructed for himself.

I personally found Dr. Erich Fromm's recent book, *Man for
Himself*, more rewarding as a study in the psychology of ethics.
The author has given us a foundation for a true ethical system based
on human values and the importance to man of the productive
character of his personality. This is a field where further study is
important.

It is interesting to observe in this summary of intellectual developments bearing on the revaluation of socialism that the most
challenging of them have not been in the field of economic theory.
True, there has been progress, principally in the amassing of rele-
vant statistical information on the way goods are produced and
distributed. But economics is still so far from an exact science that
its leading theoretical exponents have rarely agreed on so comparatively simple a task as the precise prediction of depression or
recession. The colossal failure in such prediction before 1929 was
repeated in reverse after V-J Day when the general expectation
of temporary depression, deflation, and unemployment was not
fulfilled. There were plenty of economists to tell us why after the

event, and considerable amusement could be derived by contrasting learned editorials and articles in the same papers which first told us how muddle-headed and dangerous was the demand for sixty million jobs and then boasted of the ability of our system of "free enterprise" to furnish them. They implied that they had expected this all the time.

No recent economist, not even John Maynard Keynes with his theory of spending, saving, and investment, or Sir William Beveridge, economist of social security, has produced works which have so influenced popular economic thinking as had Adam Smith, Karl Marx, or Henry George in an earlier period. But on governments Keynes has had great influence and his work is especially important in any reappraisal of socialist theory. He represents a decisive break with *laissez-faire* capitalism. In maintaining prosperity, according to Keynes, the role of the state is vital. Its fiscal policies should consciously guide investment and spending. Its own expenditures may defeat depression. In American discussion, Keynesianism, as practiced more or less unconsciously by Roosevelt and Truman, has been identified with socialism and condemned along with it. On the other hand, it has been urged as a valid alternative to socialism. Our own judgment must await further analysis of the social problem.

One conclusion, however, is immediately valid. The attempt to establish an amoral science of economics like the science of physics, independent of psychology and ethics but yet basic to them, has failed. Man makes his own economics as well as his own history on the basis of other factors in addition to the tools he invents and uses in earning his living. It follows, then, that it is not enough to work out a logical theory of politics or economics or a logical plan for society without reference to man's own nature and his reactions to the power which he is expected to exercise individually and collectively, or docilely to accept.

There are today men who, arguing the dependence of politics and economics on psychology, reject the possibility of a true science of either of them independent of social psychology. But

some psychologists argue that psychological laws of human behavior can be discovered which will be analogous to the laws of
physics. In that case freedom as a political or social concept will
be purely illusory and our rulers, following these laws, will control the masses as the physicist controls the substances with which
he works.

So completely deterministic a society would be a horrible thing.
Nothing in human history or the present achievements of psychology or sociology makes it probable. There is in human conduct
an element of will and of choice. Without it freedom and democracy are meaningless, scarcely the substance of a dream. If there is
any freedom of will, the problem of achieving a more desirable
social order is, in the last analysis, profoundly ethical.

Chapter 10

Religion and the Social Order

No STUDENT of social organization can afford to overlook the role of religion. In its multifarious forms, it has through the ages played a great part in undergirding the status quo and sometimes in changing it; in giving sanction to traditional ethics, and sometimes in proposing a loftier code. The greatest of the world's religions have professed a power to redeem the human soul. Their redemptive claims for society, short of God's apocalyptic intervention, have been less definite and more variable. Most Christian churches and sects have offered salvation out of this world. It is the church which is the City of God rather than the state which also He has ordained.

Religion, or rather religions, emerged from the cultural patterns of the tribes. Well down into historic times each tribe was the chosen of its god or gods. Gods were tribal deities. The Roman empire had a large tolerance for all sorts of cults but it superimposed on them a formal worship of a divine Caesar as head of the state.

In Christian Europe the religion of the ruler was the religion of the people. Jews and heretics were second-class citizens if they were tolerated at all. Moslem rulers followed a similar policy. The idea of the secular state, held together by a national loyalty not dependent upon a common religion, is very new. It came to strength in the eighteenth and nineteenth centuries, during which time the formal power of the churches declined to a degree that their moral and spiritual influence did not. Indeed, that influence at many periods and in many places—*e.g.*, the Wesleyan revival—actually increased.

Meantime, in the western world a fairly peaceful *modus vivendi* was worked out between church and state with varying, but on the whole increasing, degrees of separation between them. A final solution of conflict between the secular state—whose citizens are of various churches and none—and any church which, like the Catholic, claims the Keys of Heaven, is logically very difficult and has not been reached.

Historically, in their times of trouble men have tended to a deeper religious interest. Today we seek from religion different things: salvation out of this world; strength to change this world; advice in perplexity; comfort in sorrow. Perhaps the surprising thing is that this turning to religion for one or more of these reasons is as yet so small.[1] In the eastern world the secular religion of communism may for a time fill the void. But even there the dictators have been constrained to abandon or substantially modify their frontal assault on all churches. They are instead trying to make the churches docile servants of the state. In the western world there has been nothing comparable to the Franciscan movement of the Middle Ages, the Protestant Reformation, the Wesleyan revival, or the religious revivals in pioneer America in the early part of the nineteenth century.

The more significant revivals of interest in religion have been

[1] This is true despite the widespread popularity of such different religious books as Joshua Liebman's *Peace of Mind* and Thomas Merton's *Seven Storey Mountain*.

mainly intellectualist, neo-Thomist in the Roman Catholic Church, and neo-Reformist in Protestant churches along lines laid down by Barth and Niebuhr. Outside of this genuine interest in religion for its own sake, there is a more or less conscious resort to religion as a weapon against radicalism and especially communism. Some politicians and editors who talk most about the necessity of religion have very little of it. Their hypocrisy is balanced by a definite effort in both the Catholic and Protestant churches to win support of the masses by applying Christian ethics to social problems. Sometimes this is done with great and passionate sincerity. Sometimes in the utterances of the churches one feels that it is a matter of policy to bend to the winds of social change.

The excellence of many of the recent official statements of Catholic authorities from the Pope [2] to the Catholic bishops in America, and of organizations like the Federal Council of Churches of Christ, in the field of politics and economics, and in support of the ideal of peace, speaks for itself. It is a social asset for our times. The trouble has been that thus far these declarations have not had power to arouse masses of nominal believers as by a great trumpet call. Organized Christianity in all its various forms is a considerable but not a mighty force toward solving the problems of freedom with security and peace.

Too often Christianity is loved as a way of escape from the world rather than salvation of the world. It is thus that the Protestant sects, which lately have seemed to be gaining faster than the older churches, conceive religion. Within the older churches some of the new zeal for theology is escapist, a desire for salvation out of a world irredeemably lost. By no means do all the admirers of Dr. Niebuhr's theology share his social zeal, and it isn't easy for the layman to see a logical connection between Niebuhr's theology and his admirable economic and political suggestions.

Henry Luce has made his publications, notably his *Time*, preach-

[2] From this praise of recent encyclicals I except the encyclical of Pius XI on education and some other dogmatic utterances, especially Pius XII's utterances in *Humanis Generis* on relations of the church to science and to non-Catholic Christians.

ers of a return to religion without too much discrimination concerning the nature of religion. Mr. Luce is one of the better-known spokesmen for a host of editors and politicians who join with preachers to tell us that without religion—apparently religion in its rather formal sense—there can be no valid standards of ethical conduct. At worst they threaten us that a godless generation will be swept away by the tides of communism.

Before we agree that religion is necessary to individual or social ethics, we must examine the meaning given to religion. If, as an old professor of mine used earnestly to argue, "religion is a deep sense of values transcending quantitative measurement," then I think religion is necessary to the good life and to the good society.

But if religion by definition requires a theological creed or a belief in a God who has revealed His will to us through prophets and sages, it is a serious business to claim that it is an essential answer to the confusions of our time. For one thing, religion is not singular but plural. There are many religions. Within religions like Christianity, Buddhism, and Islam are many divergent if not hostile sects. In so far as there is an ethic common to all religions, it may be questioned whether they have not derived that ethic from life rather than imposed it on life. Must we wait for a decent world until all men profess something like a common theological creed? If so, the outlook is dark indeed.

That specific religions have greatly blessed mankind is indubitable. That religious faith is or may be a source of personal strength is likewise certain. But to say that there is no basis for personal and social ethics apart from one or another of the organized religions is untrue to observed fact and immensely derogatory to a God worth respect. What a strange Supreme Being it would be who would create men and put them on this earth with no possible standard of decent conduct except as it might be imparted by the conflicting revelations of rival creeds and churches!

It is, therefore, surprising to find a philosopher and unbeliever who would write as did Professor W. T. Stace in a much discussed article, "Man Against Darkness" (*Atlantic Monthly*, September,

1948): "The Catholic bishops of America recently issued a statement in which they said that the chaotic and bewildered state of
the modern world is due to man's loss of faith, his abandonment
of God and religion. For my part I believe in no religion at all.
Yet I entirely agree with the bishops."

The author goes on to develop his belief that we have "to face the
truth however bleak it may be, and then next we have to learn to
live with it." He doubts, however, the capacity of men in general
to accomplish this difficult task of living creatively, while facing
truth, in time to save themselves or their civilization.

Certainly the task is immensely difficult. Certainly the right sort
of religion, if it could be universally accepted rather than imposed
by coercion, would be a mighty help. But our efforts to derive an
ethic from the experience of life are not so meaningless to thoughtful men or even to the multitudes as to justify Professor Stace's
gloom. One may take a pessimistic view of man's fate in this universe as does Bertrand Russell in his well-known essay, "A Free
Man's Worship," and yet believe with him that in our cold, impersonal universe we little men can find dignity and reason for
living and loving through our capacity for understanding and
fellowship. Certainly there is more hope in achieving a unifying
loyalty of men in the service of a great ideal for humanity if it is
based on life's experience and not dependent on one of the many
conflicting doctrines of God and creation, sin and redemption.

Historically, religions have hindered at least as often as they have
helped the growth of a sense of universal brotherhood and the
practice of tolerance. They have often inspired or supported outrageous cruelties and indecencies. If, in a psychological sense, communism is a religion—a secular religion—it is partly because it
has the fanaticism so usual in religion.

Few outbreaks of human hate and violence have been more horrible than the strife, in large degree religious strife, between Moslems and Hindus when the British withdrew from India. Gandhi
was religious in the noblest sense of the word but remember that
his assassin was also not only a patriotic but a religious Hindu. John

Frederick Muehl in *Interview with India* gives other illustrations of enormous evils buttressed by a decadent Hinduism. Other religions have played a similar antisocial role.

Many years ago the English historian, Lecky, pointed out the disastrous effect of the orthodox Christian doctrine of hell upon the public morality of the lords temporal and spiritual and all European society. It gave color of justification to the Inquisition as a use of lesser torture to save men from eternal hell. It was, I think, a little easier for Hitler and Stalin to revive cruelty as a major instrumentality of government because for so many centuries Europeans were taught that the final judgment of God would be expressed in the everlasting fires of hell. Religious sanction was thus given to our human capacity for cruelty and enjoyment of it.

I remember attending some of the conferences which finally resulted in the formation of that well-intentioned body, the National Conference of Christians and Jews. One night I remember a sort of experience meeting in which a number of Jews and Christians of various Protestant churches—I do not remember whether a Roman Catholic was present—explained why their religion made them more brotherly. When it came my turn I said that I did not doubt for a moment the sincerity of my colleagues but, nevertheless, it was logically and historically untrue that the religious bodies which they represented had been made more tolerant and brotherly by the intensity of their creeds. The Jews, I reminded them, were a Chosen People in a peculiar sense by the act of God. Outside the Catholic Church there is no salvation even although some who are not Catholics may, under exceptional circumstances, be saved. Each Protestant sect had been inclined in its day to believe that it had something close to a monopoly on the road to heaven. All this was a consequence of what they believed about God and His way of salvation. The terrible wars of religion had a certain horrible logic behind them, and tolerance was born of exhaustion and a turning from religious fanaticism rather than a triumph of Christian brotherhood. (Men preferred to kill one another in the name of nationalism.) Practically, I said, we were facing the necessity in America of teaching men in the name of religion to be more brotherly and tolerant than the churches had been, less cruel than the God they worshiped. I was invited to no further conferences. What I said was in no way an indiscriminate attack on organized religion but a logical deduction from the orthodoxy of our forefathers.

In these days of conflict against totalitarianism, the lover of liberty must be especially concerned with the role of the greatest of Christian churches—the Roman Catholic. We of the West owe it a debt as the channel to us through long centuries for life-giving streams of the Judeo-Christian ethic and philosophy. Unquestionably, it is authoritarian in creed and practice. Yet it has taught the dignity of the individual and the worth of each human soul. It has shown some capacity to live with democracy. Its claim for the infallibility of its head is carefully limited—as communism's is not. Therefore, the Church can be accepted as an ally in the struggle against the totalitarian state.

But it cannot be accepted completely or uncritically. In its struggle against the Kremlin, the Church or some of its spokesmen have seemed to come close to advocacy of war, a holy crusade of the atom bomb. More definitely the leaders of the Church, but not all Catholics, have seemed to have a double standard of humanity and justice, one for Catholics in communist countries, another for the enemies of that son of the Church, Franco of Spain.[3] The Pope and some German bishops were at times very critical of Hitler, born a Catholic, but, like the great majority of Protestants, they managed for years to get along with him. They were less critical of

[3] Catholics often defend Franco, especially in his treatment of Protestants, by the *tu quoque* argument. They cite the establishment of the Lutheran Church in Sweden and discrimination against all other churches, especially the Roman Catholic, which cannot own property in Sweden without special permission of the government. A "Dissenter Law" committee in 1949 recommended six desirable modifications in the law but would still leave the Lutheran as the Established Church. It is abridgment of freedom of worship that there should be any established church or any restrictions on churches outside those applicable to all associations. By no means can democratic Sweden be equated with Franco's fascist Spain. But Sweden should go much farther in establishing true religious freedom.

Mussolini, who reestablished the Church in Italy for which Pope Pius XI, even in the encyclical *Non Abbiano Bisognio* (1931) in which he criticised certain fascist acts and doctrines, again reiterated "perennial gratitude."

The Popes could not accept statism in its extreme fascist form and they have been a force against absolute nationalism. Yet the support of the Church has been essential to many South American dictators; the Church was a major factor in the fascism of Dollfuss in Austria; it stands behind Salazar and his fascism in Portugal; the Pope has blessed Franco without openly rebuking his cruel regime in Spain.[4] The Church is still regarded as the ally of the great landlords in Italy.

Against active communists, the Vatican has imposed an excommunication never threatened against the Nazis, much less the Italian fascists. Togliatti and the Italian communists must think this a poor reward for their vote for perpetuating in the new constitution the privileged position of the Roman Catholic Church in Italy—a piece of strategy which temporarily brought extra peasant support to the Communist Party.

The effect of the excommunication remains to be seen. In cold logic it is true that the opposition of communist philosophy and Catholic theology is absolute. But in hundreds of villages in Italy, Poland, and Hungary peasants and workers have been communists politically without rejecting the Catholic religion. Will excommunication force them to choose? If so, how?

Not only in politics but in religion the Vatican is giving disquieting emphasis to doctrinal rigidity, notably expressed in the papal encyclical *Humanis Generis* (published August 22, 1950). This document almost equals certain decrees by the Kremlin in the dogmatic and obscurantist restraints it would impose upon free spirits in search of scientific truth.

In general, the Catholic Church is at its best in countries like the

---

[4] The Pope, who blessed Franco, later was reported as having asked mercy for one of Franco's victims named Nadal, a fighter against Nazism in France, condemned to death in his native Spain for trying to organize a union. Franco in his great mercy reduced the sentence to thirty years.

United States where it is not dominant. But even here its attempt to force upon all of us through the state its concepts of birth control, divorce, and education raises problems that we shall have to examine in a later chapter. Undeniably, the Church has a real hold on large numbers of the workers and is developing a powerful interest in workers' rights and social justice along lines of recent papal encyclicals.

One can hardly turn from a discussion of the role of religion in our society without mention of Arnold Toynbee's essential religious interpretation of the rise and fall of civilizations in his popular *Study of History*. His theory of the rise of civilization in response to challenge is both sounder and more convincing than Spengler's in rejecting a theory of civilization as organic. He makes an inspiring case for the role of creative minorities as the pioneers whom the masses follow by "mimesis" (imitation) in building a civilization.

But the fall of civilizations, according to Toynbee, follows a rigorous and uniform pattern, a "seven-beat process of rout, rally, rout, rally, rout, rally, rout." That is, civilizations in falling would seem to be governed by a more deterministic pattern than in rising —a philosophic position involving elements of unresolved contradiction. Nor am I altogether persuaded that Toynbee's theory of the fall of civilization is so much derived from evidence as imposed upon it—a task made easier by our relative ignorance of most of the civilizations which have perished. Before Toynbee, many Marxists showed how easy it is to impose a plausible theory of history upon partial reconstructions of the past. I grow increasingly skeptical of interesting but inconclusive attempts to discover a rigid pattern in history, whether they are made by Hegel, Marx, Spengler, or Toynbee.

I would be more hesitant to make these criticisms in a field in which Toynbee's learning is so vast and mine so small were it not that I find his theory of communism and its role in Russia so inadequate to the evidence as to suggest that its author is not infallible. (Mr. Toynbee saw communist philosophy as a western Hegelianism derived by way of Marx and he thought that Stalin's communism had become conservative and national, and the Soviet Union no longer an "outlaw society.")

What is of more importance to this study and the crisis of our times is Toynbee's conclusion that what hope we have lies in the "reaction of gentleness" rather than of violence; in the way of Christ rather than of Caesar. It is a glorious hope. But in his unfinished *Study of History* he does not implement that conviction with any workable program for the salvation of our civilization or the rise of a better. His writing was interrupted by World War II in which he, like most of the rest of us, played an active part suitable to his abilities. It was scarcely a reaction of gentleness. Since the war, I cannot find in Toynbee's published statements any new or important elements of a program to arrest the drift to a war or series of wars in which not only our civilization but the human race itself may perish.

The challenge, as it needs no Toynbee to tell us, is present. To meet it requires a conscious acceptance of "values transcending the material." In so far as religion helps us to find, to measure, and to serve those values, it has a great role to play.

Chapter 11

The State

Today as never before the national state is a dominant factor for human weal or woe. It has many forms. It is justified or attacked in the name of conflicting theories. Belief in some sort of world state as a necessary expression of the unity of one world tends to grow. Men very critical of every existing state and of statism as we now know it are often blissfully sure that one world state, usually of a federated order, would guarantee our earthly salvation. But, meanwhile, everywhere amid the hates and confusion of war's aftermath, the power of *national* states is growing and so is man's dependence, however reluctant, upon them. Of the Marxist withering away of the state, there is less than no sign anywhere, least of all in that vast nation whose rulers claim that they have already achieved socialism.

For our discussion we shall accept the usual definition of the state as "any body of people occupying a definite territory and politically organized under one government, especially one that is sovereign, or not subject to external control."

The state is a development within history. In our sense it did not exist in primitive tribes or cultures. Every state has been created with some use of force and demands for itself a monopoly of force in maintaining internal order and organizing defense of the national security. The totalitarian state claims to be the exclusive expression of society; other organizations, including churches, exist by its consent. Democratic states recognize rights of association not derived from the state. But in all states eternal vigilance is the price of liberty.

It is possible to classify states in various ways and according to various principles of division. Thus there are or have been city-states, nations, and empires; monarchies, oligarchies, republics, democracies; and in our day highly centralized or federalized states. Some of the terms we have used are overlapping; thus, republics have been oligarchic, aristocratic, or democratic. Often they have been governed under a combination or compromise of conflicting principles, oligarchic and democratic.

To add to confusion political theorists have not always meant the same thing by the same words. Aristotle, for instance, would not accept democracy as the description of any modern national state. In his conception of democracy he had in mind the assembly of the citizens of a city-state, which assembly was above the law and decided each question independently. He says that to elect magistrates is oligarchic; to appoint them by lot is democratic. Many of his criticisms of democracy can be understood only in the light of this definition. Interesting as are Aristotle's observations, I think the value of his *Politics* for our time is smaller than his admirers claim. His whole discussion is based on his observation of the working of Greek city-states under kings, tyrants, oligarchies, and democracies. It is one of the many curiosities of history that so great a thinker, who had himself been Alexander's tutor, should have lived and written without the faintest conception of the significance of Alexander's conquest and the rapid obsolescence of the states he was studying.[1]

---

[1] Bertrand Russell makes this point very ably in his *A History of Western Philosophy* (Simon & Schuster).

Aristotle, however, as a champion of the organic theory of the nature of the state is significant in these days of conflict between totalitarian and democratic ideals. Involved in that conflict is the important theoretical distinction between concepts of the state as an organism which grows and the state as a machine, a mechanism or organization which was created by and is subject to its citizens. Under the organic theory of the state individuals in it are as cells to the body. The well-being of the state is the highest good and the good man is first and foremost the good, that is, the obedient, citizen. Under the latter theory government rests on consent of the governed; however powerful it may become it is still the creation of its citizens or subjects either by their conscious consent or their docile submission to a particular group or economic class which gains and maintains control of government.

I think the organic theory of the state—or of the larger and vaguer concept, "civilization"—untenable. Men under the state do not act like cells in the body or bees in a hive. Social evolution has on the whole developed a greater sense of the dignity and value of the individual than existed in primitive society. The rejection of the organic theory does not compel belief in any specific act of men in setting up the state in its early form by contract or otherwise. It developed despite its abuses in answer to certain obvious needs of men who felt themselves bound by some "consciousness of kind."

Hegel held an extreme organic theory of the nation-state which has had great influence in Germany. Marx, his pupil, rejected the Hegelian doctrine in favor of a mechanistic conception of the state. But in accepting it Marx by no means accepted the theory that government was derived from the consent of the governed. Government, on the contrary, he held, is something imposed by force by a dominant class and in its interest. Men, Marxists believed, lived in societies before the rise of the state; the state itself became necessary to support the economic interest of the master class in the ownership of land and slaves, and later of the capitalist class in the ownership of tools of production. The capitalist class supplanted the feudalist class by revolution; so in turn would the working class come to power. Its government would be its executive committee and it would use vigorously the state apparatus until the final disappearance of economic classes and class divisions should deprive the state of reason for its existence.

All existing governments and laws in 1848 were class institutions with no claim on the obedience of workers, except in so far as weakness, prudence, and the tactics of the class struggle might dictate. "The laws," says the *Communist Manifesto*, "have been contrived by our enemies . . . in the interests of the wealthy and propertied classes. We who possess nothing can only be bound by the law as long as we are too weak to set it at naught." [2]

It did not follow, therefore, that workers should be indifferent to the kind of government which exploits them. In Marxist theory reforms under capitalism and under capitalist governments may not only be accepted by the workers but actively sought, but only in the degree that they might make the workers stronger for the eventual and inevitable revolution which Marx and Engels conceded might in some countries not involve armed violence—a concession which Lenin denied. Sound tactics would require workers to reject reforms that might delay revolution.

Lenin's theory and practice of the dictatorship of the proletariat was, I am now inclined to think, a plausible but not inevitable interpretation of the Marxist doctrine. He was also influenced, consciously or unconsciously, by the Russian tradition, stemming from Nichaev, which openly accepted "deception, calumny, and murder for the attainment of their objectives."

As we have already seen, Marx never explained his passing allusion to the dictatorship of the proletariat. It is conceivable that he might have interpreted it as Rosa Luxemburg did rather than Lenin, or he might have held that a working class in control of government could allow some democratic practices much as did

---

[2] Quoted by T. D. Weldon in *States and Morals*, p. 99. I owe much to this clear and incisive study but, as will appear, do not accept all its findings. Weldon's treatment of Hobbes, Locke, and Rousseau is admirable.

the capitalist class in "liberal" or "democratically" governed countries. One thing, however, is certain. To Marx democracy under capitalism was necessarily illusory. The force by which a dominant class held power need not always be naked and violent. It could and did contain large elements of cunning. It could strengthen itself by tradition, education, and the propaganda of false philosophies. Nevertheless, in the last analysis, the state had no sanction but force. Law is the expression of the interest of the dominant class.

For myself I have to confess that I never could quite see how social-democratic parties professing orthodox revolutionary Marxism could reconcile their beliefs with their current reformist practices in democratic countries before and after World War I. Karl Kautsky and other anticommunist Marxist theoreticians were able to make a good case that Lenin did not so much interpret Marx as substitute his own doctrine of the road to power for Marxism. They were not able to make an equally good case for the use of democratic procedures to achieve socialist ends if democracy was necessarily illusory and every government must be fundamentally controlled by the dominant class. It was one of the weaknesses of the German social-democratic movement and a partial explanation of its failure that on the one hand it could not altogether escape the pervasive influence of the Hegelian theory of the organic German State, while on the other it gave allegiance to a Marxist doctrine of the state which was more or less incompatible with the democratic techniques which it tried to follow.

It must, however, be pointed out that Marxist socialists who accepted legal and democratic political techniques had the high authority of Engels who, near the end of his long life, wrote in *The Class Struggle in France:* "History proved us in the wrong and revealed our opinion of that day [1848–50] as an illusion. . . . The time is past for revolutions carried through by incoherent masses. . . . We, the revolutionists, we strive much better with legal than illegal means in forcing an overthrow."

The Leninist interpretation of Marx led to the establishment of a totalitarian state far better justified by the organic than the mechanistic theory. Unquestionably the Russian people accepted the Leninist totalitarian state more easily because it appeared to them as a natural successor to the organic state of the Tsars. They were not widely imbued with the doctrine of government as something that citizens can make and citizens can change. Nevertheless, I think that T. D. Weldon (to whose excellent book I have previously referred) and others make a grave mistake in finding the Stalinist state the natural continuance of the organic, authoritarian state of the Tsars. In the Russia of 1914 were areas of liberty now lacking and a principle of liberal democracy fermenting among the people which the totalitarian (not merely authoritarian) Stalinist state has all but destroyed.

I definitely disbelieve Mr. Weldon's interesting contention that the Soviet Union in the opinion of its own rulers has become an organic state. One seriously misunderstands the world situation if one believes with Mr. Weldon that "it has, indeed, been clear for a long time now that Russia is not a Marxist state and has no intention of becoming one. Her interest in world revolution as such is negligible, though her interest in revolution in other peoples' countries as a means to an end remains considerable." Indeed, I wonder if the author still holds that opinion.

It is only defensible on a sharp and at this point misleading distinction between "Russia" or "the Russian people" and the Soviet dictatorship. There is no reasonable doubt that Stalin and the Politburo consider themselves Leninist and hence Marxist. Their interest in world revolution is very strong. It is easy to prove that Russia is not socialist but rather state capitalist in an economic sense. The government is, nevertheless, Marxist in the Leninist interpretation of Marx. If the destruction of the capitalist class in Russia has not led to a withering away of the state, Stalin can always argue that the dictatorship must be maintained not only for defense against attempts of capitalist and imperialist states "to encircle" the Soviet Union, but also positively to aid in the process of world revolution which is necessary to the final security of mighty Russia.

In other words, Lenin's dictatorship of the proletariat has developed into a totalitarianism practically indistinguishable in its burdens upon citizens from Hitler's, despite great differences in their original theories of the state. Hitler was, of course, at this point a Hegelian and a believer in the organic state in its most extreme and mystical form. That theory provided him with a logical justification for his abuse of minorities rather sounder than Stalin today possesses. Yet Stalin, out of the tactics of totalitarianism, aided by the background of the Russian people, has developed in practice a god-state as powerful and more enduring than Hitler's creation. The Soviet god-state has denounced the extermination of racial minorities in the interest of the higher good which is the state's, but in that same interest it is continually practicing the extermination of political minorities and of dissident nationalistic groups.

The logic of totalitarianism, as we have seen, led avowed Marxists, complete disbelievers in the role of the "hero" in history, to canonize Lenin and preserve his body as a holy relic because such tactics helped the dictatorship hold power. The logic of totalitarianism has led professed Marxists to bestow upon Stalin in his lifetime a power and adulation never exceeded, if indeed it was equaled, by that which was the portion of the Japanese emperor in the organic state of Japan or of Hitler in his sacred German State. The conclusion is inescapable that, while the organic theory of the state logically makes easier the sacrifice of the individual to it and the moralization of cruelty in its service, the Marxist theory can be made to support very similar practices.

In all fairness, it must be added that many theorists of the organic state would have found reason under their philosophy to dismiss Hitler's extreme dictatorship and his abominable cruelties with horror. Aristotle was scathing in his denunciation of the tyrant and even found it possible to give a qualified endorsement to democracy as a permissible form of government. The quality of a government is not absolutely determined by its acceptance of the organic or mechanistic theory of the state.

The one respect in which Stalinist totalitarianism has not yet taken on a color practically indistinguishable from fascist totalitarianism is in respect to the *national* (and in Germany the *racial*) quality of the sovereign state. As yet Stalinist communism has manipulated nationalism without theoretical surrender to it. It is a question how long that will remain true. For its own reasons, in the war and in its fight against the Marshall Plan, the Kremlin has made a point of supporting nationalist sovereignty to a degree which would have horrified Lenin. Not even an almighty dictatorship seeking the power of a world government can play with the fire of this nationalist doctrine without being burnt. Witness Tito's revolt.

We shall best deal with the problems the state presents if we remember that man evolved in a social group and has always existed in society. The state, we must never forget, is not identical with society. It developed as a political organization for defense or aggression against other states and the preservation of internal order. These functions required a degree of coercive power. The state was not primarily or simply the creation of a master class for its own ends but that class used and manipulated it for its own advantage and was able largely to shape its institutions in accordance with its own class interests. As life has become more industrialized and more complex, the functions of the state have necessarily expanded. It has had to take on more positive services for its citizens and subjects. Its government, even in totalitarian countries, has had to profess and to some degree display interest in popular well-being, going beyond the immediate interest of the dominant economic class or the administrative elite which controls it.

Especially in the democratic or partially democratic countries the state renders services in the fields of public health, education, and the control of regulation of economic processes, which may be well or poorly performed, but are nevertheless indispensable. In our complex society men cannot perform these services for themselves or by any feasible voluntary associations. Imagine a city's plight before fire or plague without governmental agencies for water supply, sewage, sanitation and fire and health departments!

It is true that the state, whatever theories its citizens or subjects may hold of its origin and nature, tends to become a thing in itself, the sole and sufficient expression of society, so that its interests are apart from and superior to the ordinary, every-day interests of the people who live under it. But it is not true, even in our age which has seen specimens of that most terrible leviathan, the totalitarian state, that the state is the mother of all evil, and that to get rid of it or provide substitutes for it would simplify the problem of achieving plenty, peace, and freedom. It is important to distinguish between the state and the people, but the contrast in their relative morals is not so great as antistatists assume. There is no worse government than that of the mob into which the people all too easily degenerate. Let the communal strife of Moslems and Hindus in 1948 bear witness.

Anarchy and anarchic syndicalism as popular forces declined in strength from the First World War on. There is today a new and extreme libertarianism arising which, justly outraged by the concept of the god-state, goes almost to the length of anarchy in rejecting any state. It professes a great, if somewhat hazy, faith in decentralization and voluntary action through unions, cooperatives, and other groups. At its worst this sort of antistatism seems to assume that if only "the state" in name, at least, can be done away other organizations may absorb its functions and yet be saved from the curse of the power that corrupts. There is no ground in human history or psychology for such a hope. It happens that some of my antistatist acquaintances are among the most intolerant of men in their own groups and the most Machiavellian in tactics. Few human organizations have asserted more totalitarian control over individuals, their thoughts and actions, than supposedly voluntary communist communities under religious sanctions.

As for syndicalism, that is a form of social organization in which labor unions would take over most of the functions of the state.

There could be no blinder road to freedom. Unions are a necessary and valuable expression of the interests of workers, particularly wageworkers. But men's interests are not summed up in their interests as workers. We work to live, not live to work. Our interests as consumers are enormous and may become more unifying than our interests as workers.

The class solidarity of our time is solidarity against another class and will be weakened as the reason for that negative unity is lessened or removed. As I have repeatedly pointed out, makers of pants and makers of power today have much in common as users of electricity. In a socialist society they might have more in common as consumers than as workers. There is no easy reconciliation of their claims on the national income simply because both groups are workers. There is no preordained rate of exchange for pants and power. Electrical workers, thinking only as producers of electricity, can hold up the rest of us far more effectively than clothing workers. One can patch pants but not so easily produce electric power or do without it.

The breath-taking growth of technology steadily reduces the importance and permanence of crafts and increases the importance of leisure. The one big union or any conceivable federation of unions would be a more vulnerable and generally unsatisfactory expression of men's common interests than our existing imperfectly democratic states.

Not only is this true on theoretic grounds but on the basis of examination of the unions themselves. In America they avowedly reject syndicalism as held by the I.W.W. but have strong syndicalist tendencies in action.[3] By and large, they have given no guarantees of democratic rights to their own members, still less to workers in general, Negro as well as white, which are as adequate and well enforced as is the Bill of Rights of our Constitution. I do not insult labor leaders or ignore exceptions when I say that as a class, largely because their power is newer, they are often more domi-

[3] On the relation of this to socialism, see Chapter 18.

neering within their own organizations than public officials or corporation presidents. A syndicalist organization or society would make the problem of individual freedom far more difficult than it is today in democratic countries.

The same line of reasoning applies to the idea of "consumerism" peculiar to that American pioneer of cooperatives, James Peter Warbasse. He argues that consumers' cooperatives could and should take over useful functions now performed by the state. Actually, they would lose their voluntary character and become coercive. Valuable as cooperatives are in our economy, a public authority is a better agency than any cooperative for handling such a generally used service as the water supply or the New York subway.

Once I believed in Peter Kropotkin's Communist Anarchy as an ideal, although not an immediately practicable form of society. Experience with all sorts of organizations makes me doubt its ideal value. I have more hope for achieving a democratic control of the state and for making it a genuine commonwealth than for supplanting it or outgrowing it.

The extraordinary danger of statism today, both to peace and freedom, arises from two related evils. (1) The state tends to consider itself the sole expression of society, the one form of human association from which all others derive whatever rights they have. (2) Every existing state thus claiming absolute sovereignty is national and stands ready to sacrifice human interests to national greatness.

Hope lies in abolishing war, working toward limited federal world government, and insisting always that civil liberties, including the rights of association, while they should be guaranteed by the state, are not derived from it but, like the state itself, are products of social evolution, conditions of human welfare, and necessary to the realization of a fellowship of free men.

Obviously if the state, any state, national or world-wide, is to be safe for the people, it must be subject to their control through democratic process. But that easy statement of itself solves no problem. Democracy is not even self-defining, still less self-generating, once men have been led to shout its praises. Democracy in action is a large part of the problem we must solve.

Chapter 12

Democracy

FEW WORDS are used with greater variations of meaning and significance than democracy. Its definition runs the gamut from a mere numerical rule of the majority to Walt Whitman's lofty equalitarianism:

> "I give the password primaeval, I give the sign of democracy,
> By God, I will accept nothing that all cannot have on equal terms."

That statement is somewhat rhetorical since all of us of necessity begin by accepting great inequalities in natural endowment. It is, however, a notable repudiation of man-made inequalities.

More soberly, we speak of political, economic, and social democracy. The word in its fullness implies Christian standards of brotherhood and finds for government its ultimate sanction in group decisions reached through common counsel. In the current conflict between the United States and Russia, both claim to stand for democracy. Neither of them practices it in Whitman's sense.

To the American, democracy means primarily representative—

not direct—government wherein representatives are chosen by the majority under a system which permits a minority by persuasion to become a majority. In Soviet and communist parlance, democracy is a convenient synonym for antifascism and antiracism, perhaps, also, for collectivism as opposed to private capitalism. It is often said that communism believes in government of the people and for the people, but not by the people. This is far too optimistic a picture of the regime of the Soviet dictatorship. The absence of private capitalism, plus an approximate equality of all races in subjection to the totalitarian state does not constitute government *for* the people, not in a land where there is a growing inequality of income, a land entirely without civil liberty, wherein millions of men and women are slaves to the state.

On the other hand, concentration of wealth and economic power in the United States, racial discriminations, and defective techniques of government designed by its founders for a republic which was to be a limited democracy, make the practice of democracy something very different than our boasted theory of it. The growth of the power of the workers under the democratic political theory contradicts the extreme radical belief that there can be no democracy under private capitalism because those who own will rule by job control and mastery of the means of communication. Nevertheless, in practice, capitalist democracy is very imperfect.

One thing is clear from the lip service on the one hand of the capitalist class and on the other of governments including the Soviet dictatorship to some version or perversion of democracy: that is the passing of the day when the many could be made to assent to the government of the few under concepts of the divine right of kings or the intrinsic fitness of aristocracies to rule. The assent to government which is necessary even to dictatorships may be wrung from the people largely through fear of a ruthless police state, but, in the long run, it requires some pretense that rulers are functioning for them or in their name. Men may be dissuaded all too easily from the intelligent assertion of democratic rights but not to a conscious renunciation of them in deference to an admitted superiority of any self-perpetuating governmental group or caste.

For the purposes of this discussion, I shall accept the American ideal of democracy as government of the people, by the people, and for the people. In modern usage a government may be called democratic in which the ultimate power is in the hands of the people rather than of any one class or any sort of elite.

Obviously modern democracy cannot function in so pure a form as in the town meetings of Greek city-states and New England communities. Government must be representative. It is quite too complicated a business to be carried on by a series of snap votes by the people. As democracy is increasingly concerned with economic controls, this becomes increasingly true. And if democracy is not to be mobocracy, the rights of minorities, including the right of a minority to become a majority under an orderly procedure, must be guaranteed. The rules of the game, the techniques it employs, are of primary importance in a democracy and attention to them and respect for them are essential.

Any worth-while democracy must be truly liberal in the correct sense of that much abused word. But democracy and liberalism have not been identical. Historically, democracies have by no means always guaranteed the rights of the individual which are dear to the liberal. The democratic party was in control in Athens, and democratic rule by free men—a small minority in comparison to the slave population—was in force when Socrates was condemned to drink the hemlock. On the other hand, Voltaire, pioneer of modern liberalism and champion of the rights of the individual, was not even a republican but rather an advocate of constitutional or limited monarchy. In our own day the most vociferous advocates of the right of "the people" to rule are rarely distinguished by intelligent devotion to civil liberty. To that curious but widely distributed modern phenomenon, the American totalitarian liberal, as to the more blatant demagogue of the Huey Long school, "the people" is something to be flattered and manipulated with a very selective support of true civil liberty. Witness the pages of the newspaper *PM* during and after World War II.

In the process of becoming a war cry, an organizing myth in two world wars, democracy in America tended to lose reality. It became something to believe in rather than to understand, to die for in war against a foreign enemy rather than to apply in practice as against its enemies at home. And that is no new experience in its checkered history.

Indeed, the assumption that democracy is the natural state of man stands the tests neither of historical nor psychological examination. Belief in it and the attempt to practice it are for human beings acquired habits, something further to set them apart from the rest of animal creation. In the hierarchical and tightly organized life of ants and bees, the individual's place is determined by birth. Herds of animals have leaders who gain and hold their place by strength, skill, and cunning, but no wolf pack indulges in town meetings. Even among hens there is said to be the right of the first peck and in every well-ordered kennel one male is chief. (To all of which decent dogs might reply that the institution of leadership among them requires no such cruelty as Hitler practiced.)

Primitive societies of men took various cultural forms but none of them was democratic in anything like the modern sense of the word. The practice of democracy has been always imperfect, occasional rather than customary in history, and the defeat of democracies has been more usually a result of their inherent weakness than of the strength of an enemy. Today, after two world wars in which the "democratic" forces won total victory, democracy as we have defined it exists with a fair degree of security in few countries. It is not certain how many Latin American republics can be numbered among those few or how long the democracies of western Europe will withstand the pressures of communism; not even in the English-speaking and Scandinavian countries is the future of democracy absolutely assured. Self-government ideally requires in our complex society a fairly high degree both of intelligence and economic security widely distributed among citizens; its practice bores a great many people; they crave leadership; they tend to seek the solidarity of the crowd rather than the unity of fellowship; in short, the freedom with self-discipline and a sense of responsibility without which democracy becomes the tyranny of the mob is something which men fear as well as love.

It follows that justifications for democracy, or rational grounds for faith in it, are not to be found in eulogies of "the common man"—the best Lincoln could say for us plain people was: "You can't fool all the people all the time"—still less in sentimental nonsense that the voice of the people is the Voice of God. Sometimes it is the voice of a demagogue, an advertising agency, or some other propagandistic group.

Occasionally, when the crowd mind is dominant, "the people" or large sections of them are guilty of crimes from which even their governments would have restrained them. Race riots in our own country have sprung from the popular mob rather than from government at any level. Of recent years both the President and the Supreme Court have led rather than followed "the people" in progress toward racial equality of rights. In view of such situations confined to no one race or continent, there is something a little sad, a little ludicrous, and more than a little demagogic, about the oratorical presentation of the "common man" as always innocent and virtuous, but misled, enslaved, betrayed, or otherwise put upon by wicked priests, politicians, editors, bankers, or what have you. The acute observer must say: If you act like sheep you can hardly blame the butchers for treating you like mutton—or, at any rate, shearing you of your wool. And we sheep are capable on our own account not only of great apathy and stupidity but at times of great madness and cruelty. The voice of the people has sometimes been the voice of Satan.

In reality there is no single voice of the people. And the faith of early advocates of democracy (as applied through universal suffrage) that individual and group interests would cancel each other out and automatically add up to the public good has been discredited in practice. Pressure groups too often find a formula for their mutual advantage, at least temporarily, at the price of a more or less inarticulate public. The man in the group to which only one thing matters, whether it is a subsidy or a prohibition law, has an obvious bargaining advantage over the rest of us in the game of pressure politics.

The pragmatic case for democracy, even in the oversimplified form of majority rule, is that it is better to determine issues by counting noses than breaking heads. The acceptance of the nose-counting method in place of violent determination of preponderant force is a definite gain, a step in the long process of substituting rational cooperation for coercion as the dominant feature of government in organized society. Moreover, nose counting gives rather more stable results than simple army revolutions or *coups d'état* on the South American model. Where government by brute force is relatively stable, it is by virtue of monopoly of effective violence in an age when barricades are obsolete before bombers.

More positive justifications for democracy are these: (1) It is the way of life that best conforms to what men ought to be and do; what at their best they want to be and do. (2) In practice, with all its imperfections, it has provided better government than any substitute for it. (3) By its nature it permits its own improvement. These justifications apply only to a democracy which is liberal, that is, which respects the basic rights of the individual and safeguards the right of a minority to become a majority by persuasion.

For the believer in the dignity of the individual, there is only one standard by which to judge a given society and that is the degree to which it approaches the ideal of a fellowship of free men. Unless one can believe in the practicability of some sort of anarchy, or find evidence that there exists a superior and recognizable governing caste to which men should by nature cheerfully submit, there is no approach to a good society save by democracy. The alternative is tyranny.

This logical conclusion is supported by the history of human societies. We have admitted the imperfections of democracies, yet they challenge comparison with any other form of society.

What is at stake is man's capacity to maintain a tolerable social order. If it cannot be done under democracy it cannot be done at all. Under no other system can the power which in this interdependent age government must possess be kept from corruption or subordinated to the service of the common good. Let us look at the record.

Democracies, it is truly charged, often permit mediocrities or worse to rise to the top. But the famous observation, "Behold, my son, with how little wisdom men are governed," is general in its scope and by no means limited to democracy. The relentless postwar investigations and exposures of the Nazi ruling clique revealed no superior men, unless one should regard complete amorality in pursuit of power as a type of superiority. By and large, the rulers of democratic or comparatively democratic states, *e.g.*, the Scandinavian, French, and English-speaking nations, in the nineteenth and twentieth centuries compare well in ability with their predecessors in aristocratic or autocratic stages of their countries' development or with their contemporaries in nondemocratic states. And the latter produced no such figure as Abraham Lincoln.

The same general answer can be made to the charge that under democracy government tends to be corrupt and venal. American municipalities were, perhaps are, more corruptly governed than German cities before 1914. Financial integrity was high in the old German civil service. But there were more elements of democracy in the Germany of Bismarck and Kaiser Wilhelm II, imperfect as it was, than in Hitler's Germany when standards of honesty in office fell disastrously. Consider the loot collected by Goering from his own people even before World War II. Meanwhile honesty and efficiency in local government and in administration generally increased in Great Britain directly with the growth of democracy. It was indeed the rising tide of a liberal democracy which abolished the rotten borough system and all that it connoted in England.

Hayek's much touted argument in *The Road to Serfdom* that

the worst would come to the top in a socialist society cannot be dismissed as an absurd impossibility. But it must hold, in so far as it holds at all, in the democratic political order as well as in a socialist order or an industrial democracy. Yet Hayek writes as an avowed champion of the liberalism which in Britain had become definitely connected with political democracy and had grown with it, without bringing the worst to the top.

To the cure of the sickness of our times conventional democracy has thus far proved itself unequal. But the active enemies of our peace have been totalitarian, not democratic. The civilization which failed from 1914 on to meet the test was not primarily to be characterized as democratic, but as acquisitive, capitalist, nationalist, imperialist. Democracy was not immune to the virus of extreme nationalism but it did not originate it. And, in its most extreme fascist form, nationalism became totalitarian, a support for a dictatorship wholly antidemocratic.

The relationship between democracy and capitalism under the modern alias of free enterprise requires examination. The more or less intellectual champions of "free enterprise" in America stridently insist that on it depend both democracy and individual liberty. It is true that in its struggle against feudalism the rising bourgeoisie had to proclaim a freedom of the individual not determined by status or fixed at birth. That process was good even though it tended to weaken the sense of responsibility of the individual or group to society. As against mercantilism and other forms of state control of economy, the devotees of the profit system sought liberty of economic action by individuals and voluntary groups. Democracy, or some approach to it in politics, was a political weapon against a feudal autocracy. In America, where capitalism grew strongest, the conditions of pioneer expansion were peculiarly favorable to the theory that that government is best which governs least. Yet Jefferson himself, still more the Jacksonian Democrats, turned to the state to provide education for the people, thus markedly extending the function of government.

And very definitely there was another side to the historical development of democracy and capitalism as allied forces. Your bourgeoisie by no means welcomed workers or peasants to a share in the government except as concessions were forced by them or granted to them to hold their support in the struggle against the landed aristocracy. Workers were "hands." Labor was to be obtained in the market like other commodities. And the nineteenth century was far advanced in Great Britain before it could plausibly be argued that the masses had gained rather than lost by the Industrial Revolution. Not they who invested their lives, but those who invested their money, were rulers of industry. In politics, as in industry, government spokesmen for the new class in power wanted property qualifications for suffrage. As late as 1842 the liberal Thomas Babington Macaulay, opposing the second Chartist petition in the British House of Commons, declared: "I am opposed to universal suffrage. I believe universal suffrage would be fatal to all the purposes for which government exists and for which aristocracies and all other things exist, and that it is incompatible with the very existence of civilization."

Modern champions of capitalism would probably say as much if universal suffrage had not become in England and America an accomplished fact without destroying civilization. They still resist the notion that men good enough to vote for the President and congressmen might be good enough to vote for directors in the corporations where they work.[1] And they fail to see how a growth of private monopoly or oligopoly in control of the press, radio, and movies, as well as other business, denies even the qualified democracy of the *laissez-faire* economy. To argue, therefore, that democracy and private capitalism are Siamese twins and that democracy must die with the death of private capitalism is to flout past history and present-day facts. Historically, it has been the death of the old order under the strains of war and depression in Russia, Italy, and Germany where democracy had not been

[1] Note that modern democratic socialists do not suggest direct choice of foremen or managers by the workers under them.

very strongly established which has led to totalitarianism.

What I have been doing, perforce, is to defend democracy by comparison. Most of us love it today in the degree that we hate totalitarianism. And the democracy which has only this negative support has little dynamic quality and many grave weaknesses. Class interest like greed for profit, and popular passions like nationalism, may be the active causes of most of our social sins of omission and commission, but it is undeniably discouraging to think that in America, where the final appeal is to "the people," so many of them are ill informed, apathetic, and prejudiced. It is a situation only partially to be explained or condoned by the imperfections of our educational system. Mere information or formal education won't save us, but certainly wisdom is not derived from ignorance, much less from apathy. The shocking ignorance of American history discovered by the famous *New York Times* survey, the easy acceptance of a Bilbo or a Hague by the masses, the facts that on so controversial an issue as the Taft-Hartley Labor Act 75 per cent of those interviewed in the Gallup Poll, though most of them had strong likes or dislikes, could not name a concrete provision that they liked, and 85 per cent that they disliked, do not breed confidence in our democracy's ability to face triumphantly the crisis upon which the fate of our civilization, if not our human race, depends.

A Sunday issue of the *New York Times* (September 27, 1947) carried two contrasting stories. Editorially, the *Times* quoted a study by Dr. Max Radin, Professor of Law at the University of California, concerning the reaction of voters to referenda placed on the California ballot between 1936 and 1946. Sixty-eight proposals were rejected by the people and forty-eight were approved. Dr. Radin concluded: "The danger of quick nostrums in public policy being forced on the voters by demagogues is demonstrably nonexistent. The representative legislature is much more susceptible to such influences."

The same issue of the *Times* carried a vivid account by Gilbert Bailey, one of its staff writers, of his experiences accompanying

Congressman Joe Martin—then Speaker—on one of his systematic tours for meeting the people of his Massachusetts district. Plenty of them talked to him but not on the issues which threaten disaster. The writer concludes: "And I couldn't help but wonder at what state in a supreme crisis the pulse of the constituency one heard so much about really begins to beat." The answer would not be found in mechanically increasing opportunities to vote. Legislation in California as contrasted with legislation without the referendum in New York does not justify that conclusion.

It is correct but not very helpful simply to urge "better education" as a cure. What sort of education and by whom in this age of high-powered propaganda? If—as is clearly the case—no elite, no class, no individual is our predestined Messiah, how shall we be saved?

The beginning of the answer may lie in a breakdown of the general indictment of democracy's inadequacies so that we may see what are its specific weaknesses and what may be done to cure them without renouncing democracy itself. A list of problems might go somewhat as follows:

First, the necessity for a common purpose underlying inescapable conflicts and permitting constructive compromise. It has frequently been said that ability to compromise diverse opinions and interests is the lifeblood of a successful democracy. That is true and the fact has implications both for good and evil—evil because some issues need a comprehensive and forthright handling of which politicians and people trained in the arts of compromise and without unifying purpose are incapable. Compromises on fundamental issues like slavery postponed a realistic facing of the problem at the price of making inescapable a civil strife which possibly a definite program adopted in time might have averted. Only in the United States did the emancipation of chattel slaves require a civil war.

On the other hand, the peaceful existence of a modern non-totalitarian society depends upon its capacity for intelligent or constructive compromise. There is no other way in which a society can carry on so long as there is no detailed uniformity of belief and interest. In modern society there is no such uniformity. Certain tolerances and accommodations are imperative unless we want either perpetual strife or submission to authoritarian rule. Few governments have been as tyrannical or, in the long run, as unsuccessful as those in the hands of sincere men who believed that they were acting for God or in the name of absolute truth. The belief which must unite men in modern society sufficiently to permit democracy to work must include tolerance of differing opinions, and faith in persuasion—faith, that is, in a method which often requires compromise but not compromise which violates the basic integrity of democracy.

The classic Marxist doctrine of *the* class struggle unquestionably raises difficulties for democracy because it suggests a struggle which cannot or should not be compromised. The socialist song, "The International," makes the workers of the world, described as "the prisoners of starvation," declare: "We have been naught; we shall be all." The process by which one class becomes and remains *all* is scarcely democratic. Whether and to what degree class conflict can be settled by democratic process has been a point of discussion and controversy among socialists, especially orthodox Marxists. It becomes less of a problem to the degree that the line of division becomes less sharp.

In any event, it is absurd to imagine a society without tensions and conflicts. But there are conflicts on very different levels and of different sorts of intensity. The struggle between a master and a slave class arises from the fact of slavery, a fact in itself the negation of democracy. But the end of major class conflict between master and slave, landowner and serf, or capitalist and worker, would not mean the end of differences of opinion and interests. Even in a society no longer dominantly acquisitive, a society free from present-day exploitations by private owners or the police state, there will be differences of opinion on the way the national income should be divided. Justice cannot be reduced to a mathematical formula whose obvious and total correctness will demand and receive universal acceptance. There will always be managers, farmers, industrial workers, and other groups not only with special interests but points of view partially shaped by the nature of their work.

That is one reason why there never can be a genuine dictatorship of the whole proletariat or working class. To equate such dictatorship with democracy because the workers are the majority is to assume a nonexistent identity among workers of interest and opinion. It is a semantic solution. Dictatorship can only be exercised by a disciplined group, an elite, a company of true believers themselves under leadership.

The fact of conflict between groups is itself a potential bulwark for democracy against stagnation or dictatorship. No one group, unless it is organized under a dictatorship based on complete control of the apparatus of a police state, will be, or at any rate remain, powerful enough to dominate society or the state. Today, when the class interest of workers tends to unite them in a struggle for a more abundant life, it has not been able to unite them in any monolithic economic and political organization. In America we have the C.I.O. and the A.F.L.; in England the one trade union congress is far from being a strongly centralized, monolithic body. Few things are more certain than that industrial workers, uncontrolled by a dominant elite, will not operate as unified monopolists of power intent upon imposing their single will upon society once the commanding heights of the economic order are socially owned and controlled, not while there is even an imperfect democracy. The unity of economic classes, such as it is, is mostly a unity of opposition against another class—negative, not positive.

Democracy will be the healthier when individuals will not be units lost in one vast society but will function usually with and through one or more groups to which they belong as producers and consumers. These groups must be held together by conscious concern for the common good. There will be no *final* conflict in a healthy society nor, indeed, in any society unless and until the severity of the conflict and the nature of the weapons employed should destroy civilization, if not mankind.

In emphasizing the potential value to a healthy democracy of differences between groups, I am not reinstating in somewhat different form the old radical doctrine which earlier in this chapter I rejected, namely, that there is an *automatic* cancellation of selfish interests under democracy. We have seen enough of pressure politics in America to know better. I am merely arguing that there is hope of safety and health for democracy in the improbability that any great mass majority will act—at least very long—as a unified whole at the expense of minorities, with no concern for individual right.

The process of conflict and compromise which must characterize democracy, we must always remember, will be safe only so long as deep down individuals and groups are held together by some unifying loyalty, some common purpose. Nationalism within states has been such a unifying principle. The tragedy is that it has worked primarily by exalting hate or fear of other nations rather than love of one's fellow citizens. The supreme necessity for successful democracy must be a loyalty, akin to the passion of patriotism in war but uncorrupted by hate, to a society which seeks consciously to function as a fellowship of free men.

It is in education of men in this concept of the common good, the inculcation of a loyalty to it, that there lies hope for man. That is the education which H. G. Wells believed was the alternative to catastrophe and of which, at the end of his life, he despaired. For democracy, purpose is even more important than program.

The second major problem for democracy arises from the disparity between the magnitude and complexity of the decisions governments must make and the interest, intelligence and information possessed by the democratic electorate.

One could illustrate this problem at length. We have said enough in other connections to make it superfluous to prove that democracies dependent upon the majority vote are not endowed with wisdom by adding together the follies, prejudices, and interests of the voters. Indeed, under the compulsion of the crowd, the result may be a collective intelligence less than the intelligence of the average individual. Reinhold Niebuhr wrote a provocative book, *Moral Man and Immoral Society*. He might have written another along similar lines of reasoning on intelligent man and unintelligent society.

In both cases there is another side. Men will often vote at the polls for better laws than individually they would impose on their own conduct; for social standards and services to which as individuals they would give little active support. The Ten Commandments and even the Sermon on the Mount would get a big vote. Sometimes certain nations seem more mature than the average citizen of them. But it remains a serious fact that most men function as voters, even as they function as husbands and fathers, with less thought, less concern for reliable information, less direct education for their task than they demand in preparation for their favorite sport.

Clearly, a successful democracy must improve the quality of its education. But that is not the whole answer to our problem. It can be simplified and made more soluble if in organizing and operating our democracy we will do these things:

First, learn to avoid or minimize the use of techniques which make us act like a crowd rather than as comrades in the strange business of living who must seek rational answers to our common problems.

We socialists have frequently been reproached because we did not copy and use for good ends some of Hitler's techniques of organizing parades, meetings, and demonstrations so as to create a sort of mass hypnotism. One must admit that there is a legitimate organizational skill which we American socialists, and democratic socialists generally, have not learned and applied as well as we should—as well, perhaps, as fascists, communists, or American demagogues like Huey Long or even Henry Wallace. But increasingly I am persuaded that no party concerned for the integrity of the democratic process can deliberately resort to the techniques of fascists and communists for mass hypnotism and get that modicum of rationality without which democracy is doomed.

It would be as undesirable as it is impossible to discuss great issues or to appeal to men for effective action in terms of cold reason without emotional warmth. I do not know of any infallible formula for laying down a line between a legitimate appeal to human beings with emotions as well as reason and an illegitimate attempt at mass hypnosis. But a line exists and certain practices made familiar in our time by their nature threaten democracy even if employed allegedly (as in many religious revivals) for good ends. Against such practices, unless they involve the creation of private armies and the commission of overt acts against peace, democracies cannot safely legislate prohibitions. The attempt might bring in repressions worse than the evil at which they were directed. Here, education is our one hope.

A further essential for successful democracy which follows on what we have said is such organization of its structure as will protect civil liberties and minority rights but permit the majority in control of government to act and act decisively in matters where delay is serious. The American Constitution tends to tie up effective action by government or people in a network of checks and balances far in excess of what may be desirable to permit an appeal from Philip drunk to Philip sober. Theoretically, the absolute supremacy of the British Parliament opens up opposite dangers of precipitate action and the tyranny of the majority. Practically, however, these dangers for England are lessened by the strength of custom in a nation with singular reverence for custom and historic precedent.

Finally, a successful modern democracy requires us to make a sound differentiation between basic decisions and choices of rulers on which the electorate must pass and decisions on subsidiary matters which should be entrusted to administrative agencies or specialized groups particularly concerned and hence familiar with the problems.

In our American society, very considerable powers are now entrusted to regulatory commissions like the Interstate Commerce Commission, to administrative authorities like the Tennessee Valley Authority, and to nongovernmental agencies like bar and medical associations. To such a list one might fairly add the controls inherent in the industrial order and collective bargaining agreements which govern large segments of our economic life. The Bar Association and John L. Lewis' United Mine Workers (both of which groups may resent this bracketing) are imperfect group democracies concerned in controlling the jobs by which they earn their living, but the arrangements they make affect us all.

Our experiments under the New Deal and in the war with administrative regulation or law have not all been successful, but if Congress had tried to enact all necessary regulations there would have been complete governmental collapse. Justified but often exaggerated complaints against red tape, pettifogging and arrogance in administrative office call attention to the need for change in attitude and simplification of machinery in governmental administration.

It is equally true that the self-government of the bar and medical associations in its effect on the public leaves much to be desired. Their motto isn't *noblesse oblige*, much less the greatest good for the greatest number. Yet there again the remedy certainly does not lie in referring all their present control over their own members to town meetings, state legislatures, or Congress. Neither is that the solution for the evils suffered by the public when monopolistic labor unions work out agreements with great corporations, sometimes at the public's expense. The problem here is education in proper attitudes and a clarification of the areas in which these group democracies may legitimately and effectively act.

Much of this discussion boils down to the necessity of far more attention to the techniques of democracy and must be postponed to later chapters.

Important as is the increase of knowledge and understanding and the improvement of democratic techniques, we cannot afford to forget that where governments, both democratic and undemocratic, most flagrantly and dangerously go wrong is not in handling complex problems but in the relatively simple field of moral issues. And the classes err as much as the masses. It is on moral discrimination that peace or war, the nature of peace after war, fraternity between races, even the correct distribution of the national income primarily depend. The immense complexity of our problems was a factor in the bitter mistakes made at Teheran, Yalta, and Potsdam; it is a factor in the comparative impotence of the United Nations. But basically the decisions that perpetuated slavery and displaced some twelve to fifteen millions of Europeans after V-E Day sprang from simple moral failure: the triumph of vengeance and hate and a completely ruthless nationalism. The failures of the United Nations arise not from the stupidity of its delegates or the national masses behind them but from rival drives for power which are the more dangerous when directed by men with high intelligence quotients. The requirements for successful democracy are basically moral.

Chapter 13

***

The Failures of Private Capitalism

THE SORT of "one world" in which we live is something which neither nineteenth-century socialists nor capitalists correctly predicted. The Second World War gave the final death blow to the capitalism of Adam Smith but, in dying, that system did not give birth to the socialism of Karl Marx or of any other systematic thinker. *Laissez-faire* economics has yielded supremacy even in America to a high degree of confused collectivism which has not yet achieved the material or spiritual objectives of socialism. State intervention in the economic process, and varying sorts, kinds, and degrees of planning, are universal commonplaces. In America labor unions and the farm lobby have great power over our economy. Private monopolies flourish. But there is still much competitive capitalism and belief in "free enterprise" is general. The practice of it is another matter. As one student put it, "The only example of pure free enterprise I can think of in America is boys playing marbles for keeps."

In countries neither communist nor socialist the extension of state activities in the economic sphere is in part the result of two world wars and anticipation of a third, in part an effort to forestall socialism by some brand of the "welfare state," in part a necessity under our nationalist system because of lack of private capital within the nation. Thus, Tillman Durdin reported in the *New York Times* (November 27, 1949), from Hong Kong, that state-owned business in Red China is expanding beyond the original plans of the communists themselves largely because "Chinese economy has been in such a state of collapse that only state resources can deal with many of the operations required." In great degree that will be true of the processes of development in all underdeveloped countries, many of which will look for international aid under the control of the United Nations or some agency established by special agreement.

In Great Britain, as we have seen, the Conservative Party actually boasts that it fathered the welfare state, generally identified in America with socialism.

In America itself, where private capitalism is still strong, it has in action almost abandoned its logical *laissez-faire* justification. Senator Taft, a vigorous and intelligent champion of the older economics, has felt obliged in his battle for "free enterprise" to accept degrees of control utterly anathema to the teachers of his—and my—college days. He supported a law for federal subsidy and direction of housing completely inconsistent with his faith in the adequacy of private initiative and the automatic equilibrium of markets. Our supposedly conservative farmers not unreasonably demand a support of prices quite inconsistent with true "free enterprise." The phrase itself on the lips of private monopolists, autocratic chiefs of powerful labor unions, and manipulators of that potent lobby, the farm bloc, has become at best an incantation, at worst, sheer hypocrisy. Socialists can better prove the plight of private capitalism in the country where it is strongest by the words and deeds of its friends than by their own arguments.

It is impossible today to contemplate any victory over the world's hunger save by a degree of planning and social control at war with *laissez faire* and the market economy. Theorists most opposed to "statism" and socialism advocate fiscal policies, tax programs, and legal limitations on size in the interest of competition which necessarily will exact the continuous intervention of an alert and vigorous government. Their proposed controls at once to force competition, and inconsistently to guarantee a fair price while protecting the public from the worst exploitations of capitalism, would require about as much of the state as we socialists have demanded of it without providing adequate grounds for belief that in the process poverty could be conquered or depression averted. It is not hard for socialists to point out the intellectual bankruptcy of our curious confusion of an economy of private monopoly (two hundred corporations control half the business wealth of America) moderated by the existence of large areas of competition, by the pressure of powerful labor unions, and by the intervention of government to deal with emergency situations and protect the interests of groups like the farm bloc. The frantic efforts of capitalist spokesmen to justify their system by appeal to a freedom never heretofore the concern of capitalism is a sign of its decline.

It may also argue a guilt complex in that capitalism's defenders thus seek some ethical justification of a system which Lord Keynes (not himself a socialist) described as "absolutely irreligious, without internal union, without much public spirit, often, though not always, a mere congeries of possessors and pursuers." [1] Private capitalism cannot indefinitely be saved by an appeal to the dignity of man which it has so ruthlessly disregarded by its impersonal system, or by frantic appeals to fear of the state. There is a real danger in the insincerity of men who are indifferent or worse to concrete denials of liberty in the United States and yet declare

[1] Quoted by Francis Williams in *Socialist Britain* (Viking), p. 6.

capitalism to be its only defender against "Communism, Fascism and Socialism," all of them, as one prominent congressman belligerently told his audience, "out of the same bottle—statism."

The advantage of *laissez-faire* economy theoretically was that it was dynamic, progressive, and, at the same time, self-regulating; that it did not require the intervention of the state in behalf either of the strong or the weak. If that had been true, we might perhaps have forgiven or condoned exploitation by King Profit and his crass estimate of human values in terms of dollars and cents. Planning for the common good is difficult, and if "God and nature" had so "planned the frame" that "self-love and social are the same," life would have been easier. That nothing of the sort is true is attested by every day's experience.

The uncompromising *laissez-faire* liberalism, the economic system so dear to a Hayek or a Von Mises, never really existed in a pure form, and its reign was limited. Its tenets were worked out of the great misery of the Industrial Revolution; its golden age was short. It assumed an economic order which would function independently of political groupings and politics—unless prevented by positive governmental interference; and a universal, self-regulatory law of the market which ought to be global in extent. Logically it required an international fiscal system—the gold standard; free trade; the self-regulating market within liberal (not totalitarian) states. It depended upon freedom from great wars, a freedom partially guaranteed in the nineteenth century by a balance of power between strong nations. Compared with the practices of totalitarian states, it had its virtues. But in its conception of the economic man and the supremacy of a pure and undiluted profit motive it was inhuman and contrary to agelong human experience under various civilizations.

The balance-of-power system collapsed in two great wars. Gold lost any great intrinsic value for civilized men so that the gold standard became an artificial thing impossible to maintain in the face of the confusion of the world after 1914. Free trade was never fully achieved in the face of national interests which interests in a warlike world required a high degree of national self-sufficiency. In practice free trade, or an approach to it, meant a considerable exploitation of the resources of economically backward nations and the "export of topsoil," an unbalanced economy in which production of food and of manufactured foods were widely separated, in the long run to the hurt alike of England, the mother of capitalism, and of colonial regions. The repeal of the corn laws in 1846 was an immense blessing to the poor workers of England but its maximum long-range advantages required an international security and a balance which the market economy by itself could not bring. Polyani acutely observes: "As a result [of the application of the industrial-agricultural division of labor of the planet] peoples of distant zones were drawn into the vortex of change, the origins of which were obscure to them, while the European nations became dependent for their everyday activities upon a not yet ensured integration of the life of mankind." [2]

The socialist indictment of this capitalist system in its present state of confusion is by no means dependent upon an orthodox acceptance of a Marxist theory of increasing misery. We socialists may or may not believe (as Marx did) that technological development out of a feudalistic handcraft economy was inexorably tied up with private capitalism and inconceivable without it. But historically it was capitalism of a *laissez-faire* type which broke the feudal yoke. The release of productive energy passes therefore as the achievement of capitalism. The extraordinary progress of science made this release of energy productive beyond the expectation of capitalism's friends or foes.

An owning class or management in its behalf did not have to keep wages on a subsistence level to provide profits. It could afford real wage increases either to anticipate labor troubles or to end them. More than that, as we have seen in discussing socialism in America, there came a time when obviously profits depended upon mass consumption else the achievements of mass production were in vain.

[2] *The Great Transformation*, p. 181. This book of Polyani's is a remarkable study of the development of capitalism.

Mass consumption depended upon wages well above a subsistence level. It became definitely to the interest of the owning class— which often was exceedingly blind to that fact—to support a high-wage policy. This fact, however, introduced difficulties in the automatic regulation of a market economy which we shall later examine.

Under capitalism this productive process gave us along with more goods for consumers the assembly line for workers with its depersonalizing consequences. Aldous Huxley's *Brave New World* is a familiar satire upon the effects of mass production of which he makes Henry Ford's name a symbol. A dreary appraisal of it as it seems to many workers is given in a recent book, *The UAW and Walter Reuther* by Howe and Widick.[3] Unquestionably this method of production, apparently necessary to abundance and the end of a stunting and crippling poverty, raises problems that no political or economic system can automatically cure. Yet the ill consequences of the assembly line on the workers can be diminished by certain applications of psychology to the alleviation of the process, by making men citizens in the industry in which they invest their labor, and by increasing and enriching leisure. In any case, Huxley's factory worker would have little cause to envy Markham's "Man With a Hoe."

In prosperous America, blessed beyond all other nations in facilities for providing abundance, it is not the assembly line which is the major grievance. It is the failure of the business of production and distribution, bitterly evident in the fact that in the very prosperous year 1948 almost ten million American families, between a quarter and a third of the whole, received incomes under $2,000 a year. One million seven hundred thousand farm families had less than $1,000. At the prevailing prices that meant that Franklin D. Roosevelt's famous statement is still approximately true: one-third

[3] An experienced official of the United Automobile Workers who himself hated work on the assembly line told me that during the rush of war work most of the complaints from workers whom he had to represent (especially women) were against being transferred in emergency from the repetitive processes they had learned.

of our people are ill fed, ill clothed and ill housed. And it doesn't help them much to tell them how much worse off are the people of India, China, or Russia, or to deafen them by shouting figures to prove how much richer we all are collectively than our forefathers who subdued the American wilderness. They had compensations which we lack.

I have spoken of the resources which have blessed America. Under private capitalism they have been exploited in a carnival of waste which still continues. It is a natural, even a necessary, accompaniment of our American conception of the righteousness of the private ownership of natural resources and their development for private profit.

Under this concept, our topsoil in most agricultural counties has been mined out. Our magnificent first-growth forests were ruthlessly burned and logged. Over great areas, not a tree was left to an acre for reseeding. No heed was paid to the effect of deforestation on soil conservation, floods, and the climate itself. Only recently, and then mostly by government, has any action been taken for forest conservation or restoration.

The same sort of thing has been true of our mineral wealth. Coal is so plentiful as to seem inexhaustible. But millions of tons are wasted. And beautiful and entirely practicable plans for turning coal to power near mine mouths, its by-products being scientifically utilized, its ugly mining villages cleaned up and made comfortable, and smoke and soot conquered, remain dreams because competing private owners can't possibly afford thus to reorganize the industry.

As for petroleum, the whole principle of property in oil wells is a legalization of robbery. Oil prospectors strike oil on, or rather under, A's land. He, or the company to which he leases the land or sells it, claims the right to all the oil that may come up through that well. The landowner did not make the oil, the pool which is drained through his well may under modern conditions of drilling be more than a mile below the surface of his farm or lot. It may extend far beyond the surface area that he owns, yet his by legal definition is all the oil which may be pumped up through the well. There is nothing for it but for his neighbors B, C, D, and the rest of the alphabet, at once to drill, or permit others to drill, through their land to try to strike the same pool before it is too late. Hence it is that great oil fields are forests of unnecessary wells. In eastern Texas alone, in spite of an effort by the state to assert some social control and to prorate the oil, an effort enforced for a while by militia, the number of wells increased from 1,625 in the summer of the depression year 1931 to approximately ten thousand in the spring of 1933. I shall not soon forget the impression made upon me, a greenhorn, when in eastern Texas for the first time, I saw a cloudy winter's sky, at dusk, lurid from the flames of gas burning from the top of pipes. It was dangerous, I was told, to let the gas escape into the air and it did not pay the profit seekers to store or ship it, hence they burned it. This process has meant not only an actual waste of natural gas running into millions of cubic feet but also a very inefficient utilization of the pressure of the gas in helping to force up oil and to keep out the encroachments of water. The competitive drilling of unnecessary wells is in itself an immense waste.

The average man thinks of petroleum in terms of monopoly such as Standard Oil established out of cutthroat competition. Today there is competition which usually doesn't affect an agreed price for gasoline, a kind of competition which hurts us consumers. In the dark year 1932, Glen B. Winship, writing in *World's Work*, said that unnecessary duplication of facilities cost the motoring public two cents on every gallon of gas that it buys.[4]

A stock excuse for this wasteful exploitation is that it had compensations in the pioneering energy it stimulated. Perhaps, once. But today the pioneers who count are trained soil experts, foresters, geologists, and engineers. Petroleum isn't discovered or developed by lucky hunches, nor are deep wells driven by industrial enter-

---

[4] I have quoted here somewhat freely from my book *Human Exploitation*, published in 1934. The facts about coal, petroleum, etc., have not greatly changed.

prisers who take their own risks, but by experts. These experts should be working for us all.

The great petroleum companies are not the only ones to make the public pay through the nose for wasteful types of competition. Middlemen, high-pressure salesmen, and the advertising business get an unduly large part of the consumer's dollar. Decent salesmanship has social value but lower prices would do more to distribute certain goods than the excessive pressure salesmanship to which we are subjected. No wonder ulcers are an occupational disease for the gentry who have to discover new stunts to advertise nonexistent superiorities of the same sorts of soap and cigarettes. Much of our frantic advertising not only wastes money but breeds an ominously cynical distrust of the spoken and written word.

Along with waste, the great economic crime of private capitalism is that it has given us chronic unemployment. The evolution of capitalism in the western world has not put all but a handful of us into a proletariat permanently half-starved. It has periodically put millions of us out of work and, between 1929 and 1940, depression tended to become chronic. While the number of unemployed in our own country fluctuated widely from the high point of the first quarter of 1933, it was always numbered in millions. In September, 1939, at the outbreak of World War II, it was estimated at ten million. War and only war brought full employment and then, as Broadus Mitchell remarks in his *Depression Decade*, "if the nation had ten million unemployed when the war began, a few years later, when it was well into the conflict, it had three times as many not productively employed."

Roosevelt had provided a fairly decent subsidization of the unemployed through various devices. Necessarily, this process, a variant of the bread and circuses program of the Roman emperors, menaced self-respecting democracy. When we accept a social order in which large numbers of men are dependent upon the bounty of government rather than upon their own labor in a going economy, we shall have accepted a situation fatal to a progressive democracy. Believers in "free enterprise" profess terrible alarm lest workers under any sort of socialism be directly dependent on government for jobs. That result can be minimized under proper planning and the correct mechanisms of social control. It is in any event less dangerous than when able-bodied adults are dependent upon government to be able to live without jobs except in made work.

It is a simple fact that unemployment as a widespread phenomenon was created by capitalism. It was not characteristic of the old agricultural and handcraft society in which men and women found something to do, except in times of national disaster, as long as they had strength. (The idle proletariat of the city of Rome were something of an historical exception to this rule.)

Before cyclical or chronic unemployment could become common, it was necessary that machine production should be able to provide something of a surplus over effective demand. It was also necessary that effective demand be something different from the total of human wants and needs. Unemployment originates in the fact that the whole body of workers with hand and brain receives less than is necessary to buy back the equivalent of what the workers create. A large sum is sluiced off by the receivers of profit, rent, and interest, and the administration of the whole economic apparatus is in the hands of those whose actions are controlled by hope of profit. To be sure, the receivers of profit, rent, and income are also consumers. What they do not spend they tend to invest and so provide work. If this process goes smoothly and reinvestment absorbs savings from the receivers of unearned income and the more fortunate workers, employment is maintained. But hoarding, hope of return at compound interest, and other factors seriously interfere with productive investment. Investors tend to expect their investments to be immortal and attempt to increase their total savings by reinvesting the income on them. That is, they look for compound interest. In biology "procreation within rather narrow limits must be offset by death. . . ." Similarly the offspring from money or wealth in the form of interest "must be almost equally matched by economic death—losses and bankruptcy." [5] This economic death is politically and socially very upsetting. To delay or check it even a believer in rugged individualism like Herbert Hoover rushed in with government aid through the Reconstruction Finance Corporation.

Productive investment in a complex economy with advanced industrialization depends upon the possibility of high consumption which in turn depends upon a high return to workers with hand and brain in real salaries and wages. Then under capitalism arises this dilemma. "High consumption encourages investment by the prospect of easy sales, but consumption comes from high wages and low prices—that is, from low profits." [6] Low profits discourage private investment.

There is a serious attempt in some circles to define profit merely as "payment for tools." To be sure, what is commonly reckoned profit under capitalism includes payment for tools as it also includes payment to some owners for managerial service. But profit is more than that. It is in part a reward for risk, in part of legal possession, extorted at the expense of workers in low wages and consumers in high prices, and eventually this situation discourages investment. Large profits are both a stimulus to and the nemesis of prosperity. This is a truth not contradicted by the postwar boom. At the end of 1949 there were factors which might delay depression. There were not constructive plans which would forever avert it.

Theoretically, the Keynesian version of capitalism—far removed from a logical "free-enterprise" system—might deal effectively with unemployment, especially if it should be supplemented by the elaborate plans set forth by Sir William Beveridge. We shall deal with this possibility in our positive discussion of socialism.

American capitalism, which does not accept the gospel according to Keynes, is probably better equipped to deal with unemployment and depression than in the twenties. But its principal intel-

[5] H. Gordon Hayes: *Spending, Saving and Employment* (Knopf), pp. 38–39.

[6] *Ibid.*, p. 199. In general, I accept Professor Hayes's analysis which, although non-Marxist, seems to me definitely socialist.

lectual spokesman, Dr. Emerson Schmidt of the Chamber of Commerce, calmly, almost casually, assured a Town Meeting audience (May 2, 1950) that we should need at least three million unemployed to prevent inflation. To which Leon Keyserling, chairman of the President's Economic Advisers, later made a reply which socialists would repeat with emphasis: "Our problem is to keep our economy healthy, and to keep it healthy we must recognize the fundamental responsibility to keep unemployment to minimum levels. If that causes problems of inflation because prices misbehave or because wages misbehave, we must deal with those."

From a different approach, there is evidence that unemployment is far from conquered. The magazine *U.S. News and World Report* in the spring of 1950 gave reasons to support fear of an army of twelve million unemployed by 1955 even if production should remain very high in America provided (1) that the present rate of increase in population should be maintained; and (2) that the increase in the uses of labor-saving machinery be continued. Under the latter head, it did not take account of a catastrophic use of electronic robots such as are now under development. But neither did it take account of new war as a cure for unemployment.

Obviously to deal with this situation in a peacetime economy requires planning, control of the rate of introduction of labor-saving machinery, and studied expansion of production, all of which private capitalism has opposed. No one can contemplate a happy democracy in which the unemployed are numbered by millions even if they are somehow kept from starving. Such a society would dangerously enhance that sense of alienation, of not belonging, which is already so disquieting a fact of our times.

Some sort of welfare state we are bound to have and any welfare state, however far short of the socialist ideal, requires such a degree of government intervention in economics as to constitute proof of the decline of private capitalism and a massive qualification on free enterprise. Protestations by "liberals" and labor leaders, ardent propagandists of their own version of the welfare state, that they devoutly believe in "free enterprise" are, I insist, stupid or dishonest. They may not be socialists but they ask of the state and demand for labor unions degrees of control over the production and distribution of goods completely out of line with the logic of free enterprise.

At that our Fair Dealers have not saved us from depression and unemployment by the welfare state but by the warfare state and the magnitude of its expenditures on arms. American capitalism was propped by an arms economy even before the Korean war.

This development was not directly and solely the result of capitalism but rather of the cold war. It does not adequately support the strident communist contention that capitalism faced by catastrophic collapse in chronic depression must in any strong nation like the United States become imperialist; that its desperate need of foreign markets to take care of surplus production at home cannot be satisfied by fair trade between peoples; that profit for traders and investors in underdeveloped areas will require some degree of political imperialism. Hence, communists believe, rivalries of strong nations for markets, sources of supply for raw materials and opportunities for investment will lead to war, which may also come from the cumulative resentments of exploited peoples.

We have acknowledged that the First World War was in large part a result of this sort of rivalry between sovereign nations. The explanation of the Second World War was somewhat more complex. The Third World War, if it comes, will be even less the inevitable consequence of the last or imperialist stage of capitalism. Its main cause will be the aggression of organized communist totalitarianism.

The Leninist dogma of capitalist imperialism is central to communist doctrine and profoundly influences its practice. It must be understood and not merely denounced by those who would correct it. Communists loyal to that dogma believe that American capitalism is already necessarily and consciously imperialist. The Marshall Plan, they think, was a deliberate effort of capitalists to postpone depression by dumping surplus goods abroad.

Thousands of Europeans and Asians, not members of any communist party, more or less accept this theory,[7] partly, perhaps, out of conscious or unconscious envy of American good fortune and partly out of suspicion of the capacity of any nation as a nation to act generously.

What, then, are the historical facts about imperialism in America? On the whole, our country has not been imperialist. Once the United States had conquered the Indians and consolidated its continental territory through the Mexican War, it turned its major intention to developing what it had. Its economy had no such need of foreign supplies of raw materials or foreign markets as the British, French, and German capitalisms which by that need had been spurred toward empire.

Americans were not completely immune to the imperial tendencies of their times. Pride as well as some economic interests urged important sections of our population in this direction. We had our fling in the Spanish War and dollar diplomacy. The financial rewards were not great. Our domestic economy was capable of great expansion and, in the final tests, America thus far has refused to follow the imperialist road to a dubious profit and a power attended by more trouble than it was worth. She demanded no concessions in China and used the Boxer indemnity for Chinese scholarships. She had fixed the date for Philippine independence before World War II and fulfilled her promise—not without attaching, unjustly, some economic strings to her gift. What is more extraordinary, under Republican Presidents Coolidge and Hoover she refused to back up American enterprises and investors in Mexico by force. Still later, under Roosevelt, when Mexico confiscated American oil holdings and the Latin-American nations generally defaulted on the loans of American bankers, there was not only no military aggression, but small outcry for it. Once more, after World War II, America sought no imperial rewards.

Although European relief by 1948 had become a prop to an in-

[7] Their belief is sharply to be distinguished from the Soviet propaganda of the Big Lie that the United States was the aggressor in the Korean war, but it makes easier the acceptance of the lie.

flationary economy, so far were American capitalists from feeling any compulsion to tax themselves along with the rest of the people in order to dispose of surplus abroad that even after recession had set in, very powerful sections of the American business community demanded cuts, not expansion, of that Marshall Plan aid which European leftists had persuaded themselves was nothing but a self-interested device of an imperialist America. That it had elements of self-interest is true enough and that some of that self-interest was stupidly selfish is also true. But that was not the outstanding fact about the plan. What was significant was the enlightened understanding it displayed, and the degree of cooperation with European nations in its administration. Surprisingly, capitalist America did not dictate terms to them.

From the beginning of the long argument on aid to Europe, as I found in various debates, the arguments of the *Chicago Tribune* and spokesmen for the NAM point of view had some curious resemblances to those of the Wallace-communist alliance.[8] Isolationism dies hard. The Marshall Plan has not to date replaced it by a dictatorial American imperialism.

If American conduct in respect to imperialism did not conform to a conventional Marxist forecast, still less did the conduct of nations conform to the Marxist idea that imperialism was merely and inevitably a stage of *private* capitalist development. The years have proved that the manipulators of state capitalism, fascist or communist, may be at least as strongly impelled toward war for national advantage as the private capitalists whom Lenin regarded as predestined war makers. No explanation of modern war has weight which does not reckon primarily with the organization of men in nationalist states and with the deep concern of men and nations for power as well as profit.

States or their governments in modern times do not project *major* wars for profit and power. Not even Hitler planned his war on a global scale. But governments do go in for militarism and imperialism for the sake of national "security," profit, and power. I

[8] Broken in 1950 by Wallace as a result of communist aggression in Korea.

doubt if today militarism and imperialism could be forced on the American people, except for fear of communist imperialism. That fear—witness the Korean crisis—is justified. Disarmament is at the moment impossible.[9] It is infinitely desirable. We must face the fact that once a nation starts on the road of the armament race in a cold war it is likely to undertake appropriate imperial obligations. It finds that the arms economy may for a considerable time be a successful form of boondoggling against unemployment, but if indefinitely continued and expanded it tends toward bankruptcy and makes certain a grave decline in living standards. Meanwhile, rival militarisms and imperialisms, the politics which support them, and the tensions they engender, breed wars which cannot be guaranteed to remain small any more than a forest fire in dry weather can be kindled and then confined within a small area.

Certainly atomic war is not consciously desired for economic reasons by any considerable number of people anywhere in the world. The people didn't want the wars that we have survived. *But so long as war did not bring with it invasion by land, sea, or air,* it was in the preatomic age far more complacently accepted than most peace lovers like to admit by a civilian population which gained jobs and a certain relief from boredom. In our recent history it was not Roosevelt's "Dr. New Deal" but his "Dr. Win-the-War" who turned chronic depression into prosperity and unemployment into manpower shortage.

The postwar boom was directly the result of purchasing power stored up during the war and a tremendous backlog of economic wants and needs which could not be satisfied during the war. Moreover, our boom economy, as former President Hoover and President Truman's economic advisers seemed to agree, had two crutches: one, an abnormal foreign trade, the result of war's destruction; the other, military expenditures in preparation for the next war. In the economic sense military expenditures are pure boondoggling, worse than leaf-raking. Yet on them, without sub-

[9] But see Chapter 19 on a drive for universal, enforceable disarmament.

stantial protest, the American government has felt compelled to spend annually many times more billions than it ever spent on Roosevelt's relief and work projects which aroused such outcries of anger and alarm in the thirties. It took war, in an America vibrant with unsatisfied wants, to put men, money, and machines to work. It was one war's aftermath and preparation for another which by 1949 kept men at work and moderated the depression—or, more optimistically, the recession.

This is the truth which compels us to consider capitalist decline and socialist construction in terms of a program for all mankind. As Americans we face an economic as well as a political situation beyond our powers of control by purely domestic policies. Our growing armament economy requires a degree of control and planning wholly inconsistent with a free enterprise economy, and at the same time Mr. Truman's current budget is 6 to 8 per cent welfare and 75 per cent warfare for conflicts past and to come—this before the Korean crisis. A peace program hence becomes vital to socialism. The Leninist dogma of inevitable catastrophic destruction of capitalism in violence requires more than intellectual refutation or modification. It requires a positive program for the world and a substitute for the arms economy not yet developed by any anticommunist nation. And it requires a nobler philosophy than capitalism's.

We cannot turn from the general subject of capitalist decline without more specific mention of certain arguments of defenders of free enterprise, "the American Way," against socialism: (1) the allegation that socialism can only work under the control of a police state; and (2) that only capitalism will offer inducements to make men work except under conscription.

The first allegation is discredited by the facts of socialist development in Scandinavia and Great Britain. Its complete refutation must lie in the success of socialism in introducing those varieties of instrumentality and mechanisms of democratic control which are logically possible and will be further discussed in our positive statement of socialism.

The second allegation is obviously absurd on the basis of present performance in America.

In the strict economic sense of the word, profit today is enjoyed mostly by absentee owners; the men who do the real work from managers down are paid by salaries and wages.

In the loose sense of profit as material reward, it is not true that it is the sole motive for productive labor. Men work for many other reasons: because they must in order to live; because they want to "keep up with the Joneses"; because of an inner creative urge; and because of an obligation of service, or more accurately, mutual aid.

The compulsion of necessity as a reason for able-bodied adults to work in order to live, or at least to live well, might easily be increased by a system which ended or extraordinarily limited the possibility of living well by picking one's ancestors, the right corner lot, or the right shares of stock. In the process, the resentment and jealousy which now tend to impede productive work might be greatly lessened.

The creative urge is today the motivation of the most valuable work that is done in science, pure and applied, and the arts. Our great inventors, with a few exceptions like Ford and Edison, have notoriously been failures at getting and keeping great wealth. Pure science even now has to be socially supported by governments, universities, and foundations. Comparatively few corporations maintain pure research laboratories with an eye to ultimately profitable applications of truths discovered.

As for the service motive which I have heard lauded at the same Rotary and Kiwanis clubs which then wildly applaud the profit system disguised as "free enterprise," that also is powerful. We expect it to govern the conduct of soldiers in battle. They risk life itself not for profit but for their comrades and their country. Upon mutual aid the cohesion of the family and the rearing of healthy children depend. In short, by no means is all the world's work done in hope of profit.

Nevertheless, the socialist can afford to admit that in the present stage of society there is place for material incentive. Differentials in material award can be allowed without continuing the profit system. They can be made far more closely to approximate the value of the work performed than today when a sober inspection of the records of America's two hundred wealthiest families would by and large warrant as an answer to the question, "What have they done to gain such wealth?" the simple statement, "They have done us!"

In sum total, this review of the decline of private capitalism does not warrant faith in the automatic success of socialism. It does show that what socialism seeks—plenty, peace, and freedom—are in no sense mere class interests. They are of universal concern. The classes which have escaped proletarian status have not been immune to unemployment, much less to war. They share the spiritual poverty of the acquisitive society. The appeal of democratic socialism should be peculiarly strong to industrial workers. Its deepest strength must lie in the appeal to the whole community in a world made increasingly interdependent not only by its highest ethics but by the compulsions of its way of life.

Chapter 14

The Socialist Answer

Implicit in what I have been saying is the fact that the contrast between the existing American capitalist hell and any probable socialist heaven is less absolute than it seemed in Gene Debs's day. His answer to capitalism was everlastingly right in its warmth of brotherhood and its hatred of exploitation, but the application of his faith seemed simpler then than it does to us.

When we modern socialists state our answer we have to remember that before our eyes total collectivism in Russia has been accompanied by total tyranny. Democratic socialism in Britain has kept freedom but it wrestles—on the whole successfully—with difficulties absent in more fortunate America. Hence we are confronted with the incorrect and unfair but widely propagandized syllogism, "America is capitalist; Britain is socialist. America today is more prosperous than Britain. Therefore capitalism is better than socialism."

Here at home there are those who say that the answer to the

failures of capitalism is not socialism but a pragmatic series of reforms, most of them appropriated from original socialist demands.
A few of Mr. Truman's highbrow friends try to impose a Keynesian pattern on his pragmatism. Others, like Stuart Chase and Irwin
Ross, call in varying accents for a "mixed economy." Mr. Henry
Wallace (who is not Mr. Truman's friend) calls his very mixed
economy "progressive capitalism."

Against all this we socialists insist on a more definite philosophy
of cooperation and integrated planning. Some labor union theorists
are beginning to say what in practice most labor leaders generally
believe: namely, that it doesn't matter much who owns the natural
resources and great aggregations of tools if labor partly by direct
economic pressure and partly by political action can control the
division of income. This notion the socialist emphatically rejects
for reasons which will become increasingly clear as we state our
answer.

Meanwhile, on all these differing pragmatic programs of well-
being as well as on true democratic socialism the Republicans after
the 1948 election officially imposed the name "socialism" or "state
socialism." Their analysis went like this: Truman's Fair Deal equals
socialism; socialism equals or leads to communism. Communism
is the complete foe of freedom; socialism is its enemy only in less
degree. Therefore, said they, the issue is "socialism versus liberty."
And they proceeded in their discussion to show how little they
know about either—except in so far as liberty is interpreted as
the right to exploit. To make confusion worse confounded, most
of these same Republicans had rejoiced that in Britain Churchill
and the Conservatives (whose program was well to the left of Truman's) have stopped socialism by reducing the majority in the
House of Commons to a precarious margin.

I have already in another connection referred to *Fortune's* contention in an article entitled "Socialism by Default" (March, 1949)
that both Truman's and Attlee's programs were examples of
"soft socialism." The nub of the argument was thus stated:

"Collectivism under whatever guise—communism, socialism, or

statist planning of production and distribution—means that the state, the creation of man, becomes his master; and once his master blankets him with an infinity of paper directives. . . . Then at length comes 'the knock at the door'—the pistol-point order of obedience."

This is to affirm that it doesn't matter whether one clings to private profit as king or accepts the philosophy of cooperation; whether, like Truman, one rejects, nominally at least, large-scale social ownership or, like Attlee, seeks to bring it to pass. Likewise, it is to affirm that differences in kinds and degrees of collective ownership are unimportant; and, finally, that historically, totalitarianism has evolved through socialism.

The falsity of this last contention we have had occasion to observe. As for the similarities between the Fair Deal and British socialism, certainly some exist. But the differences are great and important.

They are strikingly illustrated in the fact that the Labour government had a philosophy and a drive which enabled it to carry out its platform of 1945, whereas Truman's promises of 1948 were almost completely unfulfilled by the Congress which his party nominally controlled. Part of the reason lay in the nature of our political system but more of it lay in the failure of Truman's pragmatism in drive and power.

To the degree that the Fair Deal is consciously or unconsciously Keynesian, it shows the weakness of popular or political Keynesianism. That doctrine asserts the possibility of an adequate control of our economy without bothering much with social ownership or a philosophy of cooperation. Government may control inflation and deflation, prevent depression, and guide expansion by its policies of taxing and spending and its direct and indirect controls over investment. Some Keynesians would add an elaborate program of social security on lines laid down by Sir William Beveridge. Others like Professor Jewkes of Manchester (England) reject this as necessarily a part of the "ordeal by planning" which they oppose.

Keynesian ideas and techniques have their value, but on the American record the outlook for the success of Keynesianism as a savior of society in time of depression is not bright. Government spending did not end the great depression until it became the terrible spending of men and money in war. Lord Keynes said that Roosevelt did not spend enough, but under the capitalist psychology it was a victory that the President could persuade Congress to give him as much as it did. Whatever the reason for the New Deal failure, it will be remembered that there were almost ten million unemployed on the eve of Pearl Harbor.

Even after the experiences of depression and war, the Truman Administration would be hard put to it to get enough to spend, or permission to spend it in the right way, to end a real depression should one develop—unless its spending should be for an intensification of the arms race or war itself. On the other side of the picture, if 1949 and 1950 with their high levels of income despite recession and some growth of unemployment require deficit financing, what years won't? As a practicing Keynesian, the President was handicapped because in January, 1949, his advisers led him to forecast a continuance or renewal of inflationary trends. Keynesianism, conscious or unconscious, does not produce infallible prophets.

The enormous size of the national debt is psychologically another discouragement to deficit financing. The attitude both of Congress and the public makes very dubious the process of compensatory taxation in which good years pay for bad. Socialism won't magically and instantly solve this problem of democratic responsibility. It will at least raise it honestly and supply other motivation to meet it than the profit system offers.

The President's more resolute followers are unafraid of debt. In 1949 they urged upon him legislation permitting a very large use of government credit or money for economic expansion through public works and other devices including loans to private enterprises to avert depression. The Murray bill for economic expansion embodying these ideas was introduced in 1949, with some liberal and labor support. It got little attention and the Korean war submerged it altogether. The President had suggested earlier a plan for the government to finance expansion of steel facilities either by loans to the steel companies or by direct construction of marginal plants. This might be revived in terms of war economy.

On this whole theory of putting private capitalism on a dole, the socialist must look askance. The time-honored justification of the profit system was that profits were the legitimate reward of risks taken by private investors, and now, at times when there is much investment capital in private hands, theorists of the dole urge that the government assume most of the risk while the investors reap the benefits. Our socialist proposal for economic expansion to end unemployment, which antedated anything suggested by the President or Senator Murray, proceeded on the assumption that if public money must finance new enterprises, it must be on a cooperative or nonprofit basis. There are all sorts of dangerous pressures implicit in the financing of private enterprises with public money. Our socialist alternative will be further developed in the next chapter.

It certainly is no part of a socialist plan to make the government a kind of auxiliary to steel corporations, big and little. Even Senator Taft complained that when the steel trust raised its prices it should have consulted other interests, since its action was so far-reaching in its effects upon our whole economy. Is it not reasonable to socialize anything that so vitally affects all our interests as to have a power over us greater than some governmental agencies have enjoyed, far more reasonable than to put it on dole?

These differences between socialism and popular Keynesianism are quite too important to permit the Olympian editors of *Fortune* to lump the Truman plan and the British Labour government's actions together as "soft socialism."

Socialism provides for the people a unifying principle with a practical and moral power that all versions of Keynesianism and all purely pragmatic "mixed economies" sadly lack. It insists that if we are not to be torn asunder by a narrow vision of conflicting interests, there must be a basic acceptance of cooperation as the price of plenty, peace, and freedom. Socialism respects the moral power of the indictment of private ownership of natural resources like petroleum, iron, and coal, as well as uranium, which no man made and which nowadays no man merely as an individual entrepreneur discovers or develops. To a socialist it is evident that the vast extension of absentee ownership, almost wholly stripped of managerial function, not only stands in the way of planning production for the common good, but creates passions of possession and of envy which enormously impede progress toward the only good society: a fellowship of free men. Moreover, it is obvious that variations in public spending can be far more intelligently carried out if society itself is the owner of great industries and completely controls the system of money, banking, and credit.

This sort of socialist answer to our problem requires an emotional loyalty but it requires more than mass emotion. It cannot offer absolute and certain salvation by faith or through the automatic and dangerous mechanism of a revolutionary mass movement, however admirable may be the direction in which the mass juggernaut at first begins to roll. It requires sustained intelligence in action.

Basic to it must be a point of view or a philosophy which wins emotional and intellectual support. The good society of the socialist is something different from and better than an acquisitive society in which material benefits might be made more abundant. It is a society of which men feel themselves actively a part. The conquest of poverty itself requires an active sense of fraternity and a practice of cooperation in which is to be found part of life's joy. A universal Hollywood would be a dreadful Utopia.

A socialist ideal and a philosophy of cooperation are even more important than a socialist plan, and they are essential to its strength. Our lives are enriched by variety of loyalties and our actions may be variously motivated. But in the hierarchy of loyalties not individual self-seeking but cooperation must be chief. There are no golden towers of material well-being in which the individual, the group, or the nation can find security, peace, or true satisfaction in our storm-tossed world. Primary emphasis must be on mutual aid and conscious practice of it. This ethical ideal is a scientific necessity in the successful and peaceful management of our highly interdependent economy.

The first insistence, then, of democratic socialism must be that free enterprise is not enough. Freedom, yes, and enterprise are essential. But "free enterprise" as a euphemism for a capitalist economy under the supremacy of private profit is not working and cannot work to solve the problems of peace and plenty or to establish true liberty in the modern world. It is very dangerous to permit a philosophy of the adequacy of capitalist free enterprise to go unchallenged while in practice every group flouts it. The right sort of loyalty is essential to the right sort of economic and political plan. It is not a mere by-product of any inevitable movement in history or any change of the tools of production. It must be consciously taught with intelligent reference to the power of modern technology and the growth of interdependence among men and nations. If we are incapable of this cooperative loyalty we or our civilization will perish.

Nevertheless, no high devotion to the good of men bound together on this strange and beautiful planet by common destiny—or common doom—will absolve us of the necessity for planning and for organizing to carry out our social plans.

Chapter 15

Socialist Planning

Planning is essential in modern society. It is a grim and bitter necessity in war; it is in peace an essential to prevent war and conquer poverty. But there are various kinds of planning. Much of the current objection to planning by government rests on the false analogy of blueprints for buildings. Society is a growing thing. It is not a static organism. It is made up of men with wills of their own. Planning must be in terms of life in which the planners are involved, not of man's controls over inert matter. Plans must be concerned with the directions in which we should go, the goals we should seek, and the roads toward them. It should never be based on a dogmatic acceptance of an abstraction like collectivism as a good in itself. Always the question should be how much collectivism and what sort will serve mankind in pursuit of plenty, peace, and freedom.

In this spirit let us start our discussion of planning by asking what should be socially owned. That has always been a basic question in socialism. I believe it is still basic in spite of the facts (1) that social ownership is not of itself the panacea for all social ills, and (2) that a sufficient degree of overall planning by no means requires such complete collectivization of capital goods as exists today in the Soviet Union. Other governments in war and even in peace have established a considerable degree of control without ownership. Nazi Germany went very far in that direction. In the process it illustrated one of the dangers of the method. If the state is not to be largely the tool of the great interests it nominally controls, it will be under grave temptation to develop extremely authoritarian attitudes and apparatus. For effective control over industries still legally owned by private individuals requires a more arbitrary exercise of political power than the state operation of these industries by public authorities under a system of social ownership.

Moreover, the bureaucracy which watches other people work is even more likely than any public authority which actually works to adopt those attitudes and habits which we associate with bureaucracy at its worst. This statement is supported by experience with bureaucratic controls even in wartime when the stimulus of danger was a spur to action.

Sound democratic socialism will seek public ownership under democratic control of the commanding heights of the modern economic order. It is neither necessary nor desirable, so long as there is unity of purpose in the main direction of our economy, that there should be a monolithic type of ownership and control. There is a wholesome stimulus in competition, or emulation, and in diversity of functional apparatus. There is large room for private ownership when the owners are serving a useful function, provided that their ownership does not give them undue control over our social life. Public ownership need not be of one type. Generally speaking, the state should be the agency of ownership, and public corporations or authorities of somewhat various types its administrators. But there will be a large place for cooperatives, especially consumers' cooperatives, in the good society.

Often it will be advantageous to combine different types of

social ownership and sometimes of social and private ownership. Thus, we have already made a good beginning in setting up co-operatives to distribute electricity in rural areas. These could be linked to a publicly owned giant power system administered under public authority.

A way of combining public authority and planning with co-operatives and with private enterprise was found when the Tennessee Valley Authority was set up. It has been so successful that it is amazing that no more river-valley authorities have been created either by the federal government or by treaties between states such as that which established the successful Port of New York Authority. The constitution of these authorities we shall discuss after we have examined what we mean by the commanding heights of the economic order.

Broadly, they fall in three divisions: (1) natural resources; (2) the system of money, banking, and credit; and (3) the great monopolies or oligopolies in which already most ownership is absentee ownership, there is no effective competition, and the initiative of the engineer and manager has superseded the initiative of the owner or enterpriser. These three divisions require further comment.

Land, including the minerals in it and the forests on it, is, except for the fish in the sea, still the basis for the supply of our needs. On it and by it men must live. The defense of its ownership by individuals and corporations is (1) that men deeply crave land they can call their own, and (2) that collective ownership and use of land in Russia has been maintained by a continuing coercion of a sort that society should not afford.

If our American system of ownership of land and other natural resources was supposed to promote the state of Biblical bliss where every man lives under his own vine and fig tree, it has been a sorry failure. With few exceptions American farmers under free enterprise in all regions have ruthlessly mined out the topsoil and subjected it to erosion. A new country peopled by free settlers who acquired their own farms, often under the Homestead Act, is today, to a great extent, a country of tenant farmers. California is known for its "factories in the fields." The plantation system of the South is responsible for the lowest form of cultural and economic well-being in America and one of the lowest in the world. Even under our so-called system of free enterprise it is now generally agreed that soil conservation must be a concern of the state.

To be sure, agricultural poverty and waste in America, like the poverty of the city slums, has other roots than private landlordism. That fact does not invalidate Henry George's classic criticism of allowing individual landlords to take to themselves values in the form of rent, which values are a social creation. His remedy of expropriating by a tax the economic rental value of land in behalf of the society which has created it is both just and useful. It is not, however, an adequate panacea either in town or in country. It is a basis for proper planning in cities and for the best use of the soil in the country, not a substitute for such planning. To apply Henry George's tax to mineral lands would encourage a rapid competitive exploitation of them which would be socially detrimental.

The extraction of mineral wealth involves something very different from the use of land for homes or farms. Mining exhausts the store of the mineral that is mined or the oil that is pumped. There is a sense in which we can speak of the conservation of coal by proper mining, but not in the sense that soil can be conserved or forests restored. Mining and oil production are large-scale industries in which the key man today is not the owner, the prospector, or the promoter. He is the geologist, the engineer, and the manager. Few things are more absurd than the American law that the man who owns the surface of the earth should also own the oil a mile below it. When Clare Boothe Luce voted for social control of the entire process of producing atomic energy, including ownership of uranium mines, she admitted that it might mean letting socialism in "through the back door." She spoke more truly than she knew, for if society's good compels this socialization of atomic energy, it logically compels a similar process in the case of iron, petroleum, and other resources not as dangerous in private hands as uranium but as necessary for the social good. Democratic socialism, therefore, in America proposes the following principles for the ownership and administration of land, forests and minerals:

(1) Where family farming is the way of life it should be recognized and protected, but title should depend on occupancy and use, and private landlordism should be abolished by a land-value tax. Farm cooperatives should be encouraged for ownership of machinery and marketing products, and standards of soil conservation should be enforced. Corporation farms and great plantations should be transformed into agricultural collectives, cooperatively run.

(2) Land in cities should be controlled not only by a land-value tax but by zoning and large-scale planning. Until the wage structure is radically raised upwards there will have to be subsidized housing for low-income groups. The proper housing program involves more than the control of land. It involves the correct use of government credit; it requires drastic reform in taxation and in the building industry, including some of the practices of the labor unions as well as of the bosses.

(3) Title to all mineral wealth should be vested in the government as the agent of society. This fact should be specified in all future deeds to land, and that mineral wealth which is now in private hands should be acquired by the government. The occupying owner of the surface of the land should, of course, be compensated for any loss of its value to him arising from the extraction of mineral wealth. The federal government is in far the best position to organize a socially owned coal, iron, copper, or oil industry and should be the principal agent of society rather than the state governments, but the latter must participate in working out a plan because of their ownership of much land where minerals exist and their present dependence on the taxation of the land for education and other functions of local government.

(4) Large stands of forests and large acreages of reforested land should be socially owned and socially used, not only for supplies

of lumber and wood products but for protection against floods. Under American conditions, federal, state and municipal governments must cooperate in a comprehensive plan for the development of the use of forests. Wood lots of any considerable size on family farms should be subject to regulation as to use and perpetuation by proper planting.

The second major essential to an economy of abundance is the proper management of money, or more accurately, of money, banking, and credit. The invention of money was one of man's major achievements, but like others of his other inventions, man has used money to his own hurt. Properly speaking, money has two and only two functions. The first is to facilitate the exchange of goods, and the second, to simplify cost accounting, on which any dynamic society must depend. The trouble is that men have considered money as in itself real wealth, and they have speculated on it on terms which make those who manipulate it masters of us all.

Politicians and bankers have been the principal manipulators. Often they have worked at cross purposes, neither group having in mind the real welfare of society. For a long time money manipulation was more or less restrained by the quantity of the precious metals, gold and silver, used for money. Shortage of this supply of hard money helped to bring down the Roman Empire. The increase of the supply of precious metals in the western world, as a result of the discovery of America and later of the British conquest of India, helped to finance modern capitalism and imperialism in their career of expansion.

Today gold and silver have little or no automatic regulatory power over currency. Most of the world's currencies are "managed," usually rather badly managed at that. Economic wars have been fought by nations through juggling currencies. Gold has value only as fetish and as a fetish is useful chiefly as a corrective in the international field to the nationalist manipulations of money. The proper management of money will be one of the chief items in decent economic planning and "one world" will be somewhere nearer reality when it has one fiscal system. Some years ago, in attacking both the Roosevelt silver purchase plan, which is a subsidy to mining interests in a few American states, and the Roosevelt gold purchase plan, which did so much to finance the Japanese in preparation for war against us, I wrote:

"Theoretically I believe in a managed currency directed solely to the maintenance of a stable medium of exchange and cost accounting. The management of currency should never be allowed to be a private function. Practically, I think that Congress and Treasury officials need some protection against manipulative tendencies. I am therefore strongly attracted to the idea of backing the dollar by reserves of actual commodities accumulated according to a weighted index of relative values already worked out by statisticians. 'Open market' transactions of the public officials in control could then consist of the necessary purchase and sale of various commodities of use to men in such a quantity as might be necessary to stabilize the dollar." [1]

The one thing that seems most vital in the regulation of money is the ending of the outrageous system under which generation after generation pays interest to private banks for no other service than what ought to be the social function of the creation of money in the form of credit. A large part of our staggering national debt represents a logically unnecessary payment of interest on bank-created credit, not backed by any actual savings of individuals or corporations. It is preposterous to believe that government is essentially incapable of creating money parallel to the creation of goods on terms that will not invite inflation. Yet to hold this defeatist conviction is the only excuse for turning over to private banks so large a share of the creation of credit, that is, money, in war and peace. No nation fights a war with men or goods not yet in being. Every war debt is essentially a bookkeeping transaction by which fortunate sections of a population and their children after them are able to draw interest from the general public. Privately owned banks of issue or those which virtually create money by setting up credit are chief instruments in this process.

Any modern monetary system is bound up with the whole busi-

[1] *We Have a Future* (Princeton University Press), p. 143.

ness of investment, and upon wisely directed investment a dynamic economy emancipated from the recurrent cycle, boom-to-bust, must depend. Increasingly the control of investment must be directed toward social ends. Here in "free-enterprise" America we have seen the persistence and growth of the Reconstruction Finance Corporation, an instrumentality originally set up by that rugged individualist, Herbert Hoover, to save great corporations from the fate to which they were condemned under a *laissez-faire* economy. The very existence of RFC marks the surrender of a basic principle of private capitalism. Under better and more democratic controls RFC could become an instrument for achieving and operating a socialist economy.

The third category of commanding heights in the economic order includes the public utilities and the other monopolies and oligopolies so characteristic of the American economic order. There is today a strong movement to make private monopoly the scapegoat of our economic system and to seek salvation through a return to competition by means of deliberate imposition of limitations on size. All monopoly needs to be watched because bigness can be a disease, and monopoly, even under social control, may paralyze economic development. Private monopoly, especially in the era of finance capitalism, has permitted a concentration of control dangerous alike to true freedom and plenty. It is, however, absurd to argue that we shall be saved from these evils by an indiscriminate and, in view of the historical record, impossible return to competition. It was out of competition that monopolies grew. If they should be broken, they would probably grow again except for state intervention of a sort which the United States has conspicuously failed to develop satisfactorily under the Sherman Anti-Trust Act. Some of the worst conditions in respect to wages and prices exist in the textile and other industries in which there is the least monopoly. In the last two decades of the nineteenth century, J. P. Morgan and others thought, with some justice, that they did a public service by ending or policing cutthroat competition. The classical contention that monopoly would tend to stifle production as compared with competition has been refuted by the history of production in America, a fact of significance for a socialist-planned economy.

In such an economy, there will still be a role for competition of various sorts. But competition can never be the dominant principle for the organization of an economy directed to the conquest of poverty. That requires the ethical and practical sovereignty of the principle of cooperation. The size of operating agencies and the degree of monopoly will depend upon conditions. Most of what we now call public utilities are natural monopolies and direct public operation of them under proper control is preferable to the attempt to regulate them. Contrast, for example, even in capitalist America, the superiority of municipally owned water systems to privately owned companies, or the electric power rates under the Ontario Hydro-Electric system, or the Jamestown, New York, system, with similar rates in New York City, which is dependent on regulated private corporations. Rates under private ownership of electric power are about 40 per cent higher than under public ownership. Our public utilities—even the well-run telephone industry—would be able to give us cheaper service under public ownership if for no other reason than they could get new money cheaper. The recently increased rate for telephone service in New York State was justified partly by the plea that the company had to pay up to 10 per cent to get new capital. Government now pays far less.

There is a popular argument for capitalism that under it bad management can be punished and checked by bankruptcy as it cannot under public ownership. That is doubtfully true of big corporations such as those which President Hoover felt that he must save through the RFC in the early thirties. It is not true at all of public utilities which must be kept going. In the late forties, the remedy for the badly managed Long Island Railroad was not bankruptcy. Nor was receivership an answer to its problems in dealing with its workers or its passengers. As I write, conservatives are beginning to say that the road must be put under some sort of state authority. The state, it appears, is always useful for salvaging what isn't profitable! Then if the state finds the job hard, it can always be alleged that its troubles prove the folly of public ownership! There is a field in which responsible private ownership permits easier change and adjustments to new conditions than public. But that field is not the field of public utilities or basic resources.

Look, for example, at the coal industry, to which I have previously referred. Bituminous coal is produced under competitive conditions very wastefully. The marvelous picture which *Fortune* once presented in detail of what could be done by proper management of coal to eliminate the smoke nuisance from cities, to utilize all by-products and to avoid present wastes of coal and the very lives of the men who mine it, requires a comprehensive control of the whole industry such as could be committed to no private group without great danger to democracy. It is only when engineers work for society in this field that we can reasonably hope to utilize for the common good their knowledge and their skill.

Just how far in this industrial field social ownership should go is not a matter which one generation can absolutely determine for the next. In the peaceful achievement of democratic socialism a happy medium must be found. Piecemeal nationalization or even socialization won't get very far in a society still dominated by private ownership and the psychological attitude it breeds. Successful operation of, let us say, socialized coal mines would be easier as part of a planned socialization of commanding heights than as an individual experiment. On the other hand, wholesale socialization of almost all industry would impose a crushing burden on government and any apparatus it might set up. I suggest, therefore, that when a socialist government has decided what industries should be socialized and what left to private enterprise or cooperatives, the decision, while not immortal, should not be subject to capricious revision. The managers in every type of industry should have an assurance of reasonable time to show what they can do under whatever setup is adopted.

One advantage of the socialization of major and basic industries is that it will simplify the conquest of depression. In every dynamic society there will be changes in demand. No economic order can successfully continue for decades if it is frozen into a pattern, no matter how admirable that pattern was when it was set. Changes in population, changes in the relative growth of different geographic sections, changes in methods of production, and changes in the wants of men require a flexible system. That flexible system can be better guarded against depression if the great basic industries are in public hands and their output and investments in them can be varied according to the state of the economy as a whole. Control over the rate of interest which Keynesians consider so important can be more fairly exercised by public authority if such a dominant industry as steel is socially owned.

We Americans have already accepted in theory the idea that government spending in public works should be pushed in relatively dull times. There are severe limits to the usefulness of public works as checks on depression. Those limits would be greatly widened if the same principle could be used in the operation and development of public utilities as a whole and of such basic industries as steel and coal, under conditions of public ownership which would not involve the subsidization of private owners.

Two questions always arise in the discussion of socialization of industry: the first, "How will you pay for them?" and the second, "How will you run them?"

Socialists themselves, even democratic socialists, have been divided on the question of compensation. "Why," it is asked, "should special privilege be continued and income diverted to nonworkers on the basis of ownership through payment in bonds or otherwise for the great corporations that are taken over?"

There are several parts to the answer. A policy of compensation is worth its cost if it promotes peaceful and orderly transfer. Nothing would cost the people so much as bitter confusion. Compensation, moreover, is fair in equity when certain industries are socialized and others are not. There would be no particular justice in expropriating the owners of coal mines and steel mills while the owners of the cosmetic industry or of printing plants were untouched. It is a much fairer device to offer reasonable compensation and then to tax the wealth derived from such compensation and all other wealth on the same basis. Inheritance taxes, income taxes, and, if necessary, *a carefully graduated capital levy* can take care of our problem more equitably than expropriation.

The principle of compensation, of course, should never be interpreted so as to permit private owners to unload on the public. No compensation should carry with it any lingering control over the industry. If compensation is on the principle of the substitution of bonds for the outstanding securities, the rate of interest should be low and the bonds should be amortized within a reasonable period of years. Generally speaking, the bonds should be a charge upon the industry itself rather than directly upon the government. Under no circumstances must the owners of sick industries be allowed to profit by government bounty in fixing the purchase price.

Admitting that payment for the properties the state takes over represents a real problem, it is very naïve to say, "How can any government anywhere at any time afford to buy out industry?" The public now pays, very often through the nose, a great reward to the owners of industry, a reward by no means to be explained as a mere payment for tools. The public would pay less, always provided the industries were efficiently operated, for the capital charges, including purchase price, of socialized industries. A proper substitution of bonds under public ownership could squeeze a good deal of water out of the capitalization of some private industries and the necessary replacement of tools or purchase of new tools could be more cheaply managed than through the manipulations of the stock market.

These financial manipulations, whether in the stock or in the commodity market, have more than an economic cost. Defenders of free enterprise can argue until they are blue in the face that gambling in commodities—wheat futures, for instance—at a time when children are starving for bread, really adds nothing to price. Ordinary men will never believe it. Grain should be sold by those who raise it to those who use it without intervention of an elaborate gambling apparatus. This is especially true at a time when the production and probable consumption of grain and other commodities can be as well estimated as it is today. President Truman's friend, Ed Pauley, holder of high governmental posts, may not have made any illegal use whatever of inside information in cleaning up nearly a million dollars in wheat "to protect his family" in a world where millions of families can't get enough bread for their children. In the process, in the eyes of the whole world, he dishonored democracy and bestowed upon the communists an illustration of inestimable value for their propaganda. Reasonable compensation emphatically does not mean the continuance of opportunities for lucky men to make vast fortunes by gambling on the basic necessities of life. The work of the world will be better done when men do not see its material rewards distributed to speculators who have made no single contribution to the creative work of the world.

In the administration of socialized industries, there should be considerable variety and flexibility. The general pattern should be the public authority of which TVA is a successful example, rather than the Post Office Department. I still prefer the latter to the American Railway Express, but it is not the type of democratic administration which socialists desire, and the Postmaster Generalship has too often been the reward for partisan political service. Every public authority, unlike TVA, should be organized on the principle of direct representation of consumers and of the workers, with hand and brain, in a particular industry. Whether there should also be representatives of the state or the government as such, I rather doubt.

In general the dominant interest ought to be the broadest common interest and that is our interest as consumers. But until the end of time there will be special knowledge and special interest possessed by different categories of workers who invest their lives in socialized industries and they are entitled to direct representation in governing boards. I do not think that we need to assume that representatives of the workers and representatives of the consumers would always, or indeed usually, vote as a bloc. With the growth of socialist responsibility they would often vote their individual convictions concerning administrative policy. I should like to see workers' representatives chosen by the workers directly, as workers in the industry, rather than through the medium of their unions. Unions will continue to have a function in a socialized society, but it will be as representatives of special interests of workers rather than as administrators of industries.

How representatives of the general consuming interest shall be chosen is a problem upon which I am not ready to be dogmatic. In time associations of consumers of particular commodities, coal or steel, might be formed for the election of consumers' representatives. In the beginning it would probably be necessary that representatives of consumers should be appointed by the President, but, I suggest, out of panels presented by various engineering and civic groups.

The plan which we have outlined for democratic administration of socialist industries will not of itself solve all the problems of a bureaucracy which on all levels of government does tend to breed excessive devotion to slow, unimaginative routine coupled with a curious sort of arrogance toward the public.

This aspect of public service has been greatly exaggerated by propagandists of free enterprise. They forget that the arrogance of petty officials toward the public exists under private monopoly. I have never seen worse examples of it than in the offices of public utility companies in poor districts of great cities. (It must be admitted that the bad manners of petty bureaucrats, public and private, are often provoked by the manners of those with whom they must deal.)

A worse offense against truth is the studied forgetfulness of critics of public service of its many great achievements. A conservative study of water supply systems in New York State acknowledged the great superiority of municipally owned systems to those under private ownership. Industry and the public owe an immense debt to experts in the Bureau of Standards, the Agricultural Department, the Public Health Service, and to engineers in the Bureau of Reclamation. Public service may sap the quality of dynamism, but the career of Robert Moses, administrator extraordinary of New York's park system, overseer of the building of the Triborough Bridge, conspicuously proves that public servants can escape the paralyzing hands of "bureaucracy."

Nevertheless, an honest socialist must admit that increases in government control tend to magnify the ills we associate with bureaucracy.

The petty little French bureaucrat has long been the object of literary description and satire. Once when time was precious I waited on these gentry for about a week in order to get the stamps on papers which would permit me to go to Loyalist Spain, to which I had been invited by the Spanish government and clearance for which I had been given by the American government and the French Foreign Office. That, I thought bitterly, was characteristically the French way.

Since then I have matched this experience by adventures with some of Truman's bureaus, notably his Bureau of Immigration and Naturalization.

Part of the trouble lies in our comparative failure to work out in civil service a balance between the discipline necessary to efficiency and security from arbitrary political interference and removal. On the higher levels administrators like David Lilienthal are bedeviled by politicians and underpaid in comparison with men enjoying similar responsibility in private business.[2] More-

---

[2] It is, however, a question whether private salaries are not fantastically high. In a decent society, there should be other ways of honoring and rewarding good managerial service than Hollywood salaries.

over, the processes considered necessary to prevent fraud, corruption, and political favoritism often slow up action.

This situation is by no means exclusively a problem for socialists, but socialists who would expand public activities must consider improvements in the technique of civil service. Problems are different in the police department and the public library, the State or Treasury Department, and New York's municipally owned subways. Public authorities over socialized industries will have to deal with unions [3] which are already strong.

But in all cases administrators must find ways to induce and honor enterprise. The main qualifications of public servants at all levels cannot be avoidance of mistakes at the cost of paralysis of action. Nations as different as Russia and Great Britain reward and stimulate specific service by honors to which we have no equivalent; in Russia by various orders, in Britain by the King's honor list which in recent years has more and more bestowed titles on men and women for conspicuous service rather than for contributions to the funds of the party in power.

Payment of public and private administrators must be more nearly equalized, in part by further reduction through taxes of the extravagant salaries paid in certain industries. Perhaps even more than on an improved technique, we must depend on the diffusion of a new attitude of loyalty to the common good in a relentless war against hunger, ignorance, and disease. A new spirit will inspire public workers in proportion as it infuses public attitudes. This, I confess, is a subject to which we socialist planners have given too little attention.

By no means is social ownership the beginning and end of a socialist system. Proper planning for the common good will require as a fundamental basis an authority which, as need arises, can

---

[3] This fact is strangely overlooked in Charles S. Hyneman's generally comprehensive and suggestive book, *Bureaucracy in a Democracy*. He doesn't mention unions.

determine priorities in access to materials. It will also involve a constructive use of taxation and labor legislation. It will provide cradle-to-grave social security. It will set up special agencies to deal with the prevention of unemployment by guiding and directing new investment in those functional lines and those geographic areas where such investment will be useful in meeting human wants and needs.

In no field will planning be as essential as in feeding mankind. Today two-thirds of the people of the world are chronically undernourished and half of them are face to face with gnawing hunger. Yet the population is rapidly increasing. Education in voluntary birth control is a necessary part of the answer, but so, even more emphatically, is an increase of food supply completely beyond the power of uncoordinated "free enterprise" to bring to pass. Already governments are active agents in the war on pests, the improvement of seeds, the control of floods, and the provision of electric power so necessary for the production of fertilizer. Governments must take more responsibility for controlling floods and reforestation. They must enforce soil conservation and improve processes of marketing. At many times in many places they will have to determine what must be grown or raised. Increasingly the fight for food must be the concern of the United Nations or a world government.

Already in the United States it is commonly agreed that to keep farmers on the job prices must be supported. The question is, how? Socialism should favor subsidies along the line Charles Brannan, Truman's Secretary of Agriculture, is proposing. In theory it would make more food available at a price consumers could pay than today when excess food is wasted or piled in warehouses because the price under the parity scheme is too high for the hungry here or abroad to pay. Any plan must be directed toward getting food (which is today destroyed in great quantities in order to keep up prices) to the low-income groups of the nation and the world.

Necessarily, any support plan requires a calculation of the extent to which production should be supported. The support given to potato growers in 1948 was a public scandal—as neither Governor Dewey nor President Truman nor Henry Wallace had the courage to say during the Presidental campaign. That was left to socialists who, because they believe in planning, believe in standards of honesty and common sense. Today any aid to farmers must be directed, among other things, to restoring to grass the land plowed for wheat during the war and now blowing away in dust storms.

The most desperate impact of this problem of food is not in the United States of America. That half of the world's population which lives "face to face with want" is outside our borders and can't buy what it needs. Hence with the progress of recovery in Europe by the fall of 1949 large American surplus food crops were piling up which could not reach those who needed them most. Even a beginning of an international approach to this problem is to be encouraged. No organ of the U.N. is potentially more important than the F.A.O. (Food and Agricultural Organization). More and more attention must be paid to feeding the world in trade agreements and such beginnings of planned marketing as the international wheat pool.

The kind of taxation that governments employ and its incidence on various groups are vital elements in the struggle against hunger and for abundance. Sales taxes bear very unfairly on low-income groups who have to spend almost all their current income on food and other goods subject to such tax.

The main dependence of government, local, state, and federal, should be on land value taxation, income and inheritance taxation, and a capital levy. The last named, in a carefully graduated form, can be useful in wiping out excessive public debt and aiding socialization. The fairness of very high inheritance taxation is obvious. So is its usefulness, properly handled, in helping to achieve socialization.

Income taxes should be the major source of revenue. They should be so levied that state and federal taxes can be combined and paid on the same basis of calculation. Income taxes should apply primarily to the ultimate receivers of income who can't pass them on as can corporations, to a large extent, in the price structure. Income taxes on corporations, plus taxes on individual incomes of owners of the corporation, are a form of double taxation and tend to befuddle understanding of the true picture of profits and tax burdens. Nevertheless, because corporation taxes are easily collected and can be levied so as to deter the accumulation of excess profits through unnecessarily high prices, they should not now be completely dropped. On the contrary, with the coming of new war in Korea excess-profits taxes on corporations became an imperative necessity for ethical and practical reasons.

Both in respect to individual and corporate taxation, some place may be given to encouragement of incentive in lines where that is important by variations in the rate of taxation on income from useful enterprises in which incentive is important and risk is great. There will long be legitimate room in this field for private enterprise under broad overall planning.

Socialized industries, as a rule, should not be exempt from such forms of taxation as apply to nonsocialized industry. It will always be necessary to support many services of enormous social usefulness (*e.g.*, education and public health) by revenues derived from productive enterprises. Hence, there will always be need of taxation or its equivalent.

Labor legislation will claim more of our attention when we examine the role of labor unions in our present society and under socialism. Here it is important to stress the necessity of setting a minimum wage adequate to health and decency. Any branch of industry or agriculture which pays less is parasitic. It counts on supplementing the fund by which it maintains labor by public charity. It depends upon a reservoir of unskilled labor which it can brutally exploit, leaving to public and private philanthropy such care as may be bestowed on the wreckage it creates.

Unemployment insurance, we are coming to see, will always be necessary in a dynamic society because of changes in demand and industrial process that will affect the number of workers needed in various employments. During a time of replacement and possible reeducation, unemployment insurance should provide security.

Nevertheless, the monstrous evil of large-scale unemployment, second in hurtfulness only to war, and itself a factor in the breeding of war, cannot be dealt with safely in a democracy merely by unemployment insurance even if it is supplemented by the boondoggling of militarism or made work which does not compete with productive industry. Here is manifest the outstanding need of planning and herein lies the test of any specific type of planning.

In the social ownership and control of the commanding heights which we have discussed lies no mechanical prevention of depression but a valuable means, intelligently used, for greatly reducing the swing of the pendulum from boom to bust. The increase of purchasing power in the hands of the masses will also be a somewhat automatic factor in avoiding wholesale and chronic unemployment. But this is a field where more specific planning is necessary. A beginning has already been made in the setting up of a committee of economic advisers to the President and Congress to report on trends. In the Seventy-ninth Congress Charles La Follette, at the request of the Socialist Party, introduced an important bill to which I have previously alluded. It would have set up an authority with power to do more than advise. It would be authorized, as a means of checking or forestalling unemployment, to lend money without interest, except for carrying charges, to properly organized cooperatives or nonprofit corporations for investment in new enterprises in geographical areas and in industrial fields in which the economic survey would show a need of goods.

The inflationary boom diverted attention from full discussion of this type of measure for dealing democratically with what has been the worst disease of our economy. But in 1949 recession led Senator Murray and some of his associates to introduce a comprehensive bill for economic expansion. With many of its provisions we socialists would agree, but I reiterate my previous statement of socialist opposition to loans to private enterprises as a major aid against depression. War, alas, by the middle of 1950 made this question somewhat academic.

Two fundamental problems remain. First, what about wages? What about prices? Is socialism consistent with any sort of wage-and-price system? Would not the fixing of wages and prices by public authority place upon it an intolerable burden and make of it—if it should succeed at all—a despotic instrument of power?

In part the answer to this problem must await further inquiry into the political setup of the socialist state and the role of such organizations as labor unions and cooperatives. But here I must reaffirm my increasingly firm belief that in any foreseeable future some sort of wage-and-salary system, and some sort of price system will be necessary and desirable. I can't imagine a dynamic, fully productive society in which, unless by an appalling type of conscription, men can be induced to work without definite material reward, which reward may be subject to variation to stimulate good work. While men do not work solely for material gain, least of all unrestricted gain or profit, so long as there is a floor under wages, a deliberate assurance that no wages will be so low as to make a decent life impossible, and a ceiling on fantastic salaries, variations in wages even if they do not perfectly conform to some abstract standard of justice will be a legitimate and valuable element in getting the world's work done.

Early socialist denunciation of wage slavery was justified. But the use of wages and salaries as a way of distributing the national income in a society organized primarily to obtain maximum production for use is not wage "slavery." No desirable substitute for it is at hand.

Neither in a dynamic society is there a desirable alternative to a use of a price system in distributing goods, encouraging expression of consumers' choice, and so helping to guide productive activity. There is even now a growth of social income, that is, of goods and services for which the individual does not pay directly: highways, schools, libraries, parks, and playgrounds illustrate what I mean. This sort of income will increase, but not to the extent where all of us can be provided out of a great storehouse with whatever we want by a state like Santa Claus. We shall have to pay directly for many of the things we want and need. But we need not fear that, under social planning, prices we must pay will have to be fixed in detail by a vast bureaucracy. Our recent experiences in governmental price fixing have not been the result of socialist economics but of war and postwar shortages. They have been children of emergencies, abnormalities, strains, that socialism in a peaceful world can and must avoid.

Today consumers' cooperatives utilize a price system without making profit king. Along somewhat different lines that can be done by a socialist society in which planning boards will rarely if ever have to function as did the Office of Price Administration. How prices and reasonable price fluctuations may function in a socialist economy under a high degree of overall planning and in the process help to guide that planning has been set forth in technical detail by economists like Taylor and Lange.[4] The resources of America are so great and its technological capacity so high that we shall not need the economy of rationing in a beleaguered garrison. Economic forecasting is not an exact science but, in the realm of predicting the probable wants and needs of human beings in an increasingly prosperous society, it can come close enough to accuracy to permit a policy of broad and flexible controls which will have room for effective consumers' choice under a price system.

Help in the business of forecasting and of planning can come from the more perfect mastery and correlation of information made possible by the electronic brain and what Dr. Norbert

[4] See *Economics of Socialism*, edited by Benjamin Lippincott (University of Minnesota Press).

Wiener calls "Cybernetics," the "science of control and communication." Electronic robots can make rapid and comprehensive calculations otherwise impossible. Aaron Levenstein, in articles in the *Socialist Call* (June, 1949), develops this thesis. This potential usefulness of robots should go a little way to counterbalance Dr. Wiener's own fears that these new machines will displace men on a scale heretofore undreamed of. Nevertheless, as he has emphasized, the control of these machines and the rate of their introduction will require socialism. The robot must be controlled with a regard for human values and that cannot be done, any more than the world can be fed, under the amoral sanctions and the anarchy of the private profit system.

The inescapable conclusion is this: social planning is not something to be loved for its own sake. It is desirable to keep as much individual initiative as possible and greatly to develop the responsibility of individuals in a democratic society. But planning we must have. We have forced it on ourselves by our inventions, our technology, our growth in population. It is for us to examine our democratic instrumentalities and to improve them.

As I have discussed these instrumentalities, I have in fact described one version of what is often called a mixed economy. I do not use that term in preference to socialism because it does not suggest the sovereignty of the cooperative principle or the importance of outright social ownership of a vital segment of our economy if our planning is to bring us plenty, peace, and freedom. Besides, our present scrambled economy better deserves the term!

Chapter 16

Liberty, Equality, Fraternity

THE IDEAL of socialism at its most materialistic level has always been an achievement of "liberty, equality, and fraternity." It has frequently overlooked or misconceived the relation of means to ends, and socialists were slow to recognize that there is a problem inherent in the relation of liberty to security.

But socialism was never guilty of the unreality of talking spiritual values to hungry men when their hunger was in large part the fault of a society whose comfortable priests and leaders preached resignation now with a promise of "pie in the sky by and by." Socialism knew and still knows that the good life for the individual and society requires a full measure of the daily bread for which the Christian prays.

Equality—like liberty—is not an absolute, but the concept is none the less dear for that. There is a difference between equality of individual ability—which does not exist—and equality of opportunity for each individual to do his best and to share in a self-governing community. Variations in reward for labor should be permitted—indeed they should be used—to attract men into particularly difficult work, to compensate them for long years of preparation, or to recognize and stimulate unusual service.

But those variations must never be at the price of semistarvation for the many and fantastic and irresponsible luxury for the few. No socialist society could tolerate a situation under which, as in the year 1947 (a very prosperous year less affected than later years by the arms economy), the lowest fifth of America's families received 4.3 per cent of the nation's income while the upper fifth received 46.3 per cent, or only 7 per cent less than the lower four-fifths combined.

The principal contribution to family income should always be the earnings of able-bodied adults. But, unless and until those earnings at their lowest can be raised to a level not immediately possible, there must a high degree of social responsibility for human welfare, even as today there is social responsibility for elementary education. Basic social security from the cradle to the grave must be the business of this day. So, also, must be the provision of decent housing which today is not adequately provided by any private arrangements.

The details of a housing, health, and old-age assistance program are not the concern of this particular book but certain basic observations are in order. First of all, socialists must insist that desirable provisions for general welfare cannot be obtained and maintained simply by sharing wealth or by continual government intervention to distribute the national income. We have already argued the importance of production in a dynamic society and the relation of ownership to production. It is doubtless true that workers, faced with a choice, would prefer to own a good share of the products of a great industry than collectively to own the industry. But that is not the choice with which life presents them. Actually production and distribution of wealth have to be considered together. They are necessarily related in any economy.

But there will always be a problem of distribution in any economy. Necessarily it will require planning. We must determine in a dynamic society what income can best be social, distributed through social institutions like parks, libraries, museums, and schools, and what should be individual. At a minimum we as individuals and families need our own food, clothing, and shelter. The provision of them for all the sons and daughters of this rich land in infancy and old age as well as in working years obviously requires social action. Some types of action are appropriate to present conditions which might need to be abandoned or modified in a socialist society.

Thus it is a mistake to think indefinite subsidization of cheap but decent housing is a final socialist goal. It is an immediate necessity. It requires constant vigilance (1) lest we create new and somewhat better slums for old, and (2) lest government officials manipulate housing as a favor to potential voters to keep themselves in power. Obviously the goal should be sufficient incomes so that families may house themselves with a growing emphasis on co-operative housing.

Some special problems arise in connection with our already accepted ideas of old-age assistance and the care of children. In agricultural and handcraft societies, in all of which the family is a basic economic unit, the aged, short of complete incapacity or the complete impoverishment of the whole family, had a place. There were chores and odd jobs that they could do. They belonged. That is not true in our modern economy. Neither is it true that every man simply by his own effort can save up enough to support his old age, not when old age in the sense of no job begins for the average worker well before sixty and his life expectancy, with reasonable health, continues to rise in the United States.

In our political democracy it is a moral certainty that the oldsters will demand and probably get benefits which may lay a dangerous strain on our economy. These benefits are likely to be at the expense of education and other aid to children's welfare. It is a grave question whether—short of the age of production by electronic robots—the working population can support oldsters over fifty-five or sixty in the state to which they wish to become accustomed. It is no question at all that for healthy men and women to live fairly well without contributing to the social income out of which they are paid is detrimental to the individual and the existence of a growing mass of such pensioners unhealthy for society. For a man to climb the ladder of responsible, recompensed labor until he is sixty or sixty-five and then be shoved off is a wretched fate even if he lands on the mattress of adequate old-age assistance. He may cultivate hobbies, which are always valuable to life's enjoyment, or he may seek pleasure in that travel which insurance companies advertise, but he is still an extra passenger in the lifeboat (unless, of course, he gets into the United States Senate where by seniority he becomes chairman of an important committee about the time a corporation or university would retire him). Pitching horseshoes in St. Petersburg, Florida, is no steady paradise for the closing years of reasonably healthy men.

Still another aspect of this problem arises from the pressure of strong unions to put in substantial pension schemes for old workers as a charge on the industry. They are stimulated in making these demands by the outrageously high noncontributory retiring pensions paid by many great corporations to top officials who, under capitalist theory, should have been best able to provide for their own old age. Nevertheless, to put the main burden of old-age assistance on corporations through contributory or noncontributory plans will add immensely to certain prices, tend to bind workers to a particular corporation, and still further widen the gap between fairly well-paid employees of corporations and the less well-paid employees of weaker concerns and agricultural workers.

In this situation, three principles seem clear.

1. Every effort must be made to provide work for healthy oldsters, to let them climb down the ladder instead of being pushed off. The work may well be for shorter hours and less exacting, but work there should be.

2. The main burden for basic old-age assistance should be general, taken over by government in behalf of society, and fairly

equalitarian; *i.e.*, on the basis of general human need rather than in proportion to past income. Corporation pensions should be at most supplementary.

3. Old-age assistance must not overshadow educational and other provision for rearing children to competent and healthy maturity.

We agree that our greatest national treasure and tool are children who can best be reared in their own families. Hence the reasonableness of family allotments for each child. I confess that I think such a system in a socialist society should have to be administered with a sharp lookout lest it stimulate overproduction of children in terms of population totals, often by the least desirable parents of the future race.

On no subject has there developed more passion and prejudice with less regard for facts than in the campaign of the American Medical Association and the antisocialists generally against "socialized medicine." Actually socialized medicine in the sense of government responsibility for public health began with the first health act, and the establishment of public health departments. It has continued with an increase of publicly supported hospitals and clinics. Doctors in endowed hospitals open to those who need them regardless of race, color, or creed, as well as in public hospitals, have generously contributed time and service to multitudes who could pay little or nothing. All this is in a real sense socialized medicine and it has borne with it rich rewards in the improved health of our people. Obviously, it needs extension. In recent travels I have come across doctors who in one breath curse socialized medicine and in the next argue for state support of some new medical service in which they are especially interested.

The issue is the extent and control of a comprehensive program for preventing and curing disease; in large part it must be "socialized," but how? Under what controls? How shall personal relations between doctors and patients best be maintained; malingering prevented; costs equitably distributed?

In thirty years' campaigning for an inclusive health service, I have tried to avoid dogmatizing on these questions and hoped for the cooperation of physicians. Instead, they have too largely resisted change. It is perhaps the middle class, so beloved of antisocialists, which suffers most. Its members are too well off and too proud to get free treatment; too poor to afford the enormously expensive services of the specialists who must be called in on serious cases.

Medicine is a noble profession. Its followers do themselves scant justice by imposing a tax of $25 on each member of their trade union, the better to fight what its leaders style socialized medicine, including compulsory health insurance. They do themselves less justice by countenancing such statements as the editorial statement in the *New York State Medical Journal*, August 15, 1949: "We readily admit that under it [the present system] a certain number of cases of early tuberculosis and cancer, for example, may go undetected. Is it not better that a few such should perish than that the majority of the population should be encouraged to run sniveling to the doctor?"

That sort of argument reminds me of early opposition to free public education. It hastens the coming of an imposed system in fighting disease, a system operating under rigid control by government, and makes harder the prevention or minimization of the evils which physicians fear with exaggerated emotion. It is well to remember that all parties in Britain support their comprehensive health plan, which is far better accepted by physicians, surgeons, and dentists than the American Medical Association will admit. Only Harold Stassen, president of the University of Pennsylvania and supporter of the discredited Grundy political machine, discovered how disastrous was the British law to British health. His "discoveries" involved his juggling statistics and facts. To his discredit and still more to the discredit of the *Reader's Digest*, which published his articles, he and the magazine failed to circulate corrections of errors pointed out to them.

It is quite unrealistic to argue that the sort of welfare legislation we have been discussing necessarily interferes with any valid freedom except the undesirable freedom to grab and hold great wealth without corresponding responsibility to the whole American family. Theoretically, one can imagine a danger that liberty will be reduced to equality of slavery to a paternal but dictatorial state, a society like the "contented cows" made famous by advertisements of the Carnation brand of condensed milk. Practically the risk to freedom is greater in a society that is unconcerned for welfare. Great Britain by the end of the nineteenth century had managed to combine a high degree of civil liberty with a caste and class division of society to a degree unparalleled in the history of democracy. Yet even British history attests that the tree of liberty, to achieve its most beneficent growth, should be planted in the soil of equality. The freedom which men value is indissolubly linked to a fellowship which cannot brook exploitation and the poverty and denial of opportunity that it brings. Freedom from want may be of a different order than President Roosevelt's other freedoms. It is a legitimate human desire, and freedom of conscience, speech, and assemblage are insecure in any society that will not use its technical resources to end hunger and misery.

A discussion of liberty as it affects us today and as a socialist society should interpret it is valuable less as an exposition of abstract philosophy—it is easy to prove that there is no absolute freedom—than of particular liberties which men cherish. Civil liberties are neither properly evaluated nor protected by most of the current generalizations about "free enterprise" versus "big government."

Today, our outstanding problems of freedom in America fall under the following heads: (1) the demand for equal rights for citizens of all races and national origins against any form of "white supremacy" or "Anglo-Saxon domination"; (2) the right of citizens to obtain accurate factual information and fair discussion of issues through the agencies of mass communication; (3) the rights of individual workers not only against management but against tyranny within powerful labor unions; (4) the complex of problems concerning liberty and the national security created by communist and fascist aims and methods; and (5) the impact upon freedom of the effort of any powerful church, specifically the Roman Catholic, to force upon all citizens its beliefs in such matters as divorce and birth control and to gain for itself primary influence and power in the education of children.

In dealing with civil rights the attitude of the state, while vital to liberty, is not the only factor. The establishment of fraternity between races transcends the negatives of the Ten Commandments. It requires the Golden Rule, and no society—socialist or nonsocialist—can enforce the Golden Rule. The democratic state cannot be too far ahead of popular opinion or prejudice in the enactment and enforcement of law. Witness the history of prohibition in America. It is possible, however, in a democratic society to make the effort after legislation and the enactment of good laws in support of civil rights genuinely educational. Thus the agitation for a federal antilynching law has had a most beneficial effect.

The President's temporary Fair Employment Practices Committee during the war, and the passage of a Fair Employment Law in New York—and later in nine other states—and their enforcement, have not achieved complete success but have notably contributed to the practice of justice in race relations. No socialist party and no socialist society will ever demand less of government in this field than was recommended by the President's Committee on Civil Rights in 1948. That report set a high water mark in the concept of true democracy.

In Jefferson's time the citizen's right to access to information and to participate in discussion was well guaranteed by forbidding the state to deny Milton's famous freedom "to know, to utter and to argue freely according to conscience." In a simpler society free citizens could easily organize their own meetings and publish their own papers. In our day Thomas Paine's tracts or William Lloyd Garrison's *Liberator* printed on cheap paper without illustrations would have little influence. To establish a newspaper to satisfy the curiously developed popular taste has become an enormously expensive and risky business, as Mr. Marshall Field has learned to his cost. Movies, radio, and now television offer small opportunity for hearing to the modern prophet armed only with a just cause.

In this whole field of communication through press, radio, television, and movie, one can find illustrations which give some support to the Marxist doctrine that the tools and instruments which men use determine or condition their social concepts and standards. Cylindrical presses electrically driven, radio and television apparatus, are marvelous inventions. They make possible an extraordinary degree of dissemination of information, ideas, and entertainment. In America they have given us some remarkably good service. In the world as a whole they have also been mighty factors in making possible the rule of dictators, the dissemination of misinformation, and the corruption of popular taste on an enormous scale. Radio has pretty firmly established the idea that all necessary wisdom can be imparted in five- to thirteen-minute chunks. Television insists that the chunks be illustrated. In consequence, there is a definite lowering of the desire or capacity of any large numbers of people to listen to the sustained and logical development of ideas, or to read it in books. The elder La Follette, to take only one recent example, would find it hard today to make thousands of Wisconsin farmers and workers listen to his sustained and orderly presentation of intricate problems connected with taxes, public utilities, etc. A radio version of a Lincoln-Douglas debate would have the quality of a *Reader's Digest* condensation of Hamlet.

Any concept of liberty in the field of communication requires, among other things, a positive sense of concern by individuals for its effective exercise. And that concern depends upon education.

After the Presidential election of 1948, there was considerable satisfaction that the American people had shown once more their ability to disregard the advice of the overwhelming majority of newspapers. Two comments are in order. The first is that it is almost as dangerous in a democracy for the electorate to act on the principle that the *Chicago Tribune* (for example) is always wrong as that it is always right; the second, that voters who have acquired some facility at arriving at their own judgments in domestic matters are far more dependent upon the great newspapers for knowledge of foreign affairs.

In this field some American correspondents and papers are doing a good job. There is still enough irresponsible sensationalism and chauvinism to remind me of the bad days of World War I. A small committee of which I was then a member was arguing with Colonel House that President Wilson, from the standpoint of his own policy in respect to his Fourteen Points, was making a great mistake by jailing or trying to jail all his left-wing critics while giving free scope to those on the right. Mr. Wilson's alter ego brushed our objection aside by saying that Wilson had won against the majority of newspapers in 1916 and could do it again; and that he needed no help in balance from the Left. Events justified our warning.

Our American difficulty does not arise from government intervention or censorship. No sane man would propose that we fly from the ills we have to government monopoly or regulation in the field of mass communication. In Britain a Royal Commission appointed by the Labour government has well stated a case against such action on grounds that certainly apply in America. Thus the Labour government vindicated our confidence that democratic socialism is a bulwark of freedom. But the Commission was severe in demanding higher standards from a free press and it proposed that the press set up its own council for maintaining those standards. The idea has merit for America.

Our difficulties arise very largely from the costly techniques of mass communication and the dependence of the press, and even more the radio, upon advertising. Advertising depends on circulation and the latter too often depends upon sensationalism careless of truth.

The radical critic of the press and the radio too often both oversimplifies and overstates his case by saying or implying that great newspapers or radio networks are directly bribed by advertising.

The evil is more subtle. These instrumentalities of communication are big business. Their proprietors naturally live and move in the world of big business and its ideas. Their success depends upon advertising, and advertising too generally has become a blatant and costly form of huckstering. My own experience has proved that minority opinion is by no means altogether kept off the air or out of the press. But I could tell plenty of stories of the disadvantages against which it labors.

They are perhaps best illustrated by the following quotation from the peroration of the presidential address of one Edwin S. Friendly to the powerful American Newspaper Publishers Association at its 1950 convention. Said he: "I know that in the minds and hearts of every one of you is the determination to use the all-powerful medium of honest reporting and editorial reason to bring about widespread awareness of the evils of government by directive, of the welfare state, of subsidies to everyone, of Communism disguised as democratic socialism, of all the insidious threats to the principles Americans hold dear."

It would be hard to phrase a more direct invitation to unfair, unobjective, prejudiced reporting, or to imagine a more direct, if perhaps unconscious, appeal to prostitute newspapers to the special interests which ineptly use the term "welfare state" as a short-hand for government activities which may cut into their profits.

For this bias of the owners of agencies of mass communication and this exploitation of sensationalism for profit there is no easy cure.

The situation would not be improved but, temporarily at least, worsened were all the agencies of communication suddenly to fall in the hands of organized labor or of any radical party. In any society, including a socialist society, truth must depend upon a competition of ideas. Nevertheless, legislation which sometimes has been proposed, based on the assumption that merely to increase competition by making size a crime, is not the answer. Government action against the degree of monopolization already achieved in some parts of America where the same groups own the newspapers and the radio stations is in order. But much experience has taught me that, on the whole, it is not small "independent" newspapers and radio stations which are fairest in presenting the news. Often they are financially handicapped and hence afraid. In this field small business is often more prejudiced than large because it considers itself more insecure. The *New York Times* and a few other metropolitan dailies and the radio networks do a fairer and more adequate job in the dissemination of news and ideas than the average smaller newspaper or radio station.

In a socialist society where the volume of advertising will probably be diminished it will be necessary for groups of citizens to rally to the support of their own favorite newspapers and possibly radio stations. That should be more easily possible because of an increase of income in the hands of the people.

Even now a wholesome competition in ideas might be helped if labor unions and farm organizations would improve their publications and possibly start dailies analogous to the *Christian Science Monitor*. They have begun to establish radio stations on frequency modulation.

Radio, however, presents a different problem than newspapers. Necessarily the number of channels is limited. To have the use of one is a special privilege. If in America we are to continue private operation of radios as against the British system,[1] each operator must be responsible for a balanced presentation of opinions. It was a step backward when the Federal Communications Commission permitted radio broadcasting stations and systems to editorialize. The safeguards it imposed are inadequate and dubiously workable.

What should have been done—what should still be done—is to require every radio and television user of air channels to give a minimum of x good—and the adjective is important—listening hours to a balanced presentation of issues. Definitely it should not be the business of any government agency to dictate programs, but

[1] That system of public ownership and operation, unlike the system in most countries, is under nonpartisan control and operates fairly.

the F.C.C., which now demands proof of engineering competence, should also require proof in renewing licenses that the provision for balanced presentation had been lived up to. It would still be possible for stations to develop a character of their own and to emphasize certain aspects of the many-sided service which the public desires.

The rise of great labor unions and their powerful place in our social order have raised new problems of civil liberty now and for a future socialist government. We have to consider a balance of the rights of the community to freedom from a possibly coercive and arbitrary pressure of a particular group, the right of workers to organize and of their unions to function effectively, and the right of individual workers in relation to the strong labor organizations and the "new men of power" who direct them. We cannot answer the question in terms of liberty or fraternity by absolute and exclusive devotion to one set of rights or interests. What this means in practice is so important to democracy and to the winning and maintaining of democratic socialism that I shall discuss it at length in a later chapter.

The next set of problems which confronts the believer in civil liberty now and may well confront him even in a socialist society is bound up with the rise of communism and its real threat to liberty. The Communist Party is not a democratic organization which advocates radical or revolutionary policies. It is a rigidly disciplined body under control from Moscow which is actually engaged in secret conspiracy against not only the American government but the basic principles of democracy. The Communist Party stridently demands rights which admittedly it would never grant to others should it come to power.

And that creates a new situation in a country in which the older American radicals and the later anarchists, Wobblies and socialists were flamboyantly honest in declaring their allegiance and proclaiming their purposes.

In dealing with avowedly radical or revolutionary parties which function openly and are controlled only by their own members, it was easy to apply the sound Jeffersonian principle that it was time for government to intervene to punish or prevent specific overt acts, or to check immediate incitement to them. This not only because zealous protection of rights of free speech and association are so important to the individual, but also because, in the long run, truth does a better job for its own protection when it is not under the guardianship of the policemen of the state. English experience has proved that the freedom of speech in Hyde Park is an actual protection to the peace of the community.

At first our lawmakers stupidly concluded that the principal danger of communism or of other tightly disciplined organizations lies in the advocacy of force and violence in the overthrow of the government. Rather, it lies in their conspiratorial nature. Thomas Jefferson himself at one time—rather foolishly—believed that liberty might require a rebellion every twenty years. It would have been a great mistake to have imprisoned him. Government action, as the Supreme Court has held, should require clear and immediate danger. It is one thing to tell an audience "some day there must be violent revolution, or violence in protection of revolution, in America as in other countries." It is another to say "let us gather tomorrow before dawn to take over the City Hall," or even "let us practice so that we shall be ready to take over the City Hall in the near if indefinite future."

In view of the nature of the Communist Party and its discipline, the right of the Communist Party or of communists to operate under guarantees of civil liberty is relative especially in times of national danger. It should not be assessed in terms of absolutes but only in the light of a careful judgment of the immediacy of the peril the Communist Party creates and the practicability of any particular measure directed against it. It will always be necessary to decide whether a particular punitive measure designed as a cure for communist ills may not be worse than the ills themselves.

Thus far, the federal government has been proceeding under the Smith Law, enacted in 1940. It is a clumsy piece of legislation which in general terms makes advocacy of overthrow of the government by force and violence a crime. Under that law, sixteen Trotskyist communists were convicted in Minneapolis during the war. But their alleged offenses occurred before the war. The element of danger in any of their activities was extraordinarily small and the trial judge himself imposed light sentences. Unfortunately, the Supreme Court refused to review the case. And the Communist Party, which then was vociferously loyal to the American government because it was an ally of Stalin, cheered on the prosecution of the Trotskyist heretics.

The Party did not cheer when twelve of its leaders who had reorganized the Party after the war were indicted under the same Smith Law in 1948. Eleven of them were brought to trial in protracted proceedings in Judge Medina's court in New York. The judge's conduct of the trial was eminently fair, but the question of the constitutionality of the Smith Law became acute. The evidence was very strong that the defendants believed and taught the legitimacy of force and violence to achieve communist ends whenever the party might think it necessary. There was no evidence of any specific act involving present force and violence.

When the case came before the Court of Appeals, Learned Hand, one of the best judges in American history, speaking for a unanimous court, declared: "The question before us, and the only one, is how long a government, having discovered such a conspiracy, must wait. When does the conspiracy become a 'present danger'? The jury has found that the conspirators will strike as soon as success seems possible, and obviously no one in his senses would strike sooner."

Herein lies clear and present danger. History may decide that a revolution is "right," but obviously, says Judge Hand, there is no constitutional "right" of revolution by violence. The communist record in all countries proves the kind of revolution in which communists believe.

Logically, the dubious but tough Smith Law (if finally sustained by the Supreme Court), plus some tightening of the sedition laws which the Administration sought, would have been enough to deal with any real communist menace. The Korean war saw no sudden outbreak of sabotage or espionage. But the war, preceded by the Hiss case, and the Fuchs case in Great Britain, stirred up an unreflective anticommunism and led Congress to pass, over the President's sound and courageous veto, that outrageous mishmash the McCarran Law. As the President pointed out, it will clog the machinery of the Department of Justice; it will drive communists underground where they are more dangerous; its provisions concerning immigration make an already bad situation worse in destroying America's glory as a land of asylum. The registration features which were taken over from its predecessor, the Mundt-Nixon bill, will tend to spread fear and to hurt civil liberty, but they will drive real communists into more secret conspiracy where they will be more effective. As a means to deal with sedition the law is on a par with an effort to stop burglars by requesting prospective burglars to register.

About as bad as the substance of the law is the way in which it was passed. Many congressmen admitted that they never read the long bill or the President's well-reasoned veto message. Senator Mundt, principal author of the registration features, many months ago tried to reassure "labor unions, so-called liberal groups, the Socialist Party of Norman Thomas [*sic*]" that they had nothing to fear from his masterpiece. A few months later, he assured Illinois doctors, dentists, and pharmacists that "communism and socialism are merely different stages" of "the same dread disease" which, to put it mildly, threw in doubt the value of his earlier assurances.

Some liberal senators tried to block the McCarran bill by substituting for it a hastily drawn measure providing for the internment of dangerous communist subversives in the event of war or insurrection. Something of this sort may conceivably become a sorrowful necessity. To provide for it now, even with safeguards, without public discussion or consideration of the effect of prospective concentration camps upon the present concept of civil liberty was as bad in principle as it was tactically futile in defeating the objectionable chapters of the McCarran bill. The substitute was simply added to the bill. The excuse was that congressmen who can't be statesmen without being reelected feared the electorate. What a commentary on our democracy!

When to the McCarran Law were added various municipal ordinances, a rash of loyalty oaths, and the beginnings of indiscriminate blacklists, civil liberties were plunged to a new low by the fall of 1950. In the name of defending liberty against communism, we were sacrificing the freedom and sanity which have been our American glory.

To say this is by no means to deny that the communists themselves have created the situation by their Machiavellian tactics in which the government is justified in scrutinizing the loyalty of all of its employees whose position might give them power to jeopardize national security. At this point what is to be criticized is not security tests but procedures which unnecessarily jeopardize the innocent.

The relative rights even of communists to speak their minds without going to jail should not be extended to their right to teach in democracy's schools. It is a curious fact that some of those heretofore most ardent in protecting the right of proved communists to teach our children admit no such right for proved fascists or members of the Ku Klux Klan, and they are usually bitter about the failure of the American Occupation properly to staff schools in Germany and Japan in training for democracy. One must be very cynical about any possibility of using schools to train children in the ways of democracy, or the opposite, to argue that it doesn't matter whether or not a teacher who is competent in reading and writing and arithmetic is under the control of an organization which flouts good faith and the basic processes upon which true democracy depends.

Of course, there is a real danger, already manifest, that search for communists in the school system may degenerate into a witch hunt, or that the effort to see that teachers believe in democracy may be pressed into an acceptance of a particular economic and political creed rather than a way of life. Against these dangers socialists must be on guard, as must all believers of democracy. We shall not avoid them by insisting on the right of proved communists any more than proved fascists to teach in the public schools. Any man or woman who has surrendered his allegiance to any totalitarian party is no longer free. He cannot teach anything contrary to the fiat of his party. And teachers whose minds are thus in chains cannot train others in democracy. It is indeed unfortunate that most of the current legislation on this subject like the requirement of special oaths or the Feinberg Law in New York is stupid or oppressive. Some of it would burn down the barn to drive out a few rats.

At the college and university level, as a matter of policy but not of right, democracy might be strengthened (at least in time of peace) were an acknowledged communist to be allowed to teach in a field in which he is competent and in which Stalin has not laid down an infallible line. The students are old enough to learn by discussion.

It is as important as it is difficult to see to it that controls over communists as citizens or as applicants for public employment be asserted for the right rather than the wrong reasons. In the summer of 1950, when the need for national unity was exceedingly great and when the world's fate might depend upon the solidarity of free peoples, emphatically including the democratic socialists of Britain, Scandinavia, and other countries, reactionary interests continued to push a viciously false campaign to identify socialism and indeed all welfare legislation with communism as the foe of "liberty," a blessing in which they had heretofore shown little interest. These reactionaries hate communism for advocating a socialism which in fact it has betrayed.

Teachers and teacher-training schools are particularly susceptible to the group pressures which often make of our public school teachers an order of scared rabbits. For example, in the summer of 1950, the dictate of an ultra-reactionary newspaper editor and a few like-minded folk compelled the timid faculty of Bloomsburg State Teachers College in Pennsylvania to cancel its contract with me to make an address at commencement which was to have been in no way a partisan utterance. But I was a socialist and hence obnoxious to these hypocritical defenders of "liberty" and the "American way of life." This episode was but a straw in the winds of reaction which blow through too many of our schools.

Along with our difficulties about communism and the capitalist reaction it encourages, we are confronted with problems arising from the relation of the state and church. The slogan, "A free church in a free state," is good but it is not self-interpreting. The state must legislate and enforce its laws in the field of generally approved social morality. That murder and theft are crimes there is general agreement. There is no such general agreement in modern society concerning matters like divorce and voluntary birth control. The Roman Catholic Church as a whole, and some Protestants, are completely opposed to divorce, and even more vehemently opposed to birth control—except by the dubious method of rhythm. From statistical evidence it would appear that the Roman Catholic Church cannot force its precepts even upon its own members but, nevertheless, its political influence is so very strong that in recent years the Church has been able to defeat cautious proposals for legalizing the giving of voluntary birth-control information in Connecticut and Massachusetts and to block any change in the divorce laws of New York. The latter state recognizes only adultery as a ground for divorce. Hence the wealthy go to Reno; the less wealthy resort to a "divorce ring" which for a fee will furnish fake evidence; and the anonymous poor, in considerable numbers, simply practice bigamy.

The existence of groups ready to provide presumptive evidence of adultery for a fee has long been known to everybody in New York except officially to the judges who have granted the divorces. Late in 1948, however, the scandal became public and judicial machinery was set in motion to punish the purveyors of false evidence. Solemn editorials deploring the situation appeared in the press. But the Roman Catholic Church, through the presiding judge of the Archdiocese of New York, called upon the legislature to "outlaw divorce entirely" and so protect the family. (Presumably that would not check the liberality wherewith the Church itself grants "annulment"—for a price.)

The legislature was afraid to tackle the issue at all. In our democracy it is often good politics to please a determined minority by writing or keeping an unacceptable law on the statute book, like the prohibition of liquor or divorce, while appeasing the majority of the citizens by letting them break it with impunity.

It is a shocking situation. Any church or ethical association has a perfect right to hold its own members to its standards. But freedom suffers when an effort is made to impose those standards through the coercive power of the state upon a great company of men and women who deny their validity.

I regard the present epidemic of divorce with apprehension, but I do not think that the family in these changing times will genuinely be strengthened, or the interests of children furthered, by denying to husbands and wives all possibility of legal relief long after the ties of affection are broken. If there is anything worse for children than a broken home, it is a home in which hate rules. If a man or woman in loyalty to some ethical principle can master his or her emotions and hold a home together, that may be admirable; it is not admirable when the only ties are legal chains. The state can best exercise its function in protecting the family by encouraging second thought and offering constructive help through marriage counselors rather than by narrowly and arbitrarily limiting the grounds for divorce. When love, or at least mutual respect, is dead, the basis of marriage has been broken. That fact, rather than the offense responsible for it, should be the major consideration in dealing with applicants for divorce.

The relation of the Roman Catholic Church to public education presents a difficult problem. It was dramatically highlighted by Cardinal Spellman's intemperate attack on Mrs. Eleanor Roosevelt as a religious bigot.

We are face to face with two principles not easily reconciled. The first principle, which socialists and all other believers in democracy should accept, is the right of private groups to establish and maintain schools, colleges, and universities under private control and to send their children to them. Competition in education and variety in educational methods tend to prevent a deadly and unimaginative uniformity of educational procedure. There are circumstances which often make it wise for parents to send children to private schools.

The second principle is that in our modern world popular education must be the concern of the state which must guarantee it to its children. The public schools have their faults but they have been agencies of incalculable value in bringing Americans together whatever their national origins or religious and political beliefs. Among other things, the quality of ethical instruction in the schools could be improved. It might, for instance, be desirable for leaders of various religious and ethical groups to agree on a program of great readings drawn from the teachings of the world's prophets and sages.

But the support of definitely creedal instruction in schools is not the business of the state; it violates the principle of separation of church and state which has worked well in America. There is no statistical evidence whatever to prove that church schools with formal religious instruction have been more successful than public schools in preventing juvenile delinquency or in preparing our children to face life's difficulties and temptations. There is a great deal of positive evidence of the advantage of our system over that in the Province of Quebec, where tax money goes out to religious schools, Catholic and Protestant, or in those numerous countries where the Roman Catholic or some Protestant church is given a privileged position in the schools.

In view of all these facts, certainly the Catholic Church should keep its right to establish and maintain church schools. Non-Catholic Americans, however, are justified in deploring the effort to segregate children in schools along lines of religion at the very time that liberals are fighting to end segregation along lines of race. They are justified in arguing that there is plenty of time outside of the school week for churches to bring their own particular teachings to their children. If that instruction today is so often formal, superficial, intellectually and ethically unsatisfactory, the fault is that of the churches and not of the state. It is less rather than more likely to be repaired if the state should either subsidize church schools or guarantee under compulsion the physical presence of children in classes conducted by religious teachers and pastors.

Churches which want to provide schools should like other private groups support them without tax money. The state does enough when it exempts their property used for educational work from taxation. In the particular controversy over federal aid to education, it is a calamity that thus far Catholic insistence on some share in aid has blocked federal help to states too poor to do a competent job even in fighting illiteracy. Cardinal Spellman and other leading Catholics now seem ready to compromise on the basis of permitting states to use some part of federal funds to help parochial schools by supplying school lunches and other health aids to children, by providing transportation, and furnishing textbooks in "nonreligious" subjects. Those who have seen the way in which fascists and communists have manipulated textbooks even in arithmetic will recognize that state money allocated to their purchase in parochial schools would mean direct state support of a particular religion. There should be no objection, on the other hand, to federal aid for the health of children, administered through schools, except in so far as that might be regarded as the entering wedge for tax support of parochial and private schools. I suggest that such health aid be granted on its own merits outside an education bill.

Pope Pius XI in his 1929 Encyclical on Christian Education of Youth asserted: "And first of all education belongs preeminently in the Church." He went on to declare that it was the duty of the state "to respect the international rights of the Church in this same realm of Christian education." In our country that encyclical fanned the efforts of the Church at one and the same time to put all Catholic children in parochial schools with the maximum possible aid to them and to infiltrate the public schools with Catholic teachers many of whom have done admirable work. But there is considerable evidence that Catholic influence has sometimes been thrown against proper support to public schools. It is this situation which must put non-Catholics on guard.

The problem is positive rather than negative. The new society will largely stand or fall on the educational process. Every child is entitled to educational opportunity and to special advancement in fields where he shows particular aptitude. Education must be for the enrichment of leisure as well as for efficient work. It must be adapted to many needs and many temperaments. It must deliberately train citizens in the practice of democracy. It is profoundly to be hoped that the problem will not indefinitely be complicated by the effort of any church or private group to get public money to support private sectarian education at the public school level.

A disquieting fact for civil liberty is the way in which in the fight on divorce and birth control the Roman Catholic groups have used economic pressure to prevent fair discussion. Political aspirants, newspaper editors, and others who purvey ideas or information, have reason to fear what organized groups can do even when they represent minorities. In Connecticut, Catholic authorities expelled physicians from their staffs and denied them facilities because they had signed a plea to the legislature for legalization of their right to give birth-control information.

This sort of pressure is by no means confined to Roman Catholics. Many publishers live in fear of boycott on circulation or advertising if they publish material to which numerous and strongly organized religious, nationalistic, or economic groups object.

This practice of boycott seems to be growing and exceeds any legitimate use of it as defense against outrageous and scurrilous attack. Against that we do have some protection in laws on libel. Possibly the deliberate circulation of proved falsehoods to discredit any group could be made punishable as group libel, but the law would need very careful framing.

In many years of struggle for freedom of speech and the press, I have seen a diminution of danger from the police. Courts have protected freedom of speech, press, and association against the state in such decisions as that against Frank Hague in Jersey City and, more recently, in the Terminiello case. Prior to the Korean war discussion was restricted and distorted far more seriously by social and economic pressures, by fear of economic boycott, or sometimes by hope of economic reward through advertising and lucrative opportunities for speakers and writers than by the police. I could document this statement by actual experiences of persons whom I trust. Most of the evidence has not been made public.

The fate of *The Nation,* the magazine banned from many libraries for publishing articles displeasing to the Catholic authorities, was unique only in that it became a matter of public knowledge and involved officials of public schools and public libraries. "The right to know, to utter, and to argue freely according to conscience" is jeopardized by other forces than the police.

In a radio discussion with a spokesman of the National Association of Manufacturers, I was told that in our modern society more important than any of the issues of civil liberty I have been examining was "the absolute right of a man to choose for whom he would work," now imperiled by "social planners."

There is, of course, no such absolute right in the workaday world. Our jobs are to a great extent determined by social conditions, opportunity, and training. Within the larger or smaller area thus defined men have and should always have choice. That area can be expanded under a socialist system. Such a system will offer better forecasts of economic opportunity, fairer rewards for unpleasant tasks, more adequate education and advice to individuals. Thus will freedom from the coercive pressures of circumstance be increased.

Conscription in war or peace inevitably tends toward the growth of the totalitarian state. It can be justified only by the grimmest social necessity. Conscription of labor is not the necessary mark of a socialist society but of an emergency economy. The degree to which the British Labour government approached such conscription (which it has now abandoned) was slight and was dictated by an emergency created by war and the failures of capitalism. Under extreme circumstances of emergency, direction of employment for the common good can be justified rather better than military conscription, which my debating opponent accepted. The latter involves far graver problems of conscience. Nevertheless, one test of the excellence of the socialist society will be its success in increasing rather than diminishing the chance for men to work where they like and in helping them to find out what they like. Planning will have failed in the measure to which in normal times it must resort to conscription by the state in order to carry on the necessary work of the community.

On the road to an established socialist society there remains a serious problem which in times past has greatly troubled democratic socialists. Could revolutionary change, even if voted by a majority, be carried through without temporary curbs on civil rights? Would not frequent elections on a multiparty system wreck the process of revolutionary change in the middle?

Recent history suggests three comments on these fears. First, it may be true that "capitalists will never surrender except to force," but the force need not necessarily be extraconstitutional or attended by mass violence. There aren't enough capitalists to use effective physical force except as they win the support of other classes by cajolery or by exploiting the mistakes of their opponents. Already European capitalism has repeatedly been forced to take precarious refuge behind fascist demagogues who used nationalist and pseudorevolutionary formulas to seduce the masses. Fear and prejudice, horror of change, are becoming more obviously the foes of socialism than pure capitalist strength and they are not confined to one class or successfully changed by violence.

Second, in countries where political democracy is well established, drastic changes have taken place without violence or the destruction of democratic institutions. The process can be continued. A Conservative victory in New Zealand, Great Britain, or the Scandinavian nations may retard socialist progress, but no conservative party would or could restore the old capitalism. The tides are sweeping us quite beyond that mooring.

Conceivably the question on what class must fall the principal burden of a drastic readjustment to a temporarily lower standard of living in an emergency might lead to internal strife, even in a democratic country. Hunger makes neither for democracy nor peace. But with reasonable access to adequate resources, and effective economic organization of workers in unions, a nation's internal change to socialism can be peaceful and socialism will not need the destructive protection of a dictatorship or a one-party system.

Third, if to establish itself socialism must resort to dictatorship, it will lose its own soul. The dictatorship drunk on power will never voluntarily give way to democracy. This is the tremendous lesson of our times. It is no longer possible for any thoughtful man to forecast an hedonistic Utopia of the *Looking Backward* variety if it must be established by dictatorship which will never voluntarily give up power. George Orwell in *1984* has correctly foreshadowed the path dictatorial power must take. It will accept the fact that power is its own great reward. It will need war to win an easier obedience from its subjects. Hence, Mr. Orwell imagines the emergence not of one totalitarian empire but three which in shifting alliance will carry on intermittent war, deliberately refraining (after one experience of atomic war) from persistent use of the most destructive weapons. Each dictatorship will deliberately organize an economy short of abundance so that it can better bribe and coerce men and groups by differential variations in living standards.

In short, the logical deduction from the experience of our own times is that, if we cannot get peace, plenty, and freedom together, we shall get none of them. To achieve liberty, equality, and fraternity is an indivisible task.

Chapter 17

Socialism and Its Political Tools

Ｉ N THE U.S.S.R. the political
government, completely dictatorial in nature, has made itself God
over the whole of life. In Great Britain and the Scandinavian
countries parliamentary government has been successfully used
as a tool for profound social change. In our America, which
stridently protests devotion to the faith once and for all delivered
to the founding fathers, the federal government has of necessity
taken on tasks never dreamed of by the framers of a constitution
notable for its checks and balances. But despite changes forced by
the years, it is widely believed that the present state of the country
and its success in two wars are evidence of the virtue, almost the
sanctity, of the Constitution given us by the founding fathers.
There are, however, in our current performance danger signals
which ought to warn democracy that it should examine its tools.
Can we, with our present constitutional system and our present
structure of political parties which are in no sense responsible after
the British model, cope adequately and democratically with the
foreign and domestic problems of our times?

This is especially a problem for socialists since, on the historic record already cited (Chapter 8), the American political setup has been a major factor in retarding the growth of organized socialism. Concretely this problem of political machinery divides itself into two separate but related questions or groups of questions. The first concerns the adequacy of our Constitution. What changes should the socialist propose? This inquiry will also involve consideration of the role of the states in relation to the federal government.

The second question concerns the adequacy of our present party system and its responsibility or lack of it to the people. Can it be partially supplanted or supplemented by increased use of direct voting by initiative and referendum or by greater attention to the Gallup and other polls of public opinion?

It cannot truthfully be said that American socialism has given our first question the attention it deserves. Occasionally there has been socialist talk of a new Constitution or of a great increase of direct popular voting through the initiative and referendum. After World War I English discussion of "guild socialism" or government in large part through representation of economic units found some echoes in America. Many socialists at one time considered favorably the abolition of the Senate, and the Party pioneered in demanding direct election of senators. It has steadily sought a constitutional amendment for the direct election of the President.

It has looked with critical eyes on the powers of the Supreme Court. That court has played a mixed role in the history of our democracy. Under the great John Marshall it strengthened the federal government. Later its Dred Scott decision contributed mightily to the coming of the Civil War and its tendency to legislate conservatively under guise of mere interpretation of the Constitution justified Franklin D. Roosevelt's criticisms although not his court-packing plan. Circumstances permitted him to create a reformed court which no longer used the Fourteenth Amendment and the due-process clause of the Fifth Amendment more effectively to protect that artificial person, the great corporation, than human beings, colored or white. The Court has become a valuable guardian of civil liberty, with some exceptions, of which by far the most serious was its validation of the wholesale and ruthless evacuation of American citizens of Japanese ancestry from their homes on the West Coast. No American court ever created a more dangerous precedent.

Until the Supreme Court declared the Wagner Act constitutional, American socialists were greatly concerned to push the so-called Hillquit Amendment,[1] which by specific grant of power to Congress denied the Court's right to invalidate economic and social legislation, but left untouched the Court's power to curb executive or Congressional interference with civil liberties. The protection of civil liberties by the Court seemed to us socialists to have greater justification in constitutional theory and in beneficial practice than its power virtually to legislate in the fields of economics and social welfare. That power seemed to us to threaten the possibility of orderly and constitutional adoption of socialism.

With the validation of the Wagner Act and the change in the Court's position to which I have alluded, socialist concern for the Hillquit Amendment was lessened. It may yet be awakened.

It is immediately desirable that, if not by amendment, then by force of public opinion, an end should be put to the growing tendency to make political use of judges on the Supreme Court bench. Justice Jackson did the Court no good by taking the role of principal prosecutor in the Nuremburg trials. It may have been a patriotic act for Justice Byrnes to resign from the Court in order to take the difficult post of Secretary of State, but it tended to establish a bad precedent, a precedent which will become worse if other justices should continue to show a receptive interest in a Democratic Presidential nomination. The position of the Court depends upon public respect for its complete disinterestedness, and that respect will not continue if several members are regarded as receptive candidates for the Presidency. Once a man has accepted

---

[1] Drafted by Morris Hillquit, able lawyer and socialist leader, one of the founders of the present party.

the high judicial post of a Justice of the Supreme Court, he should take vows of political chastity; he should renounce all other political ambition. If he entertains the honorable ambition to become President, he should resign from the Court; otherwise he should give no encouragement to his friends even to talk about him as a candidate. Conceivably, a former President of the United States may make a good judge of the Supreme Court. But a Supreme Court judge is not a proper candidate for the highest executive office.

Except on questions of the Supreme Court and popular election of the President, American socialists, like other Americans, have taken only an intermittent and superficial interest in the problem of the adequacy of our governmental machinery to the tasks required of it.

Yet that machinery creaks badly. In foreign policy the affirmative controls of democracy are slight. A strong President can always present Congress and the people with a series of accomplished facts. Fear of Congress is sometimes salutary but too often Congress, lacking information and power for affirmative responsibility, plays an unintelligent and carping role which encourages the Executive in dubious compromises or hypocrisy.

This judgment is especially pertinent to Senator McCarthy's frantic attempt in 1950 to reduce foreign policy to the level of a hunt for communist spies, but it is also supported by the whole history of two world wars, the way we got into them, and the way we tried to establish peace.

The inadequacy of Congressional method in domestic policy is even more obvious because the Eighty-first Congress, elected in 1948 with a definite mandate, did about as badly in facing problems as the Eightieth.

In criticizing current failures to meet American needs we must try to distinguish between faults due to democracy itself and faults due to its governmental machinery. And that's not easy. We must also try to distinguish between desirable changes in governmental techniques requiring constitutional amendment and those which Congress can make under its present powers.

Much could certainly be done for the improvement of the executive branch by the adoption of the kind of administrative reforms recommended by the Hoover Committee. Congress could better streamline itself by continuing procedural reforms begun under rules urged fairly successfully by Senator Robert M. La Follette, Jr.—the last act of his legislative career. Certainly it is within the power of Congress to end the iron rule of seniority in appointing committee chairmen. It would be invidious to name the numerous chairmen of committees with vast power who through senility or congenital incapacity or both should never have had their present posts.

But there remain the checks and balances written into the Constitution under conditions vastly different than our own. In fact the Constitution has been revised in action out of all harmony with the eighteenth-century ideas of its great fathers. But it still hampers effective action. Congress is so cumbersome and administration has become so important that the national government had to become presidential to a degree never anticipated by Madison or Hamilton —to say nothing of Jefferson. The President is burdened with the ceremonial functions of the British king or the French president, plus all the major duties of a prime minister. Yet he has no such facilities for shaping a program as has the British prime minister under a system of responsible cabinet government. He is obliged to exert leadership over Congress by indirection, appeals to public opinion, the exercise of personal influence, and the pressure of patronage. He and Congress—even one house of Congress—if in unresolved disagreement, can paralyze action during at least a two-year period, which in time of emergency might be disastrous.

Our system of representation gives tremendous weight to parochial interests united most easily in pork-barrel legislation. Thus, in Bryan's time, currency had a realistic metallic basis which made sixteen to one intelligible and of general interest. The silver purchase legislation of Franklin Roosevelt's time was pure subsidy to silver interests in five or six sparsely peopled states with ten or twelve votes in the Senate. Illustrations can be multiplied in the record of every Congress. One way the President prevents deadlock is by excessive compromise with local or regional interests. He is not helped at this point by any acceptance of responsibility by the party which elected him, even if it is nominally in control of both houses of Congress. In part at least it is our constitutional machinery unmanaged by any practice of party responsibility which makes for confusion.

It is party responsibility and cabinet direction which make the British House of Commons, despite its great size, effective as well as democratic. Without that direction, our House of Representatives tends to justify a fear that the framers of the Constitution did not solve the problem which was thus stated in the *Federalist:* [2]

"The truth is, that in all cases a certain number at least [of legislators] seems to be necessary to secure the benefits of free consultation and discussion, and to guard against too easy a combination for improper purposes; as, on the other hand, the number ought at most to be kept within a certain limit, in order to avoid the confusion and intemperance of a multitude. In all very numerous assemblies, of whatever character composed, passion never fails to wrest the sceptre from reason. Had every Athenian citizen been a Socrates, every Athenian assembly would still have been a mob."

If our House of Representatives has not become a mob, it is at the price of giving excessive power to the Speaker and the Rules Committee; in no way is the House a model deliberative body and the fault lies in its size even more than in the character of its members.

The Senate, on the other hand, permits minority rule by its exaggerated devotion to unlimited debate. That is clearly a matter remediable by its own action. But the general failure of liberal leadership in the Senate in the Eighty-first Congress, at a time when it contained a very considerable number of unusually able men, raises questions about the democratic process under our sys-

[2] *Federalist*, No. 55 (Madison).

tem of checks and balances. It illustrates vividly our lack of responsible party government.

The most searching criticism of our obsolescent political machinery in recent times comes from a conservative source. Dr. Arthur C. Millspaugh presents it in *Toward Efficient Government*, published by the Brookings Institution. His remedy is drastic and provocative. He would keep a federal setup but put the real power of the federal government in a council of twenty-one elected by nation-wide suffrage. This council would elect the President and its relations to him would be somewhat those of a council to a city manager on a more complex scale. The council would be permanently in session. The Senate would be kept, constituted as it now is, but with power only to delay legislation. Dr. Millspaugh's criticisms are more convincing than his own tentative plan. The latter is worth more consideration than it will get today.

A more commonly suggested theoretical reform is the substitution of responsible cabinet government for our present system. If we could assume that parliamentary government through a cabinet could work as well as in Britain or Sweden, there would be a strong case for it. We can make no such assumption. The cabinet system does not work better than our presidential system in France or Italy. We are conditioned by our history to voting for a chief executive with power. Drastic change, if possible, would not necessarily be for the better.

When all is said and done, the Constitution has played a great role in making us a nation. Its Bill of Rights is invaluable and in recent years the Supreme Court has shown an increasing firmness in enforcing it. In general it is desirable to have a principle of continuity and legitimacy in government and that, for Americans, the Constitution supplies. Hence in the light of our present experience and the attitude of our people, socialists and all others concerned for efficient democracy should concentrate on the minimum amendments necessary to give democracy a better chance to operate in a day when Big Government is inescapable.

My own conviction is that two amendments are essential and

a third highly desirable. The essential amendments must provide (1) for direct election of the President by popular vote; and (2) for simpler amendment to the Constitution. The amendment necessary for a truly democratic choice of the President, the one man who represents us all, should lay down uniform, nation-wide standards for voters, free from racial and other discrimination, and give to Congress sole power to enact uniform and reasonable rules under which political parties may place Presidential tickets on the ballots of all the states.

The 1948 election underscored the importance of this amendment. The rigor of state ballot laws and the technicalities in them kept Truman's name off the ballot in Alabama, Wallace's in Illinois, and mine in many states. For a few hours during the counting of the votes, it seemed possible that Governor Dewey might be elected by an electoral college majority, even though Truman had a plurality of the popular vote in excess of two million, or that the election might be thrown into the House of Representatives. The fact that the country escaped so unfortunate a fate in 1948 ought to serve as warning of the need for the kind of change I have so long advocated. The election of the President is the nation's business. States' rights become tyranny over the nation when in their name (but really for the sake of white supremacy) a candidate like Governor Thurmond deliberately tries to throw the election into the House of Representatives, and to that end his supporters use every possible means to keep Negroes from the polls.

Such consideration as was given to this matter in the Eighty-first Congress centered around the Lodge-Gossett Amendment which would provide only a partial remedy for great evils. It would abolish the electoral college but it would still keep a system of electing the President by states, each of which should have a number of votes corresponding to its present representation in the electoral college. These votes, forty-seven in New York and three in Nevada, under the amendment would be apportioned according to the popular vote. No longer would the winner take all. The result would rather closely approximate the popular vote and there would be no chance of throwing the election into the House of Representatives.

This undemocratic mechanism of voting by states was proposed in the amendment instead of a straight popular vote on the theory that a fair democratic measure cannot prevail because of state pride. Supporters of the amendment argued that it would not alter the present proportionate weight of the states or their control over qualifications of parties for the ballot and of citizens for suffrage. It is precisely these latter evils that cry aloud for remedy. We ought not to concede that a quarter of our states, because of state pride or devotion to white supremacy, would indefinitely block an amendment so obviously in accordance with elementary democracy as popular election of the President.

The rights of small states are more than amply protected by equality of representation in the Senate. We Americans are notably a mobile people. Most of us openly or secretly hope to reach the earthly paradise of Florida or California before we die. It is rather ridiculous, then, that as patriots of the state of our present abode we should fight for a system under which Nevada has one vote for President for some forty-thousand people and New York for some three hundred thousand. The Lodge Amendment might have made an improvement on the present situation—even that is not certain [3]—but after being approved in the Senate it was decisively rejected in the House (1950) after inadequate debate. It may or may not be revived in a later Congress with some modification. The importance of averting the real perils inherent in the present method of electing the President remains and must not be ignored. Some amendment to the Constitution at this point is imperative. Since we must seek amendment, let us at least try to do an adequate job.

An adequate job must guard against the possibility of the election of a President with a plurality very far short of a majority. This

---

[3] It might still further increase the disproportionate influence of the Solid South, as Herbert Wechsler ably argues in the *Journal of the American Bar Association*, March, 1949. But see my comment in the 1949–50 issue of *Debate Handbook* (University of Missouri).

could happen in a divided field and fear of it would be alleged as a reason for making the path of minority parties very rough. Under popular election there should be set up a system of preferential voting under which second choices would count toward a final majority or there should be a run-off between the two highest candidates. The first is preferable, the second more in accord with existing custom in the choice of governors and mayors in certain states and cities.

While we are at the business of changing our way of electing a President, it would be desirable, although not desperately important, to abolish the office of Vice-President. Under the American system, the Vice-President is usually nominated to add weight to the ticket in a campaign, or to appease a minority of the party, rather than because he is highly regarded as a possible President. Often the Vice-President has been chosen (as was John Nance Garner under Roosevelt) because he didn't agree at important points with the Presidential candidate. Once in office he has the wholly anomalous job of presiding over the Senate and otherwise only of waiting for the President to die. Heretofore, attempts to use him in executive service have failed. Conceivably they may yet succeed, but it would be more logical to abolish the office and to provide that the Speaker of the House, who presumably would come closest to representing current political opinion, should succeed in emergency to the office of President with proviso for an election the following November to fill the unexpired term. Some such plan works very successfully in New York City. It would be a rational and democratic way of handling the matter in federal affairs. Short of such an amendment, however, the present situation could be changed for the better if, as happened in 1948, the parties should exercise more care in the choice of the Vice-Presidential candidate.

The second essential amendment would provide the necessary machinery for change in the light of discussion and experience. That scarcely exists today, so difficult is the process of amending the Constitution and so far removed from the people.[4] Amendments now may be officially proposed (1) by a two-thirds vote in each house of Congress; or (2) by a convention called on application of the legislatures of two-thirds of the states. And they must be ratified (1) by the legislatures of three-fourths of the states; or (2) by conventions in three-fourths of the states. The convention method for proposing or ratifying amendments never has been used.

Various changes have been feebly urged, most of them better than what we have. It would seem to me enough of a safeguard against sudden and whimsical change if amendments could be proposed or a constitutional convention set up: (1) by vote of a majority of the total membership in each house of Congress, or (2) by at least one-third of the state legislatures; and ratified by (1) a popular majority (perhaps of at least 55 per cent) in a nation-wide referendum, or (2) by two-thirds of the state legislatures. It should be required that any proposed amendment be submitted for action without the delays which now occur in state legislatures, some of which do not act at all.

Under a reasonable plan of amendment, no party with a mandate from the people for substantial change would need to fear that the excessive checks of the Constitution would make it impossible to carry out the definite will of a clear majority.

A third desirable amendment would provide a mechanism for appeal to the people in the event of a deadlock between President and Congress on some important legislation. It has been suggested that in such a case the President be given a guarded power to demand a new election, at least of the House of Representatives. I think it would be better if either the President or Congress, under proper restrictions, could seek a referendum on the particular piece of legislation on which a deadlock might exist.

[4] The first ten amendments were agreed to as the price of ratifying the Constitution; the Thirteenth, Fourteenth, and Fifteenth were the result of the Civil War. The woman-suffrage, direct election of senators, and income-tax amendments were got by long struggle.

No socialist change should abolish the federalist principle in favor of such centralization as exists in smaller countries like Britain or France. On the contrary, democratic socialism must be concerned about the danger of overcentralization. The fact that ours is a federal union in which the states retain much power provides anything but an automatic solution to our problem. The division of powers between the federal government and the states is unsatisfactory principally because the states are not proper economic units; the disparity between them in size and wealth is great; and many of them without federal aid are unable to do a decent job of public health or education. Almost every normal economic regional area (*e.g.*, around New York, Chicago, St. Louis, and Portland, Oregon) includes parts of at least two or three states; and the difference in tax systems, labor and social security laws, etc., invites competition in escaping their burdens and complicates relations between management and workers. States' rights too often are workers' wrongs, and state governments usually are less efficient and responsive to the people than the federal government.

Something might be accomplished for decentralization by extending the use of such regional divisions as were established for the Federal Reserve Banks. By act of Congress or treaty between states (like the treaty between New York and New Jersey establishing the Port Authority of New York) these regions could be used as units for certain economic functions.

While there is merit in the cry against overcentralization, it can be overworked. Coordination, if not centralization, is an imperative need in the reform of our complex governmental machinery. Government efficiency, as well as individual well-being, requires coordination and simplification of all taxation—federal, state, and local.

In this, as in other governmental reforms, our states lag. In too many states their legislatures are worse cursed by rotten borough systems of representation, party hacks in office, and domination by lobbies than the federal Congress. The coming of socialism will require the difficult business of making its principles prevail in forty-eight states and cleaning them up and modernizing their creaking machinery in the process.[5]

More detrimental to the kind of government we need than the defects of governmental machinery which we have examined is the fact that our principal parties have no sense of responsibility to their own promises or to people who entrust them with office. This party irresponsibility is aided by excessive checks and balances in government, but it is not an inevitable product of them. While it continues we must expect government by pressure groups too little subordinate to any general mandate of the people.

The answer is responsible party government in which parties divide on principle and program and recognize a moral obligation to carry out their campaign pledges. For such party responsibility there is no substitute although it may be supplemented by occasional submission of specific issues to the people. I have suggested this as a remedy for a deadlock between the President and Congress. State and municipal bond issues are now submitted to the electorate for authorization. If it were practicable, as is not probable under present conditions, all the people should have a chance to vote on the wars they are asked to fight. There are other issues on the state level which may justify a carefully guarded use of the initiative and referendum. But more would be lost than gained by making it easy to hold snap elections on a great variety of uncorrelated proposals at any level: city, state, or national.

Short of official referenda, it is good business for congressmen to report to their people and informally to consult them. But no congressman should be bound absolutely by the results of such consultation. He should be bound on major measures by his commitments to the party platform which he accepted in his campaign, but under this broad obligation he should vote in accordance with his own informed conviction. Serious attempts have been made by congressmen and legislators systematically to poll their districts on issues under discussion in legislative bodies. Never has anything

[5] On the bad situation in our states see *Our Sovereign State*, edited by Robert S. Allen (Vanguard Press).

like a majority bothered to vote. Usually those especially interested in one particular measure reply.[6]

If slavish dependence on the wishes of articulate voters in a congressman's district makes for irresponsible parochialism, a blind following of public-opinion polls would be worse. Critically handled they should have real value in reporting popular trends and in counterbalancing the weight of special pressure groups. They do not and cannot measure intensity of conviction which is as much of a factor as extension of it. They do not follow informed discussion. Over and over citizens give answers based on ignorance which they wish to conceal; on many issues they tend to give the answer which is conventional or respectable within the group of which they feel themselves a part. In general I endorse the points made by Professor Lindsay Rogers (in *The Pollsters*) exposing false assumptions underlying this modern variant of twenty questions and warning of dangerous results which may follow from the growing habit of asking a sampling of the electorate what "it" thinks, and then declaring that its snap judgment is the Voice of the People and, as such, all but infallible.

The performance of the Eighty-first Congress strikingly illustrated our lack of responsible government. Owing to circumstances unnecessary here to review, President Truman was compelled in 1948, if he desired election, to advance a more specifically liberal program than any of his predecessors. On that basis, as well as on the basis of a party platform—which, unfortunately, there was plenty of precedent to ignore—Mr. Truman and his Congress took office with an unusually definite mandate from the people.

Moreover, the Democratic Party, by reason of the Dixiecrat revolt, seemed to be more emancipated from subservience to the Solid South than ever before. Yet the Democratic Eighty-first Congress successfully flouted the President and disregarded the mandate. The President himself partially nullified his verbal support

[6] Cabell Phillips reports in the *New York Times*, May 29, 1949, that Representative Robert J. Corbett of Pennsylvania sends out questionnaires to from fifteen to twenty thousand of his constituents every two or three months. His returns average about 18 per cent.

of a liberal program by poor leadership and by his unfortunate habit of appointing his friends to high office and then sticking by them regardless of what they might do or leave undone.

As the primary elections of 1950 came around, such was the nature of our governmental system and our traditional lack of party responsibility, that Senator Lister Hill was able truthfully to tell his fellow Alabamians that the best way to block civil rights legislation was to stick to the same Democratic Party which had solemnly endorsed it, and by sticking make sure that their congressmen, through seniority, achieved committee chairmanships. As a matter of fact, at the end of the Eighty-first Congress, Southern Democrats held ten out of eighteen important House chairmanships and nine of the ten were lukewarm on Truman's whole program as well as on civil rights.

But under our curious system they were Democrats in good standing. And Truman and his party remained the agents of progress in the minds of most of the workers and the more progressive farmers.

It is sometimes claimed by American political theorists that this party irresponsibility, due largely to lack of clear-cut division between the old parties and the failure of any third party to rise to strength, have been beneficial. New laws of importance, it is alleged, can only be enacted when American public opinion in general will support them. Thus bitterness is dulled and sharp conflict, possibly of revolutionary character, is avoided.

The argument sounds somewhat plausible but has no real weight in view of the facts we have cited in America's recent history and of the further fact that responsible parties in other English-speaking countries and in Scandinavian lands have presented clear-cut programs without evoking the specter of revolutionary violence. Actually, the tactics of the Ku Klux Klan in the twenties and some other examples of direct action in our history were encouraged by lack of real difference between responsible major parties with appropriate programs.

Short of direct action, there has been a constant magnification of the role of pressure groups in American politics. Someone has said that America is governed by shifting combinations of minority pressure groups. To be sure, much of the outcry against pressure politics is exaggerated and even hypocritical. Until it is possible for men to make a far easier and more automatic adjustment of particular group or class interest to the common interest than it is today, there will always be group pressures to which democracy must offer some scope of action. Many times I have smiled inwardly or outwardly at earnest speakers in meetings large and small who begin by denouncing pressure politics and conclude by urging their hearers to write their congressman about this or that measure.

Nevertheless, pressure politics can get completely out of hand and greatly militate against a conscious seeking of the common good. It should be the function of political parties, organized on the basis of some principle and some program, to hold pressure politics in check and to give to individuals a certain unity of purpose without which democracy is greatly jeopardized. It is no cause for rejoicing in America that socialist, radical, or even definitely progressive forces have as yet neither captured one of the major parties on a nation-wide scale nor established a strong third party as the first step in forcing responsible party government on the basis of a realistic political realignment.

In discussing socialism in America (Chapter 8) I have linked the disappointing development of the Socialist Party to the general American practice of irresponsible party government. It is a practice socialists must persistently seek to change.

One of my reasons for undertaking the rather arduous task of running six times for President as a candidate of a small minority party was my persistent hope that we could make the party a nucleus, a rallying point, a spearhead—use what figure you will—for a much larger new party on the electoral field. For many years I sought an American equivalent to the British Labour Party. Later, I strongly preferred the Canadian party known as the Cooperative Commonwealth Federation as our model. The Labour Party is too largely controlled by labor unions and their officials under a system of bloc voting at conventions, a plan that has its faults in Britain and would be more open to criticism in America. During the years I became more and more persuaded that the functions of labor unions and political parties were different and that the most a socialist party under any name should want would be the endorsement of unions and the support of their members.

Of course, I should have preferred to have our Socialist Party grow like an oak from an acorn. But only very briefly in 1932 did I think that probable. Our party was psychologically handicapped by its long association with defeat and by the natural difficulty labor leaders and others would find in coming into a party which they had long rejected. It would be more rational to expect them to join in building a new party in which I hoped that the Socialist Party could play a great educational role, much as the Independent Labour Party had done in Britain.

We had made some progress in 1948 in tentatively projecting conferences on a new political alignment after the election. But the men and women who had lent a favorable ear to this plan had predicated their action on Truman's defeat. Instead, he was elected in a campaign in which his party appeared progressive. Even socialists had to admit that it was no longer true that the difference between his 1948 program and the Republicans' was only a difference between Tweedledum and Tweedledee. The idea of conferences on a new party had to be dropped. Despite the failure of the Democratic Party to make good, there was by the 1950 election little if any sign that any considerable bloc of farmers or workers was ready for the task of building a new party although some of their spokesmen had begun again to refer to it as a possibility.

The cumulative experience of the years has raised the question for socialists whether or not a change in our tactics is necessary. For most of our fifty years it has been natural and appropriate that we should try to function on the electoral field. It is, I think, more than a desire to justify my own long years of apparently unsuccessful political effort which leads me to maintain that American workers and progressives in the years since 1900 have made a mistake in not building the Socialist Party into great strength. In these years, despite our Socialist failure on the electoral field, I believe that in the advancement of our ideas and in the political adoption of some of our concrete proposals, we Socialists did far more by running tickets than we could have done in any other way. But certain developments to which I have referred have been changing the situation. Since 1932, there has been a further tightening of the laws and rules under which Socialist tickets can be placed on ballots. The differences between candidates, if not between the old parties, has become more important to the voters, and labor's concern in politics has greatly increased.

Hence, by 1950, I became convinced that at least for the next few years we Socialists could more successfully use our limited resources in the all-important business of winning our fellow citizens to socialism by other methods than by exhausting ourselves to put tickets on the ballot at times and places where we could not wage effective campaigns. We cannot successfully win friends and influence people by insisting that, despite real differences between candidates A, B, and C, and the importance of those differences, nothing matters at election time but to keep one's purity by voting Socialist. Or, where that is impossible—as, alas, is the case in a great many elections—by furtively and secretly voting for one or another candidate with a sense of guilt for doing it.

The alternative to primary emphasis on Socialist electoral action for Socialist candidates only is not, of course, endorsement of the Democratic or Republican parties as such, much less the abandonment of the Socialist Party. On the contrary, the party should be more zealous to present its own concrete proposals and its own platform at every political level, to make them matters of public discussion, to use them as yardsticks in measuring all candidates, and to urge the importance of a mass party consciously socialist. Socialists in organizations like the Americans for Democratic Action can be more effective if, as members of the organization, having made plain their own belief in the inadequacy of candidates endorsed by the A.D.A., they can go along with the organization.

The Party itself might well afford to say: Candidate A is not a socialist, but he stands for a foreign policy or for a social program vastly better than B's by socialist standards. So loose are American laws and party customs in American primaries that in some states it might be possible and desirable for Socialists to nominate avowed Socialists in one or other of the old-party primaries.

What happens now is that individual Socialists either leave the Party in order to support the better candidate who has a chance of winning, or they vote for him and keep still about his relation to socialist principles. Either way socialism loses strength. If the Party, engaged in an educational campaign, should express its reasoned opinion on candidates and issues where it is at present unable to present its own ticket effectively, it might hasten the general process of socialist education and, at the same time, remove from its members a sense of futility at election time. Meanwhile, much of the money and energy heretofore expended in getting on the ballot could be used to send teams of speakers to the innumerable meetings in America which welcome speakers, to do more and better research, and to publish more and better literature.

This sort of program involves no imitation of the communist habit of furtively boring from within labor and liberal organizations. With complete honesty and candor, socialists may take advantage of old-party irresponsibility and the extreme pragmatism of liberal groups to press home the necessity of party responsibility through a new political alignment based on principles and program.

These new tactics have become especially important because of the development of political consciousness in the ranks of labor. If we socialists have not accomplished what we hoped, we at least have contributed toward the development of this sense of responsibility. Such agencies as Labor's League for Political Education (A.F.L.) and the Political Action Committee (C.I.O.) fall short of our socialist desires and the demands of our time. But they represent a definite and encouraging departure from the old policy of transient and casual endorsement of individual candidates and the beginning of permanently established political organization. While labor unions present problems to socialism which we shall examine in a later chapter, it has become clear that we socialists have a better chance of educating the workers by cooperating as far as possible with them in these organizations rather than by aloof criticism at a time and under conditions where we cannot present our own tickets and wage strong campaigns for them. Socialists can carry out this sort of program democratically and openly without deceitful "infiltration" of other political parties or cooperatives, labor unions or farm organizations.

Arguments like these were presented by many of us to the biennial convention of the Socialist Party in Detroit in 1950. (It was in that city in 1922 that a Socialist convention had first declared the Party's willingness to go along with the farmer-labor party idea.) After keen discussion on a level gratifyingly free from personalities or imputations of wrong motives, the majority of the convention voted to reaffirm in unqualified language the Party's devotion to absolute independence of action in elections. It would nominate candidates whenever and wherever it could, and in other cases would give neither direct nor indirect help of any sort to any old-party candidates.

For years American socialists have been conditioned to this way of thinking. It is traditional; it appears logical. To extreme leftists in the Party it seems meaningless to speak of any important differences between nonsocialists. He that is not with us is against us. In cities like Bridgeport, Connecticut, and Reading, Pennsylvania, the socialists in action are very moderate, but for tactical reasons they believe that their local success is based on sharp opposition to all old-party ticket groups at every level. It must, moreover, be admitted in fairness that the policy of shifting Socialist emphasis from nominating tickets to the conversion of more socialists through cooperation presents its own difficulties and dangers.

Nevertheless, developments almost immediately made it plain that these difficulties were less than lay in the way adopted. The New York State convention, dominated by those who had supported the winning resolution at Detroit, felt unable to place a state ticket in the field. Its action under the circumstances was not equivalent to adopting an alternative program such as we had urged but to a mere confession of weakness.

Far more disastrous was the action of the Connecticut Party's Executive Committee in allowing Mayor Jasper McLevy of Bridgeport, its candidate for governor, to accept the nomination or endorsement of the so-called Independence Party created by the ultraconservative woman industrialist, Vivian Kellems, and other dissident Republicans because the Republican Party was too liberal, too complacent to welfare legislation! It was an Alice-in-Wonderland commentary on muddled political thinking and acting. Jasper McLevy, clean-government mayor and theoretically orthodox socialist, champion of socialist purity at Detroit, justified himself by a weird hope of election and the legalistic defense that the Socialists had not nominated Miss Kellems as candidate for the United States Senate and that she ran on an independent ticket. But the McLevy Socialists did not really fight her candidacy and condoned her views by accepting endorsement from her party. The episode painfully illustrated the sterility of the old socialist tactics and the unreality of the loudly proclaimed arguments of the Socialist Party of Connecticut, one group of opponents of our proposals for new tactics at Detroit. To those new tactics, American socialists inside and outside the Party must come if they would be effective in the present situation and in hastening the day of new political alignment.

It is hopefully significant that at Detroit in 1950 there was no important controversy on the Socialist platform or on the nature of our criticisms of the old parties. Sharp differences lay only in the field of strategy and tactics; all the delegates were concerned with the best way of bringing into being a mass party, democratic-socialist in conscious philosophy and program, such as all socialists desire.

The business of establishing and maintaining the cooperative commonwealth requires deliberate and conscious planning and action; it is quite too complex to be left to drift, pressure of events, and a haphazard piling up of individual reforms. Democracy in America requires responsible party government and since the grave issues increasingly involve the attitude of the electorate toward democratic-socialist principles, it is vital that a party come into being which will be consciously concerned to make them prevail.

Chapter 18

Socialism, Labor Unions, and Cooperatives

ALMOST ALL socialists, Marxist and non-Marxist, have always regarded the wageworkers as the principal and indispensable element of the armies which were to win the cooperative commonwealth. One might compromise the absolutism of Marxist theory of the class struggle and yet admit that the industrial workers by the nature of their work were at once the most obviously exploited of capitalism's victims and potentially the mightiest agents in its downfall. Indeed until comparatively recently this socialist belief led to serious neglect of the farmers and the middle class by socialist teachers and organizers.

It was inevitable that workers should organize in the trades to which they belonged. Socialists saw in trade unions not only efficient agents of immediate improvements in the workers' lot but supporters of political change ultimately revolutionary in its extent and quality. The unions, once they were organized, would possess the economic power to back up whatever victories might be won at the polls and to defeat counterrevolution.

Naturally there were differences of opinion among socialists about the degree of socialist purity to be expected of unions and about the way in which they should be organized: simply by trades, industries, or in one big union. But, despite these differences, on the European continent socialists fairly well shaped and inspired the organization of unions which in great majority were socialist or syndicalist. Later Roman Catholic unions were organized.

This was not equally true of the organization of British unions, which were not predominantly socialist in thinking until the time of World War I. It was even less true of the United States.

The American labor union is unique in that it is consciously non-socialist and nonreligious. Nevertheless, its existence and power necessarily represent revolt from *laissez-faire* capitalism and a partially successful challenge to it. Logically, the supporters of the market economy were right in believing that under it labor must be a commodity subject to the impersonal forces governing commodities.[1] Logically, labor unions, even the most conservative and deferential of them, were a form of conspiracy against the market economy. So far is this market economy from being natural to men that in order to establish it the political state in England, mother of capitalism, had to break down the poor dignities and securities which feudalism afforded. From the beginning of the factory system down to the latter half of the nineteenth century it was necessary to drive workers into factories, first by enclosure of the old common lands and then by poor laws so bad that the worst factory conditions were preferable to any available public aid. It has been observed with truth that Anglo-American supporters of capitalism who self-righteously condemn the methods by which the Soviet dictators force men to work have forgotten that their economic ancestors

---

[1] Nevertheless, so reluctant were men to accept the complete control of the market economy for labor that in England from 1795 to 1834 the Speenhamland Law, bad as it was in conception and consequences, at least attested to a confused faith in the right to live and reinforced a low grade precapitalist paternalism. (See Polyani's *The Great Transformation.*)

successfully applied drastic compulsions by reducing the workers to the status of paupers and their labor to a mere commodity.

In the struggle against the horrible conditions of the early years of capitalism in Britain (and to a less extent America), no single force was as important as the rising labor movement. It won its victories with amazingly little violence but by a tremendous assertion of the solidarity of the workers themselves. It is a bitter commentary on our understanding of history that so many spokesmen for the middle class continually deplore the violence of strikes who support unquestioningly the violence of the political state in war. Strikes, especially in this country, have been attended by violence, but essentially the strike as a weapon of conflict has been a substitute for violence. Its symbol has more truly been the folded arm than the clenched fist. And, in terms of achievement, it has done more for human dignity than most of the wars whose heroes we teach our children to honor in schools. By contrast, labor's heroes are unknown soldiers, even to the workers in powerful unions.

In the United States various forms of labor organization began to appear early in the nineteenth century with the growth of industry, but on the eve of the First World War the growth of unions had by no means paralleled the growth of industry. Certain crafts were fairly well organized and were very conservative in their social viewpoint. That redoubtable figure, Samuel Gompers, long president of the A.F.L., was at heart a syndicalist profoundly distrustful of the power of the state. His influence was so great that the great depression was well advanced before the A.F.L. endorsed social-security measures.

The great and successful strike in the anthracite coal regions in 1902 had marked a rise of the United Mine Workers to status and power. Heroic strikes in the needle trades in 1909 and 1910 had established progressive unionism in a field that had been left to sweatshops. The leaders of these latter strikes were socialists by conviction and they helped to work out a way for the orderly government of a chaotic industry. Outside the A.F.L., at the beginning of World War I, the Wobblies (I.W.W.) were active and strong among lumber and migratory workers. Their organization was definitely syndicalist and revolutionary in purpose.

The I.W.W. was weakened by the wholesale prosecution of its leaders for sedition during the First World War. But that struggle was attended by a vigorous growth of the A.F.L. unions in membership and in status. Samuel Gompers is reported to have mourned that peace came too soon for labor to consolidate its position. At any rate, the unions lost ground after World War I under a vigorous and unscrupulous attack from the employers who were aided because the boom of the twenties permitted some rise in real wages. The depression of the thirties was disastrous to unions as it was to the individual workers. A reservoir of the unemployed always furnishes power to management in its struggle against unions and in the early thirties this reservoir was terrifyingly great. The usual weapon of the unemployed is political action or violence rather than union organization.

In the desperate unemployment of the thirties, Roosevelt prevented violence because he gave new hope and new status to labor not only by making decent provision for the unemployed but also by encouraging labor organization under N.R.A. legislation which provided for a certain degree of self-government by industry. That, in turn, logically required organization of workers. The first four years under Roosevelt, from 1933 to well into 1937, were tumultuous times for labor organization. As late as 1934 and 1935 the number of lives lost in labor struggles was estimated at fifty-one and thirty-five, respectively. Labor's victory in the automobile industry and the Supreme Court's approval of the Wagner Labor Act mark the definite emergence of unions to new power. The split between the A.F.L. and C.I.O. had and still has unfortunate features and consequences. But the split was the proof of life rather than death, and not all the features of competition in organizing the unorganized have been bad.

The Second World War was an even more powerful stimulus to organization than the First. And the postwar prosperity, the legacy of the war, made it to the interest of management to keep peace by concessions to labor which, in so far as they affected wages, could be taken out of consumers.

It must be remembered that German labor under the Weimar Republic was at least equally well organized and yet free unions were utterly broken, first, by the impact of vast depression, and then by the Nazi power. Something of the sort might happen in America. Nevertheless, depression, even on a large scale, would scarcely have the same result on our unions that it had on the weaker American movement early in the nineteen thirties. Not only are the unions better organized industrially, but they are more alert to their own interests in the community.

It is difficult to exaggerate the change in the status of labor between the end of Woodrow Wilson's administration and the beginning of Harry Truman's first full term. One should hear older workers testify to it. I myself between 1919 and 1937 was involved in many efforts to organize labor and particularly to assert the civil rights of the workers. I should like to believe that things which I saw and of which to some extent I was a part—the Passaic strike of 1926, the general textile strike of 1934, the struggle against Governor McNutt's military law in Indiana in 1935, to mention only a few instances—cannot happen again in the United States. Certainly the unions are vastly stronger and more self-consciously active on the political as well as the economic front.

This situation presents to socialists and indeed to all believers in democracy new hope and new problems.

The problems can be said—a bit melodramatically—to rise from the struggle between syndicalism and socialism for the soul of labor. Practical syndicalism speaks the language not of the old I.W.W. but of Sam Gompers; it tells the workers in his phrase that what they want is simply "more and more and more" for their unions without assuming responsibility for production or for general well-being. Mr. Gompers' successors are more ready than he to use the state and they have achieved some success in pressure politics. But with the prosperity of the midcentury they are pretty complacent in hope of winning what they want without fundamental change in the economic system.

Socialism tells the workers: you must consciously plan for the general welfare; you cannot win and maintain plenty or freedom, still less peace, for yourselves alone. Victory requires cooperative action in which the whole community—except its parasites—should be involved.

The average articulate labor man would quite honestly deny that he is syndicalist or socialist. He is, usually, Democratic or Republican and, he says, a believer in free competitive enterprise. Yet, for reasons that we have already stated, labor and its leaders are even less able or willing to act on the logic of free competitive enterprise than their bosses. What they mean by the phrase when they mean anything more than the parroting of a popularized formula is that they prefer private bosses to the state, especially since under the latter they fear their loss of the right to strike.

Sometimes they fear bigness. But labor is not the natural enemy of monopoly. John L. Lewis works with his enemies the coal operators to get something like a fixed price in coal and to keep out the competition of imports of "residual oil." The needle trades had to force the small-scale employers to bargain collectively through associations which would at least fix labor prices. In the mid-thirties labor came to an agreement with Big Steel without the bloody strike which Little Steel forced upon it. After World War II it tacitly consented to Big Steel's inflationary price rise so long as it got its wage increase. (German unions had even more definitely worked with the bosses under the work councils of the Weimar Republic to raise wages and prices at the expense of the public. This process helped Hitler to popularity, a fact never to be forgotten by friends of democracy.)

The syndicalist tendencies in American labor unions are to be seen in their drives for wage increases and pension settlements for themselves, with small consideration for the general economy and in their fondness for "feather bedding," that is, unnecessary or made work in the printing and housing trades and railroading. In 1950 the firemen actually began a strike primarily to force the employment of an extra fireman on Diesel engines after two Presidential fact-finding boards, in composition acceptable to the union, had found the practice unnecessary.

In these practices there is nothing peculiarly blameworthy. The bosses have done similar things. Labor has usually had to fight for wage increases against the assurance that "your demands will wreck our economy." Unemployment in peacetime is a haunting specter and nation-wide planning to prevent it is still very backward. To these general reasons for syndicalist lines of action labor leaders often contribute because their power depends upon their comparative skill in winning "more and more and more." A leader who can win tangible gains for his rank and file may be forgiven many sins past and present. The public has forgotten, if it ever knew, that the forceful John L. Lewis in the black years of depression was hated by thousands of miners for his autocracy and alleged indifference to their miseries. Things changed when with the coming of the New Deal Lewis embarked on a course of strategy which until the summer of 1949 won great improvements for the miners. A West Virginia miner who had been one of Mr. Lewis' critics remarked to me when better times came, "We think he's still the same old son of a bitch—but he does bring home the bacon." Therein he stated the golden rule of success for the labor leader.

It is a rule which under present conditions spurs the leader not only to seek yearly wage increases on the basis of the needs and desires of his own members but also to keep a shrewd eye on his colleagues in other unions. His relative power in A.F.L. or C.I.O. will depend upon his relative success in every contract negotiation. This is in some respects to the advantage of the workers but it tends to keep the ambitious leader from those broader and longer range considerations which are essential to the health of our economy and hence of the workers themselves.

Professor Charles E. Lindblom of Yale, examining facts like these, argues in *Unions and Capitalism* that unions are developing a monopoly power and a syndicalist attitude which threatens a dynamic economy. Our strong unions are, he thinks, gradually destroying competition and in the process exerting a dangerous inflationary influence. Professor Lindblom has no very practical or hopeful suggestions for remedying the situation since he believes both in unions and capitalism.

Socialism offers no mechanical solution. We have seen that the British unions have raised against their own party's government some of the difficulties which Professor Lindblom describes. Yet there can be no doubt that the degree to which they were socialist enabled the government to deal with emergencies as it could never have done if they were all inspired by the spirit of John L. Lewis. Socialism at least presents an ideal of cooperation and an integration of planning which make possible alternatives either to syndicalism or docile submission to bosses and profiteers.

There are, moreover, in American trade union practice elements of a socialist rather than a purely syndicalist approach to problems. The political programs of both the A.F.L. and C.I.O., while less than socialist, go beyond syndicalism in concern for the common good. Both great federations have an international vision expressed, among other things, in their formation of an International Federation of Free Trade Unions.[2]

After the U.A.W. made its excellent settlement with General Motors in 1950, including a generous pension provision, I heard two of its high officers reiterate the assurance Walter Reuther had earlier given Congress, namely that the union did not consider pensions won from each industry the final and wholly satisfactory answer to a problem which required a more inclusive arrangement. These labor leaders believe that pressure on corporations for pensions will make them favor a more generous governmental plan for the aged.

The U.A.W.—and later the Steel Workers—have come to the

---

[2] Trade-union internationalism, however, did not prevent jewelry, glass, glove, photo engraving, hat, and textile workers from leading, through their unions, the opposition to reciprocal trade agreements in the summer of 1950.

position that in arguing for wage increases they must consider the public. It is a socially responsible position to argue that their wage demands need not raise prices. President Truman's Steel Fact-Finding Board in 1949 did not find that the steel workers' case correctly stated all pertinent facts or was wholly logical. But neither did it accept uncritically the employers' case. My present point is that the very nature of the union's argument before the Fact-Finding Board illustrated the birth of a rudimentary sense of responsibility in a tremendously powerful union for something more than its own immediate interest. The fallacy of the union's position lay in its belief that it could reconcile its own and the public's interest in a near monopoly under the working of the profit system. There can be no lasting reconciliation without conscious planning and that conscious planning requires acceptance of the supremacy of the principle of cooperation.

The socialization of basic industries like coal or steel would not automatically settle industrial disputes. But the control of these enormous enterprises consciously in the interest of the whole public which owns them would provide a very different basis of action than today when unions must struggle against managers whose primary concern must be the profits of absentee owners.

These facts for the moment little trouble the unions or the public. Both are more concerned with attempts of government to regulate unions. Here the powerful labor organizations strongly incline to a syndicalist position of opposition to all government regulation. They have given many sound reasons for opposition to the Taft-Hartley Act but scarcely for the extremes of their denunciation of the law or Senator Taft. What they really want is merely a restoration of the Wagner Act.

That act was a boon in the mid-thirties. It meant, among other things, emancipation from the aggressive tactics of the bosses in fighting unions which were exposed in the famous La Follette report on civil liberties. But the growing strength of unions inevitably raised problems and the position of union leaders in rejecting all regulation in the public interest as an unsound use of state power was made logically untenable by their acceptance of state guarantees of collective bargaining rights.

Labor's hatred of the Taft-Hartley Act goes a little beyond the rational. It is an abuse of language to call it a slave act. It deprives no worker of the right to quit his job or change his job. It does not even permit absolute and permanent prohibition of strikes. It is ironic that to its principal author, Senator Taft, labor owes its escape from President Truman's draft bill urged by him to deal with the threatened railroad strike of 1946. Nevertheless, the act is justly condemned because it sought to impose restrictions on political action and set up bureaucratic hindrances to collective bargaining. It reintroduced the labor injunction, which labor had historic reasons for hating. A fresh start at labor legislation is in order.

Two thorny questions concern us and would concern any socialist government. The first concerns the right to strike and the second the closed shop. The continued existence of the right to strike and the possibility of its legal exercise are, in the light of the history of dictatorships, invaluable safeguards for liberty in general as well as for the rights of workers. But the completely unrestrained exercise of the right to strike might well invite dictatorship with its ruthless repression as the alternative to disaster. Occasionally, as in the strike of tugboat men in New York harbor in 1947, a comparatively few men can threaten multitudes. No modern society will endure this indefinitely.

In the past, the method of strike has tended to be self-limiting. Neither side would carry on to ruin. But in some industries ruin may come quickly. In certain of them, like the provision of water and power in cities, continuous operation is essential to the health of the people, and a strike may entail intolerable punishment of the innocent. No socialist, therefore, can consistently take the position that under no circumstances should any kind of government intervene authoritatively to prevent or end a strike. It is certain that any strong state will so act in an extreme emergency.

So difficult, however, is the business of drawing a law to prevent strikes, and so likely is such a law to be mostly an irritant, that legislation on this subject should be approached with extraordinary caution. The emphasis should be placed on improving processes of mediation. Beyond that, socialists will insist that an industry in which continuous operation is too urgently important to public interest to tolerate a strike is obviously too important to leave in the hands of profit-making owners. It should be socialized. Compensatory methods of adjusting grievances and fixing wages should be set up if ever in such industries the workers by contract or under law are required to renounce the right to strike. Every effort should be made to settle this question by voluntary agreement with the unions. What may compel some government action is not the iniquity of striking against the management because it is the government or an agency of government; it is the damage to society that may be involved.

The right to strike has been a sanction for collective bargaining and collective bargaining has been the most practicable approach to a satisfactory adjustment of wages. Unfortunately for those of us who would like a theoretic and ethical answer to the problem of a just wage, there is no formula for fixing it. Floors and ceilings may justly be fixed on salaries and wages but in between we shall in most cases have to look to collective bargaining. It will be highly desirable to keep any segment of industry in which that right is qualified as small as possible.

It is a fact of history and present observation that wages have not been justly determined by the amoral economy of the market or by government fiat. In our complex economy there is no accurate determination of the value of what each worker or group of workers may produce. Neither are wages easily fixed on the basis of cost of living, ability of an industry to pay, or profit sharing, although all these factors may enter into the picture. We must trust largely to collective bargaining, but a collective bargaining based on effective organization of workers in unorganized and badly exploited occupations. Without organization these workers will continue to get too small a share of the national income.

This is not to rule out the need of broad ethical determinants of fair compensation but to point out the difficulties of their application unless and until our social psychology and our economy of plenty make possible—as they do not today—the application of the great principle, "from every man according to his ability; to every man according to his need." As matters now stand, socialists must seek to conserve the principle of collective bargaining inspired by a new and growing feeling for the common good.

Collective bargaining presupposes union organization. And practically that brings us to the problem of the closed shop. Under our present conditions for fixing wages and working conditions, it would seem legitimate to require workers who accept the benefits of collective bargaining either already to be, or promptly to become, members of the union favored by the majority of their trade or industry as its collective agent.

What a great many labor leaders and some of their unions have failed to see is that this principle is only valid if the union itself is open, and if democratic procedures in it are carefully protected. It is at this point that developments in American labor unionism justify the most anxiety. The regard labor leaders have given to raising the material well-being of their rank-and-file members has not been matched by an equal regard for the rights of individual workers. Thus, there are unions, of which the most important are the Railroad Brotherhoods, which, by their constitution, rituals, or practice, still exclude Negroes or keep them in a kind of second-class membership. There are unions which completely monopolize, or seek to monopolize, their particular trades by extraordinarily high initiation fees or other obstacles to membership. The motion-picture operators have furnished examples of this.

The C.I.O. has made great contributions to democracy, notably through its interest in race equality. Its president, Philip Murray, is no John L. Lewis, but the C.I.O. national convention is less democratically run than the A.F.L. and its rules are much less democratic than those of the House of Representatives, despite the powers which the Speaker and the Rules Committee have over the latter.

In the 1948 convention, Murray prevented even the reading of minority reports of committees.

In that same year it was some of the more progressive unions of the A.F.L. and C.I.O. in which the leaders tried hardest to force their staff workers, if not their rank-and-file members, to vote the Democratic ticket. I had more complaints that year of interference or attempted interference with socialist sympathizers in the unions by union leaders than by private employers.

About the same time, an able teacher in the educational classes of one of our democratic unions complained that no teacher in the employ of a union could have written such a book as *New Men of Power*, which is essentially fair and even sympathetic to union leaders. He added that he doubted whether it could be fairly reviewed in most union papers.

A union official with a very honorable record of service once tried to justify a very extreme doctrine in action of union control over the political conduct of its members by the argument: "If you were in a minority in opposing a strike in your organization, you would go along with the majority. You ought not to scab on your unions at the polls." This is a specious but dangerous argument. It is one thing for a union by majority vote to endorse political policies, candidates, or even a political party, and try to persuade all its members to agree. It is another thing to try to coerce their votes. A strike is of necessity a war measure, greatly preferable to the resort to violence, but containing in itself some necessary elements of coercion. A strike seeks immediate and obvious economic advantage and as a rule differences of opinion about it among the workers concern tactics and not major objectives. Political questions are more complex. Democracy requires freedom of thought. The justification of a union or a closed shop is that all workers have a duty to be citizens in the industry. But citizens must not be degraded into subjects compelled to vote as the high brass of their organization may command.

This question of union control over political opinions has been made more important by the fight against the communists in the C.I.O. For a long time Philip Murray was unwilling to face the facts about the communist connections of some of his close associates. Delay in action made drastic action necessary at the Cleveland convention of the C.I.O. in 1949. There was a strong case for disciplining communist-controlled unions for their sins against democratic procedure and against the loyalty due to the general organization.[3] The action taken, however, can easily be distorted by strong-willed leaders into precedent for denying free speech on union and public policy to union members. In 1950, there were evidences that both the seamen's unions, A.F.L. and C.I.O., were using the charge of communism against any who seemed to threaten the power of the leaders. It is one of the chief items in any indictment of communism that it has prepared the way for this sort of thing by its prostitution of democratic procedures to its own ends. But the answer to a kind of communist totalitarianism in the unions should not be a near-fascist equivalent to it.

In English and American history, attitudes and institutional arrangements for protecting the rights of individual citizens within the political community were of slow and painful growth. It is not surprising that unions which have been essentially fighting organizations needing discipline should have fumbled the business of protecting the individual rights of their members against impatient and ambitious leaders. But the right attitudes and formulas must be worked out by union men and women if labor is really to serve democracy.

This is the business of the unions themselves. They should reject governmental control of their internal affairs. It would, however, be perfectly in order, since the unions gladly accept governmental recognition as an agency of collective bargaining, for government to require that the constitution and procedure of any union so recognized must guarantee to its members a bill of rights. Specifi-

---

[3] Only that union discipline is justified which deals with overt acts of disruption or breach of contract, or, in dangerous times, sabotage and sedition. Union men must have freedom of speech and political action in and outside their unions.

cally, this bill should provide that the unions must be open to workers in the industry in which it functions without restriction of race, creed, or national origin, and without prohibitive initiation fees; that every union must protect democratic procedures in it, furnish honest financial reports to its members, and, above all, guarantee them against arbitrary and whimsical discipline. I personally happen to know more cases of injustice done to innocent workers by union discipline than of injustice to the innocent in the magistrates' courts of New York City. And the penalties are less severe in magistrates' courts. Union discipline may mean loss of jobs under union shop agreements.

Only bona fide workers should be allowed to complain of violations of this bill of rights. They and they only should be allowed to bring their complaint to a proper qualified tribunal which, upon due hearing, might suspend the right of a union to act as agent in collective bargaining until it corrected its procedure in conformity to the bill of rights.

It is precisely because unions have been playing so basic and, on the whole, so hopeful a role in our changing society that their democratic development is of such concern to socialists. If free labor unions fall before communist or fascist totalitarianism, or develop a kind of neofascist syndicalism of their own, or if the unpopularity of their dictatorial leaders with rank-and-file workers should play into the hands of powerful employing groups, it would be idle to hope for any victory of democratic socialism.

Private capitalism and its institutions do not constitute so weak a force in America that we can expect them to yield solely to persuasion or meekly to accept as final a revolutionary reverse at the polls. Not unless their opponents have vehicles of economic power to support their political victory. Such agencies the unions are. The enormous social progress since the days when coal-mine and steel-mill owners maintained political and economic baronies in America has been due to more than one cause and more than one type of pressure. But without the economic and physical strength embodied in the unions those feudal holdings of industrial barons would never have yielded to more democratic social procedures.

Today the cry is going up among those who persist in identifying socialism and the welfare state with incipient communism to the effect that lovers of what they miscall "the American Way" must build "a power outside any political party" so strong that a party in office "will be compelled to yield to demands of that power." [4] Democratic labor unions must be powerful in order to meet that sort of threat. Socialists who think in realistic rather than in metaphysical and romantic terms about labor must recognize that we shall not win socialism unless we can win labor and its own organizations so that they will if necessary back political success at the polls by economic power.

Let no one think, therefore, that a desirable socialism can be exclusively the creation of labor unions. Thus far, progress in America toward social ownership and control has not come primarily from the workers as producers but from the people, including industrial workers, as consumers. At this point an American socialist cannot quarrel with the findings of Professor Seba Eldridge and twenty-nine collaborators that "initiation, growth, and consummation of a socialization movement are governed by the consumers and citizens concerned; but that leadership, technological changes, geographic conditions, imitative socialization, failures of private enterprise, and other phases of the given situation are secondary, auxiliary, or facilitating factors of much importance." [5] This truth in no way minimizes the significance of labor's growing interest in politics or the importance of its power in protecting social gains.

But the role of consumers in bringing socialism needs emphasis. So, too, does the role of farmers as producers as well as consumers. Too long were they neglected by socialist parties and their needs misunderstood. In our country farmers have an importance far beyond their proportionate numerical strength, first, because they

---

[4] The words quoted are from John T. Flynn's widely circulated *The Road Ahead* (Devin-Adair).

[5] Seba Eldridge: "Dynamics of an Emergent Economy," in *Labor and Nation*, Summer of 1950. The article is based on Seba Eldridge and Associates: *Development of Collective Enterprise* (University of Kansas Press).

are concerned in the most vital of all enterprises, the production of food, and second, because under state constitutions originally adopted when a larger proportion of our people lived in the country, the agricultural population has disproportionate political representation. To some extent this is true in the federal Congress and in the electoral college. Hence for a good many years American socialists have been talking about building a farmer-labor rather than a labor party. Socialism in Saskatchewan, Canada, came to power by its appeal to a predominantly rural population.

But farmers and workers do not constitute strictly parallel groups. Our rural population has less identity of interest than have industrial workers. Those concerned with the production of our food, tobacco, and cotton are sharply divided. Millions of them are agricultural laborers or sharecroppers—the worst exploited members of the American community. Millions more are tenant farmers. Another large group operates what we nowadays call "family-size" farms. At the top of the agricultural pyramid are the planters, and the very large-scale farmers, employers operating "factories in the field" in states like California.

Appropriately, the National Farm Labor Union is a member of the A.F.L. There are wide divergencies of interest and program between other farm organizations. As over against city folk, the rural population is given something of a common characteristic by its interest in high prices for foodstuffs and by the imponderables which rise from a country way of life even in the age of electric power, the tractor, and the automobile. Heretofore in America the solidarity either of farmers or farm employees has been less than that of organized wageworkers in towns and cities.

But there is nothing in country life to make democratic socialism alien to farmers. They who have come to depend on government price support and to use political pressure can as producers be interested in a socialist program. They, of all groups, now find it hardest to operate a pure market economy in their own interest by "free enterprise." It is extraordinarily difficult for them easily to shift production of crops to meet effective demand.

Nevertheless, our most fundamental and unifying approach to dwellers in city and country must be through their common interests as consumers. This interest has found one important expression in consumers' cooperatives. In America they have been relatively far more successful among farmers than among city workers.

To the modern socialist, cooperatives of producers as well as consumers rank in potential value with labor unions and a political party as agents for achieving and maintaining a socialist society. Producers' cooperatives are less valuable than consumers'. Beginning in the nineteenth century, considerable efforts were made in Europe, and to a less extent in America, to build producers' cooperatives into successful alternatives to corporations organized for the profit of stockholders. Operating within the capitalist system and necessarily motivated by a desire for profit, they usually broke down or transformed themselves into stock companies. One of their difficulties lay in their failure to work out a solution in cooperative terms of problems of expansion. Either the cooperators worked harder and longer to meet competition, thereby breaking union standards for labor, or they hired extra labor to which the original cooperators stood pretty much in the relation of stockholders of a corporation. It is conceivable that within a general socialist framework these difficulties would disappear or be lessened.

At present some successful marketing cooperatives of big fruit farmers in California are scarcely better than cartels. But in western Canada and the United States producers' cooperatives have made a good record with grain elevators and the marketing of wheat.

By their very nature, consumers' cooperatives where they are well established present a greater challenge to *laissez-faire* capitalism and a far greater bond to unite individuals in action. They are not run to amass profit for working owners but to reduce costs to consumers who cooperate for that end. They had their origin a little over a hundred years ago in the voluntary action of workers in Rochdale, England. Like the labor unions, consumers' cooperatives, no matter how politically conservative may be some of their members or how ostentatiously they may repudiate political action at the polls, are outside the conventional incentive of the profit system. This fact is better realized by supporters of capitalism than by many cooperators. Not the least of the services of cooperatives is that they develop efficient managers motivated by something else than a scramble for profit.

In an earlier chapter I have criticized the notion that consumers' cooperatives can be developed so as to make the state or political parties unnecessary. It should be their function in a socialist society in some cases to offer competition to government-directed enterprises—for example, in the field of housing—and perhaps to take over a large segment of the field of retail distribution.

Today the most successful consumers' cooperatives are in smaller communities and allied to farm interests, or sometimes to nationalist groups like the Finns. They handle gasoline and various types of insurance. There has thus far been comparatively little sign of progress of consumers' cooperatives in the retail field in larger American towns and cities. They cannot and should not be indefinitely supported as missionary ventures. They must be able to stand up against capitalist competition. Today they are rarely able to compete with department and chain stores. In Europe merchandising cooperatives were organized and in successful action long before the distributive businesses were comparable to American mail-order houses and department and chain stores. With us the latter first occupied the field.

In consequence, the whole socialist movement in America has suffered. In that movement cooperatives should rank with labor unions and a socialist party as instrumentalities for winning and maintaining the good society. They are in themselves something of an alternative to private or state monopoly. In the diversity of instrumentalities is one safeguard for freedom and dynamic progress.

Chapter 19

What Hope of Peace?

FIVE YEARS after the summer of victory, the nations of an alliance which had crushed not only the military might but the national existence of Germany and Japan were engaged in a cold war of steadily increasing intensity. Every nation except those compulsorily disarmed was caught in the armament race and the economy of all nations in varying degree was dictated by the arbitrary demands of that race.

The only positive gain that had come out of the war was the establishment of an inclusive but imperfect United Nations. In setting it up, all nations had condemned military aggression and created some rudimentary international machinery for dealing with it.

On June 25, 1950, this one single hope of mankind was threatened by the unprovoked military aggression of North Korean communists at the instigation or with the blessing of the Soviet dictators. The U.N., with the powerful backing of the United States, met the challenge with admirable firmness. It was greatly aided by

Stalin's blunder in boycotting the Security Council of the U.N. and thus losing his legal opportunity under its charter to veto effective measures of resistance.

It soon became plain that the U.N. was confronted with more than a police task. The nations loyal to it were caught in a war which Stalin could expand almost at will, a war for which the United States, on which most of the burden fell, was obviously unprepared. It had not harmonized its expensive military preparations with its moral and political commitments, and its intelligence service, both political and military, had been woefully inadequate in Korea. Once more the American people were caught in a war which they hated, compelled in the madness of our time to try to restore and preserve peace by a process which inevitably brought immense suffering to the Koreans to whose rescue we had come.

Yet Korea was in a peculiar sense the United Nations' ward. If the U.N. had not acted with American support, one military aggression meekly endured would have led to another until at last delayed resistance would have meant total war. The world's beginning at law against aggression would have met a worse defeat than befell the old League of Nations. The imperative task was military enforcement of the U.N.'s order to the North Koreans to cease fire and to withdraw behind the Thirty-eighth Parallel. At best the enforcement of that order could only be the beginning. The acute problems of the world in general and the Far East in particular would remain. Military preparation everywhere would be vastly intensified, and the march to total war not prevented but at best slowed down by caution. What was wrong? Could the most acute diagnosis suggest a cure? In short, could the world have hope of peace?

It cannot truthfully be said that there was an effective socialist answer to these questions on an international plane. Democratic socialists had not even fully restored their own international body for consultation and possible common action. There had been no specific international socialist program for peace. Socialists in national office had had to act under the restrictions of nationalism.

The leading aggressor was no longer the old capitalist imperialism but communist imperialism which called itself socialist.

Nevertheless, looking back on the years, American socialists could honestly say that they had consistently urged a course of action which would have given us a far better approach to peace than was possible from the day when Franklin Roosevelt disastrously substituted "unconditional surrender" for his inadequate but idealistic Atlantic Charter as the basis for peace. During the war and after, American socialists had seen rather clearly certain facts now balefully illumined by the flames of new war. Lasting peace, we said, would require an immediate and sound beginning of the achievement of political and economic cooperation on a world-wide scale. It would require the end of the old nationalist imperialism, regard for the racial and national aspirations of dependent peoples, and a universal war against bitter poverty in a world in which half the people lived face to face with starvation. We abhorred Nazi crimes but we knew that enduring peace could not be based on vengeance on defeated peoples or the appeasement of one powerful and insatiable victor.

The United States, we believed, would have to give up its old isolation, which was always far from absolute. That isolation was well justified and on the whole fortunate in its results in days gone by. It was always preferable to an American imperialism which some of its critics would have substituted for it. But by 1945 not merely the growth of world-wide interdependence and the march of the secular religion of universal communism, but our own actions, good, bad, and indifferent, had inexorably involved us deeply in world affairs.

This last fact President Roosevelt had recognized, and under him the American government took the leadership in the negotiations which finally brought into being the United Nations, an organization possessed of noble ideals but wretchedly inadequate machinery. Whether or not it would have been possible in 1945 to establish more adequate machinery is now beside the point. As it was, the U.N. might have been far more successful if there had been a decent peace settlement or if Roosevelt's gamble on the nature of Stalin's communism had been justified.

It is difficult to conceive a worse approach to peace settlement than was made by those well-intentioned leaders, Messrs. Roosevelt and Churchill. The only excuse for our rulers is that inevitably war beclouds judgment and that they were badly advised on the degree of Japanese military strength and the danger that Stalin might make a separate peace. The latter fear Stalin was able to exploit in spite of the fact that his whole career should have made it certain that he would not again risk a deal with Hitler. We witnessed a succession of blunders. At the Cairo conference, perhaps because of Winston Churchill's imperialism, nothing whatever was promised to the discontented millions of southeastern Asia except the defeat of Japan. Korea was promised independence but neither under Roosevelt nor his successor was any plan worked out for provisional government which could promptly be established. The ill-fated dividing line of the Thirty-eighth Parallel we now know was set up in a moment of victory by anonymous military officers, supposedly merely for administrative use in accepting Japanese surrender. General Hodge, the American commander, was given charge of military administration in the American zone simply because he was the general nearest to Seoul. He had no training or fitness for the job.

In 1950 the Republican and other critics of the Administration who insisted that we must indefinitely recognize the exiled Chiang on Formosa as ruler of China proposed a very dangerous policy. Some of them presented on their record an amazing combination of isolationism and anticommunist aggression in reckless disregard of objective facts. But they were at least partially right that the Roosevelt-Truman policy in China contributed to communist triumphs, first by its unconditional trust in Chiang's regime and its lack of effective pressure for reform; second, by the stupendous bribe paid in Manchuria at China's expense to bring Stalin into a war against Japan in which he did no fighting; and, finally, by its demand for an impossible coalition government of Chiang and the communists. Our government gave Chiang a great deal of aid—not enough to guarantee his victory, but more than enough to compromise its prestige in Asia.

MacArthur did a far more constructive job in Japan, but in that country America had let loose upon the world the atom bomb without any demonstration by way of warning and without that statement of terms such as Mr. Truman finally made which Admiral Zacharias, then in charge of propaganda, insists would have got Japan's earlier surrender. As the years went on, MacArthur's egotism made him a proconsul hard to reach or control.

In Europe our approach to peace was at least equally bad. Let us recapitulate the facts. The existence of anti-Hitler elements in Germany was ignored during the war. By the admission of our own Intelligence, the demand for "unconditional surrender" without clarification to the German people tended to prolong the war at the expense of American lives. At war's end, it was madness to divide Germany into zones and to leave Berlin an island in a Russian sea. The roots of the madness were to be found in a passion for vengeance against Germans plus a steadfast refusal to believe that communism was what it is. The Potsdam agreement was made worse by Russian interpretation, but in itself it invited that misinterpretation. American policy toward Germany for almost a year after V-E Day approximated the indefensible Morgenthau plan. America kept silent while the Russians after victory excelled Hitler in driving civilians from their ancestral homes.

The change began in the late summer of 1946 after the bitter experience Americans had had in trying to work in good faith with the Russians. It was then too late to redeem what was lost in eastern Europe and in Germany. The Marshall Plan and the airlift for the relief of Berlin during the long Russian blockade were positive contributions to peace of which America could be proud. But it was too late to do what might quite possibly have been done looking toward the creation of a United States of Europe not divided by an iron curtain. Granting the strength of Russia and of communism and Stalin's implacable drive for universal power, it is, nevertheless, probable that a more resolute stand by the United States from Teheran on would have made possible a very different Europe than that in which we now face the desperate business of checking further communist aggression.

It is a melancholy satisfaction to recall that American socialists, step by step, from the day of Roosevelt's first proclamation of unconditional surrender, made the sort of criticisms and counter-proposals which I have summarized. After allied victory they steadily sought universal and enforceable disarmament.

Long before the Korean war, it was evident that lovers of peace had to propose a program which could not be based on what might have been. Unless they were to live in a dream world, they had to accept communism for what it is. Obviously the ideal program would require the right sort of world government. Assuming that such government should be possessed of purpose and strength to deal with economic and social conditions which threaten peace, it would be the alternative to war.

On the other hand, the wrong sort of world government might actually provoke war. The adoption of the American Constitution ended the threat of minor quarrels between the states, but by no means did it guarantee lasting peace. On the contrary, the unresolved moral and economic problem of chattel slavery led, despite federal government, to sanguinary civil war. Simply to impose government on unresolved issues would not automatically bring peace. That would depend on the government itself and the attitude of the peoples who live under it.

In any case, it has long been obvious that there is no possibility of desirable world government unless and until there is a profound modification in the present attitude of communist states and the international communist movement. That movement seeks universal power and, on the basis of its own fanatical faith, can accept no goal short of such power. Stalin and his followers would not consent to come under a noncommunist world government unless they should believe that they could take it over by civil war. We believers in democracy would never willingly come under the control of a communist world government. That would be worse than no world government. It would mean a long night for the human spirit, a universal prison camp without cities of refuge for freedom.

Nothing is clearer than that the fairly widespread devotion to world government in the western world cannot suggest an immediate answer to the cold war except as it may strengthen the loyalty to the U.N. in stopping military aggression. We shall have to distinguish between the long-range process of establishing abiding peace on sure foundations which will require world federation and the more immediate task of averting a third world war. World government is no magic incantation. It requires from its advocates patient and persistent education of the peoples of the earth and a much more realistic approach to the exceedingly difficult problems connected with its organization and constitution than has as yet been evidenced in the practical programs of various groups of world federalists. Such a plan as that drawn up by the committee headed by Chancellor Robert M. Hutchins for the government of the world has suggestive features, but it is inconceivable that it could or should be adopted today or tomorrow. Those world federalists are wisest who concentrate their immediate attention on strengthening the U.N. so that it may more effectively provide security against military aggression. In the process may lie seeds of world government, but only by a very dubious use of words will a strengthened U.N. in itself be a world government.

In the meantime, the Korean war gave additional impetus to American sentiment in favor of strengthening the U.N. by the exclusion of the Soviet Union and its satellites. Stalin himself may force this action either by withdrawing from the U.N. or by remaining in it only to paralyze its action. But if man's dream of one world and his tentative approach to it are to be shattered, let it be by the dictators in the Kremlin, not by the governments of free nations. As long as possible, the U.N. must be supported even if on the surface it seems merely to provide a forum for bitter debate. That of itself may tend to stall off war. And while Russia is in the

U.N., the charter of which her rulers once accepted, there is a chance that sooner than we think Stalin or his successor will see it to Russian interest to adopt a more cooperative attitude in it. Any such decision would mean a change in tactics, not communist rejection of its drive for power. But in time a change in tactics might modify the nature of that drive. The existence of the U.N. makes easier and more likely a change in tactics. Moreover, on a somewhat more optimistic view of possibilities, it would probably be easier to strengthen the U.N. for effective action than to prevent war in a divided world or to create a new organization for peace.

New regional organizations might strengthen the U.N. and an ultimate world federation. The Atlantic Union, in the form proposed by former Justice Owen Roberts and Clarence Streit, would at this moment in history have an opposite effect. They propose that the nations in the defensive military alliance, the Atlantic Pact, form an organic union. But not all the nations; only the original charter members. Portugal, one of the excluded, is fascist and ineligible to a democratic union. But Italy, also excluded, is a political democracy. An official spokesman of the Atlantic Union admitted at the Colgate University Conference in the summer of 1949 that a major reason for leaving her out would be the opposition which would arise in the United States and Canada to the free entry of great numbers of Italian immigrants. Such migration would be legal in a true organic union. Yet the exclusion of Italy would almost certainly throw her into the hands of the communists—a terrible price to pay for the Atlantic Union.

Moreover, the consummation of an Atlantic Union, including the United States and Canada but not the nations south of the Rio Grande, would aggravate the difficulties of cooperation with the Latin-American countries in the progressive struggle against poverty and dictatorship which is vital to hemispheric well-being.

Even more certainly the Atlantic Union would end the dream of the United States of Western Europe toward which a little progress has been made by agreements between the ten nations which have set up a European council at Strasbourg. Ideally, it is desirable if ever we are to attain a world federation that the overweening power in it of the U.S.S.R. and the U.S.A. should be balanced by other regional federations, notably a United States of Europe. We should hesitate a long time before irrevocably consenting to a division of the European nations into the rival orbits of Moscow and Washington.

Conceivably, the Atlantic Union may become a desirable last resort. To accept it now would be in effect to discard the U.N. and thus to lose our one chance of an international organization which may be strengthened to administer a system of enforceable disarmament. In no way would it make a third world war less likely. Indeed its formation might be the signal for such a war because of the vehemence of communist opposition to it both inside and outside of the nations immediately concerned.

The division of Germany and the loss of eastern Europe to the communists have destroyed for an indefinite period the possibility of creating a logical regional federation on the European continent that might be something like an equal partner of the U.S.A., the U.S.S.R., and the British Commonwealth. The same facts and other consequences of the war create grave difficulties in the way of developing the Strasbourg organization into a true United States of Western Europe. Western Germans cannot abandon the hope of a united Germany or easily recognize the permanence of a dividing line through Germany between the Soviet bloc and the slowly emerging Western European federation. Socialists and other democratic elements in Germany look with commendable disapproval on rearmament unless under a supranational organization in which they are free partners. It was a tragic set of blunders which gave us the present situation rather than a unified, demilitarized, and neutralized Germany with which to deal.

Britain is rightly concerned over difficulties in harmonizing her position in the British Commonwealth with the closer ties to the Continent which are now clearly necessary. To the degree that practical plans like the Schuman proposals for pooling Europe's iron, steel, and coal industries would bring peace and cooperation between these ancient enemies, France and Germany, they are immensely desirable. But in its original form the Schuman plan was, as its British critics said, all too likely to create an international cartel under an irresponsible supranational authority at peril to the interests of the workers.

These difficulties are not insoluble if there is good will. Steady progress toward the economic and political federation of Europe remains a desirable goal not only for American but international socialist policy, but federation inside of a strengthened U.N., not as a substitute for it.

In no presently attainable federation is there an assurance that the present tensions will not break into a third world war. That requires agreement between the United States and other free nations on one side, and the Soviet bloc on the other, that they will not resort to war to settle their differences. Thus to avert a third world war is extremely difficult because we are dealing with communist dictators who believe on the basis of their religion as revealed by Lenin and Stalin that there can be no real peace between communist and capitalist nations and to whom every noncommunist nation is capitalist or fascist. There can be merely truces or tactical delays. This secular religion sanctifies their drive for universal power and justifies every cunning stratagem which may further it. Alliances may be made as in World War II, but only temporarily. Ferans Nagy, former premier of Hungary, in his book, *The Struggle Behind the Iron Curtain*, quotes Rajk, who was Hungary's anti-Semitic Minister of the Interior,[1] as saying in a meeting of Hungarian communist leaders, "Learn from Lenin; if you have five enemies, you should ally yourself with them; arrange to incite four against the fifth; then three against the fourth; and so on until you have only one enemy left in the alliance. You can then liquidate him yourself and kick him out of the alliance. . . . It was these Leninist tactics that the Soviet Union followed when it made an

[1] Later purged—but not for this statement.

alliance with the reactionary capitalist great powers." There was no gratitude to Roosevelt for his concessions; only anger when they were stopped.

If Russia and America were merely two great national contenders for power, the situation would be dangerous. There would be faults on both sides and accommodation might be possible. But Russia, in the opinion of its communist dictators, is more than a great power; it is the head of an international crusade for universal communism. When we noncommunists add to this fact the further fact that the same communist dictators permit absolutely no popular discussion in Russia of the road to peace on the basis of facts accurately stated, we have a situation in which the conventional tactics and programs of peace lovers are gravely inadequate. Our government could be as wise as the serpent and as harmless as the dove (which it is not); its motives could be pure as the driven snow, its love of peace equal to that of Gandhi; and the communist dictatorship in its present frame of mind would never believe it. It would see only one road to peace and that the road of surrender to communist power. The struggle to avert a third world war is not helped by the failure of so many good people in America to recognize that the primary difficulty is not the usual rivalry for power between great nations, important as that is, but the relentless drive for the supremacy of communism as a secular religion, degraded in practice to a struggle for universal power by the communist elite of the U.S.S.R.

The Quaker proposals for peace, published in November, 1949, while making some sound suggestions, suffer seriously by reason of their failure to recognize communist totalitarianism for the evil that it is. It is noble to seek to overcome evil with good. It is neither wise nor noble to reduce this principle to political measures presupposing that the evil is less or different than it is.

Some pacifists and radicals—not communists—look at American imperialism through a powerful magnifying glass, at Russian imperialism through the wrong end of a telescope. They find it easier to practice Christian love toward Stalin than toward his victims.

After the Korean war had begun, there were some Americans—not many—who thought the time had come to hold the Soviet Union responsible even if we must then carry war to Moscow. They were right to this limited extent: if we had a better accepted world law and a more powerful U.N., Jacob Malik in August, 1950, would not have been presiding over the Security Council but answering charges formally preferred against the U.S.S.R. for its open contempt of the U.N.'s cease-fire order in Korea and for its probable role in instigating war. The U.N. was clearly too weak to take such action. It had no way of enforcing its will but war—a war which it could not afford to precipitate against the Soviet bloc.

Total war in our day will be so horrible, so destructive of men and the noblest values by which men live, that the free nations dare not seem to be its instigators. The notion that the United States could enforce its own or the U.N.'s will by dropping atomic bombs on Moscow was always morally and politically abhorrent; the Korean war demonstrated its folly in terms of military victory.

Harold Stassen, disavowing belief in preventive war, got much publicity for a recommendation that Russia be warned by Congress (by-passing the President) that another aggression would mean total war. Mr. Stassen's advice was somewhat discredited by the exceedingly partisan nature of the long speech which incorporated his suggestion. He is president of a great university what time he can spare from politics. He should have remembered that the Republican record warrants no stone throwing against the Democrats. Mr. Stassen himself was responsible in his original enthusiasm for the U.N. for the suggestion that peace be kept by America's giving an A-bomb to each of twenty-five bombers, five from each of the Big Five. Worse than that fantastic suggestion has been his policy of equating or almost equating socialism and communism, his distortion of facts to that effect, and the consequent insult to our best allies, Great Britain and the Scandinavian countries.

As for his proposal itself, it was not good. The costly Korean war is proof enough of our intention to back up the U.N. The attempt to define the aggression for which the United States would go to war might actually invite Russian and communist actions just short of that point and our declaration of itself would not invite new friends or strengthen the fidelity of those whom we have. For Congress to go over the President's head would divide the country.

At the end of the summer of 1950, the Administration's policy was concentrated on commendable trust in the U.N., and a desire to strengthen it; to building up American military power and trying to galvanize the nations of the Atlantic Pact into effective action. It championed continuance of the Marshall Plan economic aid and Mr. Truman supported a weak and inadequate program of economic aid to underdeveloped regions.

It was apparent, however, that it would be economically and psychologically impossible to institute a really effective struggle for economic progress based in large measure on American help, and at the same time support the enormously costly military program which events forced on the American government. The American people had been dumfounded by how little they seemed to have got after spending approximately $50,000,000,000 on military preparation in four years. Professor Sumner Slichter of Harvard optimistically but soundly argued that we could win the economic war and yet successfully carry further arms expenditures of $10,000,000,000 a year after a possibly larger expenditure to conclude the Korean war.[2] The longer the Korean war went on, the more certain was it that this $10,000,000,000 would not be an adequate amount. Mr. Slichter took no account of rehabilitating Korea or of the paralyzing costs of rudimentary defense against atomic weapons in view of the threat of a world war. Neither did he consider in his estimate the increased costs to America in the calculated risk of sending men and arms to western Europe. He and others of his school overlooked the evidence that communist governments in general and the Soviet government in particular, despite the inferiority of Russian technical equipment to American, get enormously more for their money both in arms and men. They control

[2] *New York Times Magazine*, August 13, 1950.

masses of human beings used to a low standard of living. Those whom they cannot inspire by fanaticism they can coerce as slaves. The excellence of the military equipment of the Korean armies was something of a revelation.

The response to the Korean war heightened a fear that Russia could count more on her satellites in Asia and probably Europe than we on our allies, notably France and Italy. For entirely understandable reasons, the French and Italian people loathe the thought of an atomic war in which their lands would be devastated whoever might win. The more fanatical of their number are communists. The United States and the U.N. have inspired no such passionate support for freedom as to counteract the peoples' fear of war and their longing for neutrality. Under these conditions, which were generally admitted by honest observers in 1950, it was a gamble how far the people would back up their governments' present loyalty to the Atlantic Pact in an emergency no matter how many millions the United States might give them to rearm or how many thousand troops it might send for garrison duty. Certainly the men and money wouldn't mean much without a new spirit which a negative program of rearmament alone would not impart.

The best that can be said for any hope of peace out of a further extraordinary intensification of armament is that the Korean war left us no option. We must try to protect peace for a while longer through fear of atomic war and all its horrors. Such fear can be by no means written off as a temporary protector of peace. But the plain truth is that no race in armament in man's history has failed ultimately to end in war. It is also true that no superiority in arms achieved by one side before a war has ever been sufficient to guarantee ultimate victory. Ask the shade of Adolf Hitler in whatever hell he may be found.

The best that could be hoped from evidence of American determination to withstand aggression and to support even greater armament was that so might we gain time to put a more positive policy into effect. Under no circumstances could we regard total war in the atomic age as an acceptable element of that positive policy. In the veritable hell of that war it would be the business of lovers of freedom to stand firm to their memories of happier things and to their devotion to the peace which other military victories had not won. But men who in this hour accept a third world war as absolutely inevitable are men without imaginative capacity to serve the ideal of peace in such a war. Inevitability of total war is not established by the facts. There are things that can yet be done or tried. But there is no time to waste.

An immediate American program for peace in our kind of world must accept the necessity of further increase in our military strength. But government and people will be under solemn obligation to be on guard lest the economic and psychological effect of total mobilization upon ourselves and the communist dictators should hasten total war. To be effective or even tolerable increased mobilization must be accompanied by a more positive and imaginative program than our government has developed. That program must be worked out along three broad lines.

First, our diplomacy must make it evident that we are devoted positively to democracy and fair play rather than simply to opposition to communist totalitarianism. We undermine our own moral grounds by flirting with Franco or any other dictator guilty of the same crimes against liberty for which we oppose Stalin. We must make plain our sympathy with all peoples who live under dictatorship, fascist or communist.

We must learn that it takes something better than Franco in Europe or Chiang Kai-shek and his coterie in Asia to stop communism. Specifically, our government must do all that lies in its power to see that Stalin will not maneuver us into war with China, a quagmire in which our strength would be drained and our ideals discredited. Our support of Chiang's right to speak for China anywhere, least of all as one of the Big Five at a time when he cannot even hold Formosa except under temporary American protection, is very dangerous business which tends to alienate us from our allies. The American position in the Korean war would be stronger if our government should say that it believed that China's seat in the

Security Council should be vacant until it can be filled by a government (1) exercising real authority and (2) loyal to the Charter and principles of the U.N. The communist government of the Chinese mainland probably meets the first requirement; it has not yet met the second and cannot meet it until it purges itself of its open defiance of the U.N. orders to the North Koreans to cease fire and to return behind the Thirty-eighth Parallel.[3]

A positive diplomacy in support of world-wide democracy and peace will make effective use of every practicable means of disseminating the truth about the rival ideas and institutions which contend for men's allegiance. We Americans will forget at our peril that the propaganda of the deed is mightier than the propaganda of the word. One lynching in America may hurt us and our cause more than the loss of a great battle.

A second element in a positive American policy for peace must be a far bolder program for economic aid in a cooperative war against hunger and poverty under the auspices of the U.N. Even the arms program should not keep the United States from working out with other free nations an economic program sounder than anything communism has to offer in improving agriculture and building up industry in a desperately hungry world. The ultimate economic returns of themselves would justify the effort.

The communist program, in its first impact, is able to get immense support by its promise to deal with local tyrants, usurers, landlords, the exploiters of the peasants and low-caste people in China or in India. The immediate communist program of itself will be insufficient for new production, and to get that production communism will rapidly set up its own familiar type of regimentation and exploitation. But hungry peasants and workers, largely illiterate, see today's misery in terms of communist promise and immediate performance. Seldom have the free nations demonstrated a better way in industrially backward areas in Asia or Africa. Such demonstrations must be given, for instance in India, before it is too late. Our

---

[3] This principle would apply to Russia in like case. Her situation is different largely because she is already seated in the Security Council.

American failure out of America's bulging storehouses to supply wheat to India on practicable terms was in 1950 a blow to peace.

A positive policy for conquering poverty will cost money; it will cost more than money in terms of human understanding and capacity for cooperation.[4] It is greatly to be feared that neither the money nor the cooperative attitude will be available under the stresses of an intensified race in arms. Hence the supreme importance of our third proposal. And that is effective and enforceable disarmament for all nations.

There is no hope of peace except through the transfer of conflict from the realm of war. Conflict there must be while communism maintains its aggressive philosophy and tactics and democracy has any life at all. But the time has come when to continue the conflict on the plane of war threatens the very race itself with destruction. Hence the United States government should do now what it should have done at the first Assembly of the U.N. Its spokesman should appeal with passion and power for immediate world conference on universal and enforceable disarmament.

Such disarmament will consist of five closely correlated actions, no one of which will be successful without the others.

1. The absolute prohibition of the manufacture of weapons of mass destruction, of which atomic bombs are today the most conspicuous example. Atomic disarmament, however, will not prevent war or the use of atomic bombs in war unless it is coupled with the other measures essential to the end of the armament race.

2. The reduction of all armed forces and all armaments within each nation down to a police level except in so far as a quota force may be provided under international agreement. The business of maintaining internal order does not require the use of any of the more dangerous weapons of mass destruction, and an international

---

[4] As a fair statement of problems involved and constructive plans to meet them, I cannot too highly commend "The Bold New Program" series of eight pamphlets, edited by Anderson and Raushenbush and published by the Institute of Public Affairs, Washington, D.C. My only important criticism would be its neglect of the importance of voluntary birth control on a large scale.

armament authority should be set up to supervise the renunciation of the use of such weapons by all nations. Its actions must not be subject to veto by one of the Big Five.

3. Demilitarization of such narrow waterways as the Dardanelles and the great canals, as well as of the island bases now in possession of individual powers. This step would automatically dispose of many present causes of conflict.

4. The universal abolition of peacetime military conscription. Nations desiring to live at peace with one another will not train all their able-bodied sons for war.

5. An effective international police force should be set up under an authority established by a strengthened U.N., the mobile part of which should be recruited by voluntary enlistment from the smaller nations incapable of imperial ambition. Ely Culbertson's well-known suggestions for such a force should be carefully considered.

Coupled with this appeal for disarmament should be an American promise to spend, let us say, $10,000,000,000 a year in a coordinated program for economic construction throughout the earth, a peaceful war on poverty and hunger, preferably under the direction of the U.N.[5]

For years I have worked for this sort of appeal by the American government and I find it hard to understand why there has been so much resistance to it. It is entirely consistent with the arms program which will be necessary until universal disarmament is won. It makes more sense in terms of national self-interest than the American proposal for international control of atomic energy for peace without reference to other forms of armament in which America was and is inferior.

The occasional contention that Stalin unobserved would evade all controls is unsound. Provided that Stalin or his successor for his own interest had consented to a practicable program of enforceable

[5] Shortly before the Korean war began a group of senators and representatives, on the initiative of Senator Brien McMahon of Connecticut, introduced in both houses a concurrent resolution embodying these ideas. It was at least temporarily submerged by the war.

disarmament, he could not evade inspection without raising alarm and inspiring countermeasures.

Any agreement on disarmament should permit a nation to denounce it if it should be convinced that the machinery of inspection had broken down or was disregarded.

In the light of history, the difficulty would probably arise in working out effective controls acceptable both to the United States and to the Russian dictatorship. The latter, as we are often reminded, once proposed complete disarmament to the League of Nations. Today it talks disarmament and is capitalizing on the popular yearning for peace all over the world by its attacks on the United States as the sole warmonger. (Not even the Korean war stopped that propaganda of the Big Lie.) The Soviet dictatorship in its original proposals for disarmament was entirely silent on the subject of controls for inspection and the other members of the old League of Nations were so stupid and so involved in the race in arms that they never pressed any inquiries into Stalin's sincerity or the lengths to which he would go in establishing efficient international control.

The problem, then, is control even more than the general idea of disarmament. There is still reason to believe that, although Stalin accepts war as sometimes the Marxist midwife of revolution, he does not want global war for its own sake, especially while he hopes to win at lesser cost. It is significant that he feels obliged to appear before his own people as the advocate of peace. That fact would put him very much on the defensive should he not accept any rational proposals for controls in the interest of peace.

A case could be made to Stalin as a professed Marxist which never has been presented. He believes that the tools men use determine the way of making their living and thus, in the long run, all their forms of social organization and their ethical codes. When the tools of war become atomic bombs and bacteriological weapons, the whole nature of war is changed. It becomes no longer potentially a midwife of anything except destruction. If war invites revolution against governments held responsible for it, communism may have reason to fear such war, now that in so many countries of the world it constitutes the government. No government, Russian or American, can afford victory with its burden of rehabilitating a ruined world.

Such argument might supplement the manifest truth that Russia has everything to gain from an economic standpoint by ridding itself of the burden of the armaments race. Lenin's original outline of the road to power for his communism included violence, but not the violence of great standing armies, still less of atomic war. His faith was in the appeal of the communist elite to the working class which it would shepherd. Is Stalin afraid of conflict in terms of contrasting ideologies and economic organization?

The answer probably is that Stalin fears any sort of influence from the outside, any sort of intervention, including inspection. Dictators need foreign foes to justify their regimentation of their people. Hence Stalin rejected our reasonable proposals for the control of atomic energy.

Yet his original total rejection was modified before the Korean war. The Russian dictatorship has shown a capacity to come to terms with facts. Witness its relations with Hitler, its abandonment of the Berlin blockade in the face of the airlift, the softening of its war against the Church, and its slightly more reasonable although still basically unsatisfactory attitude on atomic bombs. Not even a communist "no" is eternal. Neither Stalin nor his associates on the Politburo are immortal. Time changes many things. No matter what agreements now exist, it is a virtual certainty that Stalin's successor will for a very considerable time lack Stalin's prestige and power to control conflicts between the major forces in the Soviet: the army, the secret police, and the rising class of industrial managers. He will have trouble in using the far-flung communist empire in a coordinated plan for new aggressions.

The Moslems never formally altered the theology which drove them forward to conquer the world. The peace of Westphalia in 1648 ended the religious wars between Catholics and Protestants without a formal renunciation by either party of its claims to sole possession of the keys of heaven. The right strategy may in time modify the global aims of communism or at least persuade it that, for its own sake and the life of mankind, it must transfer conflict out of the realm of atomic war.

It will be our business to present our appeal for universal and enforceable disarmament so consistently and persuasively that the sound of it will ring in the ears and hearts of men even after a first rejection by Moscow. Our answer to a Soviet "no" must, of course, be a tightening of defense. It must not be a preventive war, but, along with our arms program, a steady insistence that only in disarmament is there safety for mankind.

If the American appeal is made as it might be made, it will win us almost instant advantage in the public opinion of the whole world. By it we Americans should be purging ourselves of the infection of militarism inevitable in an arms race, an infection which does exist although it has been grossly exaggerated by our critics. Our appeal could be a dramatic answer more effective than any debaters' arguments to the charge that our growing armaments are essentially aggressive. It will make it far more difficult for the Politburo to persuade their own people that they must pay for military preparedness out of the poverty of their children.

It is true that the communist dictatorship can partially conceal and distort any appeal that an American president might make. But not altogether. It is a great mistake to think that the iron curtain is completely impervious, or that nothing which the American government and people can do will have any effect upon the Russian people. Even to a dictatorship it makes enormous difference whether it must lead a reluctant people in paths of aggression or can persuade them that all that they are doing is solely for defense. A mighty, dramatic, well-reasoned and continuing appeal for disarmament would immensely increase the Kremlin's difficulty in winning allies or support for a succession of military aggressions culminating in world war.

Finally, it would give a moral basis far more effective than now exists to such defense arrangements as the North Atlantic Pact.[6] Any military alliance by nations pleading for controlled disarmament would be clearly defensive. Acceptance of such disarmament would end the alliance. Our appeal, if rejected in Moscow, might stimulate courage and confidence in western Europe and help to hasten unity of action for defense.

At home this argument runs against the grim fact that once an arms economy is well established its sudden ending at any point short of bankruptcy would precipitate panic. If an angel from heaven on Sunday should proclaim the achievement of peace and the end of the arms race, there would be a panic in the world's markets on Monday; unless, that is, we Americans were ready with a planned program for war on poverty at home and abroad. That is why a bold new economic program must be tied up with an appeal for disarmament. But the latter must be made to capture the allegiance of masses of men.

Simultaneously with aggression in Korea, the communists all over the world circulated the completely insincere "Stockholm" peace petition, really directed only against atom bombs, and won millions of signatures. President Truman, Secretary Acheson, and Congress have too long resisted the obvious lesson to be learned from Stalin's desire to pose as the friend of peace. They have contented themselves with denouncing the Stockholm petition. They should have said—they should still say:

"Peoples of the earth, you are hungry for peace. Demand, then, of your governments the one requisite for peace. We offer it in

[6] I was opposed to the negotiation of the Atlantic Pact for reasons very similar to those widely publicized by James P. Warburg. I preferred American support for building up a United States of Europe and a firm but quiet statement that we should consider any act of military aggression, forbidden by the San Francisco Charter of the United Nations, as if it were against ourselves, to be dealt with in cooperation with nations loyal to the United Nations as circumstances might require. Once the pact was negotiated and signed by representatives of nations and parties on which our hope of democracy in Europe depends, its ratification seemed desirable lest we injure our friends. I insisted that Franco's Spain be excluded, direct or indirect help to French and Dutch colonialism prevented, and, above all, that this appeal for disarmament be pushed.

the name of the American people. It is agreement for universal and enforceable disarmament under a strengthened United Nations. We cannot see alike on forms of government or economic programs. We can agree to carry on our conflicts without the suicidal destruction of total war and we can make our agreement effective by supervised disarmament. There is no other road to peace. Until we understand this and act on our understanding, our security will be less than the security of men living on the slope of an active volcano and our hopes of conquering poverty or even starvation will have the substance of dreams in a world where the supreme reality is war's global destruction."

Chapter 20

Accepting the Challenge

WHEN I began this book under the spell of a desire that someone would do for our times what Marx had done for the workers of the nineteenth century I hoped for a synthesis of knowledge and aspiration which did not exist and which I knew I could not construct. As I end my task, that synthesis is still my hope, with this important qualification: it must command by its own merit the support of mankind. It must not become an infallible dogma to be imposed by the political state.

Even if Leninism were far nearer Truth than it is as a philosophy of the universe, its dependence upon the communist inquisition would make it the enemy of mankind. The sorriest pages in human history have been written by zealots for a Truth which they believe may justly be enforced by every sort of cruelty for the salvation of mankind in this world or the next. A desirable synthesis of knowledge and aspiration must be free from the coercive intolerance which usually has characterized dogmatic creeds.

Seekers after it would be helped by effecting semantic improvements. "Right," "left," "capitalism," and, most of all, "socialism," have become badly battered words far from self-defining. Every day brings new evidence of the way in which our vocabulary tends to hinder our grasp of reality or logic.

Meanwhile, we cannot wait for our new synthesis or even for the development and acceptance of a more accurate vocabulary. We must act in a world of great diversity of beliefs on the basis of simple affirmations of fraternity. If democratic socialism is to prevail, in the western world—and ultimately throughout the earth—it cannot today present itself as a complete philosophy of the universe, the universal ground of art, science, and religion. It must unite the social actions of men of varying beliefs on the common denominator of a conviction that through cooperation men may win plenty, peace, and freedom. Inspired by this faith, socialism must be experimental rather than rigidly doctrinaire. It must present itself, in Toynbee's sense, as the answer to challenge, solemnly aware that the fate of civilization is bound up in the progressive adequacy of its achievements.

The challenge itself may be stated thus: can men, so imperfectly masters of themselves but almost masters of the awful power of atomic energy, learn in time to live together in freedom and fellowship, using their enormous technological equipment only for the destruction of poverty? There is no certainty as to the answer. But we can and must bet our own lives that the answer may be yes. Admittedly that will be hard because we men are prone to rally most enthusiastically to the summons of oversimplified slogans backed with absolute certainty.

In this great experiment of remaking a world we never made, there are no infallible formulas wholly external to our wills—certainly none that we have discovered analogous to the "laws" of the physical universe. There are generalizations from human experience and tested principles of human conduct which may guide us. There are broad facts about human behavior which both limit the area in which it can be said that we and our children can make our own history and offer us guidance in the process. Let us look at some of them.

1. Men will no longer acquiesce in poverty as they did in long millenniums of time when the production of abundance for all clearly lay beyond the productive power of a society primarily dependent upon the muscle of men. What men with power-driven tools have produced in war for the purpose of destruction has proved to the underprivileged masses what might be done for abundance in peace. It has not, however, taught mankind how to produce and distribute abundance or persuaded us to renounce the passions and prejudices or to curb the national, class, and group interests which stand in the way of the conquest of war and poverty. Neither has it taught us the voluntary control of the rate of increase of population which is becoming necessary in terms of food supply.

2. There is a class solidarity which is not an absolute or exclusive principle binding men in social action but which has great force. It is an oversimplification to state class conflict in terms of *"the* owning class" versus *"the* working class" and an error to believe that any satisfactory society will be the automatic result of victory of "the working class"; even if the latter term is broadened, as it should be, to include others than wageworkers. Nevertheless, men instinctively think and, to a large extent, act on lines determined by the economic group to which they belong. Over and over they will sacrifice their own individual interests to family, class, or national interests. Even the Scotchman who prayed, "God bless me and my wife, my son John and his wife, us four and no more," recognized that fact. His loyalty was grossly inadequate. Today some labor loyalties rather magnificent in quality are also inadequate. The broadening of effective loyalties and their arrangement in hierarchical order are major tasks of our times. In learning and practicing allegiance to the noblest loyalties, men must end the class divisions inherent in the acquisitive capitalist society.

3. It is not true that increasing misery inevitably means revolu-

tion—certainly not a democratic revolution. There has never been a successful revolution made by the most miserable stratum of the population. The active agents of revolution are men with wills unbroken by misery who have had a taste of better things or a vision of them. Slavery in Egypt never yet fitted men without further discipline for the good life in the Promised Land. It is nonsense for a socialist to flatter himself that democratic socialism can be the almost automatic consequence of a revolution of desperation. Our dilemma has been this: men have rarely united to effectuate a desirable but difficult change until misfortune approaching disaster was upon them and disaster breeds not only economic conditions but a psychology extremely ill-adapted to the achievement of a true cooperative commonwealth. The answer to confusion in society is usually dictatorship which will not evolve "after the revolution is won" into a free society. For the holders of power a revolution will never be won on terms which make them or their regime dispensable. It is our business, especially in America, to develop and improve our imperfect democracy; not to seek salvation through crisis. In crisis the imperative demand is for order; our complex society must be kept going somehow; justice and democracy become secondary considerations. We must work, therefore, for fundamental changes with a minimum of disorder.

4. If man's great interest is necessarily in bread—and today a little cake—he does not live by bread alone. Economic satisfactions are not enough. Life demands human satisfactions which make it impossible for men to preserve human dignity and yet work together smoothly under direction like robots. Many schemes of social reorganization might have merit if men could be dealt with as the chess player deals with the pieces on his board, or as the engineer deals with the materials he must use. Many things might be desirable from a purely economic standpoint which would be unwelcome or intolerable in terms of human values.

Thus, a purely economic solution of the problem of feeding

human beings efficiently might abolish most home cooking. We would eat in squads as in an army. The desire of men and women for relative privacy and for intimacies of association makes such a prospect very unattractive. Public eating places have their uses, and their convenience may be a factor in the profound alteration now taking place in family life. Nevertheless, hope of emancipation from the drudgery of housework lies in the progress of mechanical invention rather than the establishment of communal eating places. Leisure is not the supreme good. It is valuable only as it makes it possible to share a fullness of life which evades material and quantitative measurement.

5. The motivations of human conduct are various. Human society cannot exist without mutual aid. Cooperation must be the dominant principle in the good society but men in general will never accept the motivation of a Francis of Assisi as sole and sufficient for the maintenance and growth of their society. No dynamic society has existed without some sort of competition. It plays a large role in human satisfaction. It has a place in the economic scheme of things. Certainly it has a place in the contests which add zest to life. Competition becomes evil when men worship "the bitch goddess, Success"; the reward rather than the deed; or when competitive victory, as in our acquisitive society, gives to the victor, and his children after him, arbitrary control over the resources and machinery by which other men have to live.

6. Social ethics are relative. Political standards are born of human experience and must be justified in terms of human experience. We have discussed one aspect of this truth in pointing out that a condition for democracy is an acceptance of compromise. But acceptance of relativity in social ethics does not require a renunciation of ethical standards or methods nor does it reduce them to a mere by-product of economics, a function in the struggle of classes. Rather is it true that there is a basic morality to which we owe a supreme loyalty, a morality derived from our common humanity, a morality greatly affected by the conditions under

which men work and live, but never to be reduced to a mere expression of personal, group, class, or national interest.

Two great ethical principles are increasingly established in human experience. The first is that ends and means are logically related in the laboratory of life, even if the relationship cannot be so precisely established as in the chemical laboratory. Bad means employed for good ends corrupt the ends. Men can rationalize their present hates by nominally dedicating them to future good, but the exercise of hatred never yet produced a cooperative society bound together by love. That will require us to turn consciously away from hate and the cruelty it inspires. I have come to doubt that any man—even Lenin—could be inspired by a true love for his fellows in the mass or in some future classless society and yet be completely ruthless in dealing with living human beings on the road to the goal. There is a profound psychological insight in the remark of John the Apostle: "If a man love not his brother whom he hath seen, how can he love God whom he hath not seen?" Substitute "the people" or "the working class" for God and you have a question applicable to many fanatics and revolutionists. May not their professed love of an abstraction—the church, the people, the working class—even though it seems to have inspired in them great and sacrificial devotion, be merely a rationalization of present hate, love of their own way and their own power, or the power of the group with which they identify themselves? Gandhi's way led him to an assassin's bullet; Stalin's to the government of a mighty empire, but may not Gandhi's method have done infinitely more to vindicate the power of comradeship and to point men toward peace with justice and freedom?

The second outstanding principle of social ethics is that in seeking or maintaining a good society, individual human beings should be treated as ends, not means. Social order and control are necessary; self-discipline must be aided and supplemented by social education and guidance, but always in terms consistent with respect for personality and the essential dignity which makes of a man something other than a pawn for governments, states, or economic and political oligarchies. There are great differences in men, biological inequalities—individual rather than racial or national—which we have to accept. None of them warrants the effort of any elite to treat men as things. It is an effort almost as damning in its effects upon a master group as upon its victims.

It is the condemnation of war that to a particularly great degree it violates both these ethical principles and of us that we have found no substitute for it. I, who write while soldiers and civilians kill and die in the brutal Korean conflict, am poignantly aware what havoc of socialism's noblest hopes will be wrought by new world war or even by a protracted period of armed and precarious peace. It is the more important, then, even while accepting the immediate and tragic necessities of the hour, to keep alive concern for what ought to be and faith that out of deep darkness the morning may break. By some such faith must socialism live.

It is a faith which will be dead without works: the discovery of a way to transfer conflict from the arbitrament of mass destruction, and the steady improvement at all times of the techniques of democracy.

That will be the hardest of all in the international field even if we escape total war. The struggle against poverty and for freedom will remain. In the abatement of poverty there is necessary place for some sharing of existing wealth not only among individuals but nations. Nevertheless, the United States will never literally divide up with, let us say, India or China. It would not conquer poverty if it did. That requires a general increase in production and a sharing of techniques. "Share the wealth" is an inadequate slogan unless coupled with success in increasing true wealth.

Hence, planning, increasingly on a global scale, and political organization appropriate to it, are the price we must pay for living in one world and availing ourselves of the marvelous but complex technology by which this one world may be able to provide its sons and daughters with abundance. I confess that there are times when I have envied Thomas Jefferson and the men of that period of American history when it was reasonable to believe that that government is best which governs least. Those days have gone, and not by reason of the theories of Karl Marx but of a necessity arising from our changing tools and the increase of interdependence. The proof is the degree to which our nation still rejecting socialism is nevertheless obliged to act on quasi-socialist principles.

In this policy of affirming a faith in free enterprise which we do not practice, lie dangers. To meet the challenge of our times there must be a sounder correlation of basic principles and practice. Our problems are too difficult to blunder through to their solution. There is no salvation in the sure and instinctive wisdom of any elite or of "the people" and the governments they elect. There is no salvation without a conscious and cooperative exercise of intelligence.

As I read over what I have been writing and think of the experiences of the years through which I have lived, I am aware that in my reexamination of socialism I have laid no emotional basis for a great mass movement such as those which have sometimes changed the face of history. I have offered challenge rather than certitude. I have been skeptical of infallible dogmas. I have assured no class, race, or nation of its own perfection or its messianic destiny. I have not found an immediate assurance of peace.

With the passing years my own study and observation have made me keenly aware of the historic fact that the emotions and convictions which generate a tremendous revolutionary mass movement by no means safeguard it against its internal corruption and disillusion and betrayal by its leaders. Witness the development of communism. Weak as man's reason has been, inconstant as has been his devotion to his highest ethics, in reason and capacity for ethical action lies his one chance for survival on tolerable terms in the world he has been making.

To say this is no counsel of despair. If history guarantees us no glowing Utopias, neither does it deny us hope. Men have greatly failed but also they have greatly achieved. There is no salvation without hope. But what can we hope? The socialist tendency has been to offer men assurance of an earthly heaven to persuade them to escape from earthly hells. Heaven cannot be thus delivered or achieved. But a far better society than any men have known is definitely attainable. We shall either win it or chaos and black night will be our portion.

After World War I, Clifford Bax wrote the oft-quoted lines:

> "Would man but wake from out his haunted sleep,
> Earth might be fair and all men glad and wise."

This is a poetic conviction rather than a scientific truth. But that such hope continually recurs in the history of our race, and that it so grips our imagination, shows how widespread and powerful in this troubled earth is the vision without which the people perish. To press toward its fulfillment is the price of life.

A Personal Footnote

WHILE in this book I have been recording my personal reactions to problems of socialism, I have made socialism and not myself the center of interest. I have discussed war only in so far as was necessary to my argument and primarily in its relation to democratic socialism.

There remains the question of my own attitude to the wars of my active lifetime, especially World War II. I am so often questioned about that subject that it may be worth a footnote—but only a footnote, for acceptance of my general opinion of democratic socialism is by no means bound up with agreement with all that I have done or advocated in relation to the wars which brought so much confusion of thought and action to us all.

World War I drove me, at that time an active Christian clergyman, to examine the problem of Christianity and the *method* of war, whatever the objective. I was constrained to accept Christian pacifism. With due respect to men who are better Christians than I and think otherwise, I am still unable to reconcile Christianity and war on philosophic and ethical grounds. If in the years following the First World War, I, to my sorrow, could no longer accept a Christian absolute of opposition to war, it was because I was constrained to modify my thinking about God, man, and the universe. (I still kept my belief that World War I was essentially an imperialist conflict which could better have been ended by American diplomatic pressure without military intervention.)

My admiration for Gandhi in the years following World War I

could not establish complete confidence in the power of non-violence in our times of trouble. His methods were exceedingly effective, given the conditions prevailing in India and the nature of the British raj. He gave his life, by no means in vain, to win justice and kindness for the Moslems whose leaders had defeated or postponed his dream of a united India. But in the hour of India's independence he had not assumed a responsible place in her government, or seriously challenged her establishment of armed forces. Against a Stalin or Hitler his method would have been ethically as noble as against the British but certainly it would have led to his early death in some secret dungeon—unless perhaps he had been drugged or tortured into a weird and terrible confession. Logically, a general application of his principle of nonviolence by masses of true disciples in all the noncommunist world might be singularly effective in ending totalitarian aggression. But in a world wholly unready for that high endeavor, it does not, I think, make for the triumph of justice or peace to preach a political program of pacifism which practically would mean surrender to brutal totalitarian might. Nevertheless, in our strife-torn world, the testimony of religious or philosophical pacifists has values which I cannot measure but can respect even though they have not established a political program for averting war.

My reluctant rejection of pacifism if anything intensified my sense of the horror and futility of the method of total war. In particular, the years following World War I by their revelations confirmed my sense of its folly and my socialist opposition to its imperialism. As I have said in an earlier chapter, no historian of repute supported the theory of Germany's sole guilt for the war and many, even those who later criticized the Nye Committee's report, went along with its explanation of America's entrance into the conflict in terms of economic interests and pressures. To help my country avoid another war became a great end in life for me.

At first I hoped much from the projected League of Nations but was disillusioned by the actual Covenant and its relation to the

Treaty of Versailles. For the America of the sick Woodrow Wilson and his obscene anti-Red crusade, or of Harding and his imperialist attitude to Latin America, to join the League without drastic modifications of the Covenant or the Peace Treaties would, I thought, strengthen the danger that the League would be used aggressively to support western imperialism and to crush the international socialism which was Europe's hope and the world's. I favored joining the World Court.

By the time I first ran for President in 1928, the march of events had persuaded me, like the majority of American socialists, that the triumph of international socialism was delayed and that the League had acquired a moderate value which might then be increased by American membership in it under reservations to prevent our being put automatically into war. This was also my position in 1932 when Roosevelt definitely declared against joining the League. I heartily supported our entry into the International Labor Office. I never thought that our entry into the League at any time would guarantee peace, and, in retrospect, I still emphatically reject the notion that it would have prevented World War II, not in view of the dominant forces in politics and economics and the conduct of the European nations most directly concerned.

During the Manchurian crisis, created by Japanese aggression in 1931, I favored American cooperation with the League or with European powers in the imposition of economic sanctions against Japan. The failure of the powers to act convinced me that effective economic sanctions would not be used by nations unless they were ready to go to war—to which such sanctions against a strong nation would probably lead. But I preached and practiced the doctrine of voluntary and concerted action by individuals not to buy Japanese, and later, German goods. That was never more than a weak gesture.

I was greatly disturbed by Hitler's rise to power but I failed in time to realize that vigorous action by France and Britain with definite encouragement from America would rather easily have checked his rearmament of Germany. I still had a little hope for a general agreement on disarmament at Geneva.

In the campaign of 1936 I was less isolationist than Roosevelt's famous Chautauqua speech and far more perturbed over the fascist rebellion in Spain. As Franco's war went on, I felt that the American embargo on arms to Spain was in effect an aid to Franco, especially since Roosevelt refused to carry out the logic of embargo and to impose it on military supplies to Germany and Italy. Both countries were involved in an undeclared war on the Loyalists. After my return from Spain in 1937, I made this point as strongly as possible to the President, with complete lack of success. After apparently ending the conversation on Spain, he suddenly began to tell me how highly he regarded Cardinal Mundelein. It seemed fairly obvious that the President felt a strong desire to carry the Roman Catholic Church with him in any action he might take on Spain. It is a matter of history that many months later he blocked a change in the neutrality law out of fairness to the Loyalist government to which even Senators Nye and Wheeler had come to agree.

Previously, and with a heavy heart, I, a former pacifist, had felt compelled to support actively a socialist effort to help American volunteers get to Spain. I played a considerable part in dissuading the government from prosecuting all groups concerned in military and economic aid to the Loyalists. At this time I distinguished sharply between the right of individuals and groups to aid a cause in which they believed and the right of the government to involve a whole nation by military intervention.[1] At no time did voluntary help to the Loyalists threaten to put the United States into war.

I dropped active support of sending volunteers for Spain when I discovered in Europe how completely the communists had con-

---

[1] In line with this principle, my wife and I willingly helped one of our sons go before Pearl Harbor as an unpaid volunteer with the American Field Service for ambulance work with the British Eighth Army in North Africa.

trol of the Lincoln Brigade and how ruthless was their G.P.U. in Loyalist Spain.

That discovery completed my disillusionment with the Bolshevik revolution from which, although I never was a communist, I had hoped so much. It was a bitter process and I still feel its hurt. In 1918, Postmaster General Burleson had threatened me with federal prison for an article I had written in *The World Tomorrow* in support of Lenin's struggling government. The next year I opened my house to a meeting for the Soviet emissaries, Nuorteva and Martens, when no hall could be found. Secret-service operatives made up much of the audience.

My hope for Russia ran high. Its revolution I thought a milestone of human progress. Slowly events like the man-made famine in the Ukraine (the truth about which I learned belatedly), the purge trials in 1936–38, and what I saw and heard in Russia and Spain in 1937, convinced me that communism was an incredibly dangerous denial of true socialism. Even so, I did not expect the cynical pact of 1939 between Hitler and Stalin.

After my return from Europe in 1937, I took the initiative in forming the Keep America Out of War Congress, which acquired some strength. It was never isolationist in philosophy and it carefully excluded fascists and communists from membership. It continued until Pearl Harbor, although it had lost many of its earlier supporters to the interventionists and had been overshadowed by the America First Committee, which was isolationist.

In many quarters it is still held against me that on two or three occasions, one of them at Madison Square Garden with Colonel Lindbergh, I spoke on an America First platform—and this by the same liberals who long since have quite rightly taken to their bosom Chester Bowles, later the able governor of Connecticut, who was a member of the executive committee of America First until its dissolution.

I always explained that I spoke for the Keep America Out of War Congress. Nevertheless, since I was sincerely anti-interventionist and sincerely convinced that the leadership of America

First could not fairly be called fascist but was on the whole surprisingly successful in keeping down fascists and crackpots, I thought that refusal to cooperate by appearance on the same platform as Colonel Lindbergh would be a futile piece of self-righteousness, a failure to use an important opportunity.

Charles Lindbergh was not an infallible military prophet or a great political thinker. He was an honest, courageous, patriotic American, hero of an epic deed, who spoke under a sense of duty, and steadily refused to exploit his enormous prestige for personal advantage. In short, he was the very opposite of the demagogue whom his enemies painted. He was very independent and he shunned advice on his speeches. Thus he blundered into his ill-fated Des Moines speech, generally regarded as anti-Semitic. I knew him well enough to believe that false. His speech was open in tense times to misinterpretation and he did exaggerate the role of Jewish-Americans in pushing the nation toward war. I issued a statement deploring that fact but I never thought Colonel Lindbergh guilty of intentional anti-Semitism. He bore with dignity the President's rejection of his offer of service after Pearl Harbor and quietly did what he could—and that was much—as an expert in aviation. I owe to him and to other honest leaders of America First, some of whom rendered distinguished service in World War II, this testimony in face of abuse going far beyond reasonable criticism. It is not healthy for the future that an honest effort to keep our country out of war should have been so unjustly stigmatized. It was not until late in 1949 that General H. H. Arnold's tribute to Colonel Lindbergh for what he had done in 1938 to "alert" our air force was made known to the public.

As for myself, when the war first broke out, I overemphasized both the sense in which it was a continuance of World War I and the capacity of nonfascist Europe to resist the Nazis. The success of the blitzkrieg profoundly shook me, but I continued to feel that America lacked the wisdom and power to play God to the world by the devil's method of total war. In the campaign of 1940 I argued—I think correctly—that unconsciously, at least, drift to war was furthered by the fact that an arms economy was a more successful answer to unemployment than the New Deal had been. I admitted that there was a case to be made for entering the war with the banners of humanity flying, even though I thought the weight of argument was against it. But ethically, I contended, there was no case at all for sidling into war, or for Roosevelt's assertions that steps logically leading to war led to peace, or for assuring the fathers and mothers of America that he would not send their sons into a foreign war. If it be true, as many of Roosevelt's champions now contend, that under a democracy the people must be fooled into a war, even a necessary war, it is a dreadful condemnation of democracy.

When Hitler attacked Stalin I did not prophesy easy victory for his arms but I did think and say that the choice between dictators in Europe was not worth the blood of our sons, and that there was more chance for American security and general decency in the rivalry of two dictators than in the absolute victory of one of them.

If this sounds like a negative program, it must be remembered that it was not based on easy confidence in our security. I did not propose unilateral disarmament. I opposed the draft in 1940 not only because of my hatred of conscription but because I thought its practical and psychological effects would be to increase the danger of our involvement in war. Evidence now available shows that so far was Hitler from disregarding danger from a "weak" America that he avoided the aggressive action against us that our open aid to his enemies invited in the hope of preventing or postponing as long as possible our full belligerent participation in war.

From 1919 on I had been insisting that I wanted for my country "the maximum possible cooperation for peace; the maximum possible isolation from war." I had steadily urged economic and political policies in Latin America, Europe, and Asia which would abolish or reduce the pressures toward war. Thus I had opposed intervention in Mexico and the insult to the Japanese and other Asians implicit in our Asiatic exclusion laws; and I had favored reciprocal trade agreements and other forms of economic co-operation.

The war which many Americans now boast that we entered when we adopted Lend Lease became an all-out struggle when the Japanese attacked Pearl Harbor. It is not to deny the guilt of the Japanese war lords to say that Roosevelt's policy was headed toward war with Japan, and that Pearl Harbor was politically a godsend to him, although he might have preferred a less disastrous attack somewhere else.

As it was, the American people were united as nothing else could have united them. Practically there were no alternatives but abject surrender on a global scale to fascism—in which would have been no lasting peace—or military action to end brutal aggression's march to triumph. No longer was powerful America an island of a possibly contagious sanity in a war-mad world. I, the hater of war, chose as between circles of hell. I chose critical but active support of the war to a point where a decent peace might be possible. For that end I worked inside and outside the Socialist Party.

The political unity in support of the war brought about by the attack on Pearl Harbor saved us from bringing serious criticism against the government and hence from the repressions of civil liberty which most of us had feared in the event of war. Even so in dealing with Japanese-Americans worse precedents were created than in World War I. I was one of the earliest and most vigorous critics of the policy which herded so many Americans into concentration camps, humanely run, but still concentration camps.

From the Casablanca conference on, I opposed "unconditional surrender" as a dangerous substitute for the inadequate Atlantic Charter.[2] I opposed obliteration bombing, the Morgenthau plan,

[2] Confirmation of my stand which brought me much abuse, especially from communists and left-wing New Dealers, is to be found in the following Associated Press dispatch from London, July 21, 1949:

"Winston Churchill and Foreign Secretary Ernest Bevin said in Parliament today they doubted from the beginning the wisdom of President Roosevelt's unconditional surrender policy for Germany. Bevin said in a House of Com-

and the appeasement of Stalin as blocking any road to a desirable peace.[3] I wanted a declaration of terms fit for peace in language that the German people could understand. (That didn't mean "a soft peace" or negotiating with Hitler.) I worked hard for a clear statement to the Japanese of the sort that I believed—even before we had the important corroboratory testimony of Admiral Zacharias—might have ended the war prior to that day in August when we loosed on the world the horror of the atom bomb without warning of its strength. A little later we added the worse crime of dropping the second atomic bomb on Nagasaki before we had had time to learn the political results of the first.

It is still my opinion that we Socialists in our campaign of 1944 and afterwards outlined the one approach to a settlement through regional and world-wide federation which might have delivered us from the cold war, or at least greatly lessened Russian and communist capacity for aggressive expansion.

To support this necessarily dogmatic summary of my position on war through long and crowded years would require at least another book. I am concerned now merely to put the record straight.

---

mons foreign policy debate that the policy had left a shambles upon which to rebuild Germany. If he had been consulted at the time, he said, he never would have agreed to it. Bevin, who was a member of Churchill's war government, said he first saw the surrender phrase in the newspapers. Churchill, now leader of the opposition, said he first heard the phrase from President Roosevelt 'without consultation with me.' He said he did not support it. 'It was not the idea I had formed in my own mind,' Churchill said. 'But working in a great alliance with loyal and powerful friends across the ocean, we had to accommodate ourselves.' He added that he doubted the British coalition cabinet would have agreed to the unconditional surrender policy if they had been able to consider it at the time."

Later, Churchill discovered that he had referred to unconditional surrender in a report to his cabinet. To his credit, he acknowledged the fact while still insisting that it had not been a subject of serious discussion and was not included in the formal joint statement.

[3] I forecast in public statements the failure of obliteration bombing in Germany even in military values and its tragic consequences on postwar policies. Later (1949) I read with some satisfaction the testimony of navy officers, not perhaps wholly disinterested, on this whole subject of obliteration or even strategic bombing. For what I said during the war and after Hiroshima I was roundly abused, especially by communists and their sympathizers.

There is a feeling, curiously widespread when one reflects on the extent of American opposition to intervention in the war and our profound disappointment with the results, that no other course than that by which Roosevelt led us into war was possible or intellectually and morally defensible. For myself I see little in the present state of the world to warrant that conclusion. I still think that America might have kept out of war on terms consistent with constructive usefulness to mankind and that, as a result, her own security and the well-being of other peoples might today be less in jeopardy than they are. My present concern is to prevent both a third world war and the triumph of communism rather than to argue what might have been. But already there is a terrible degree of logic behind the growing belief that if we could not avoid war with Hitler neither can we with Stalin.

None of us can go into the laboratory of life and by experiment prove or disprove what might have been. From 1940 on I have kept my pledge to do everything in my power to refute my own worst fears of the results of the war into which at last we went. In this book I have argued that the worst of our present dangers might have been avoided if President Roosevelt had adopted wiser political policies from Casablanca to Yalta. I do not believe that Stalin would or could have risked a separate peace from which he had to be bought at the price of American honor. Of nothing in my life am I surer than that I was right in 1944 on the policies that might have made for a decent peace. But I have neither the power nor the desire to *prove* that I was wholly right in 1939, 1940, and 1941. Some humility would also become the advocates of our entry into World War II as the road to lasting peace.

I speak from personal experience in numerous discussions and debates when I say that the interventionists told us that an Axis victory would mean an attack within a few years on the United States and that the least of its consequences would be our involvement in a terribly expensive race in arms. All of this, they said, could be averted by the victory of the "peace-loving nations" which after June 21, 1941, included the U.S.S.R.

Emphasis of the interventionists was frankly on our national security. We were to "defend America by aiding the Allies." However, war's champions usually added that by our military intervention we should once and for all end aggressive fascism and with it the crimes against humanity of which it conspicuously was guilty. The more extreme among them said that we could not if we would escape war and that any effort was at the shameful price of failure to heed the cry of our brethren of the other democracies. In the war we could guarantee victory for democracy and peace.

That was the hope of interventionists in 1940 and 1941. By 1950 communism under Moscow's leadership was spreading like wildfire throughout all Asia. Its consolidated power, already exerted in cold war against the United States, from East Berlin to Shanghai, presented a threat to our security which, by no stretch of the imagination, could have been offered by those mutually suspicious allies, Germany and Japan, neither of them supported by the loyalty of a mighty international movement. It is doubtful that an Axis victory would have advanced us anything like as far as we now are in the race to destruction provoked by our development and use of the atom bomb. It is certain that no armament race could have been more deadly or expensive than that in which we are now engaged.

The U.S.S.R. has a great hold on the respect or devotion of millions, especially among the colored races. Yet it has been and is guilty of every crime charged against the Nazis, including genocide. Its appeal lies in its propagandistic support of the underprivileged and oppressed in noncommunist lands and in its freedom from the race discrimination which Hitler so horribly exemplified in its most atrocious form. It is the cold truth that Stalin and his satellites, victors with us in a war in behalf of humanity, outdid Hitler in displacing civilians with barely clothes on their backs. They are practicing an even more extensive use of slaves in concentration camps.

It is possible that Hitler's rule in the hour of victory would have been morally even more abhorrent than Stalin's. His victory, had America stayed out of war, would probably have been less complete and his power more precarious. He could not have reduced his enemies, Britain and Russia, or his rival, Japan, to the degree of impotence to which we victors have reduced the Axis nations. Forces of resistance would probably have been stronger. Moreover, it must be remembered that the most abominable of Hitler's crimes, his deliberate and cold-blooded liquidation of Jews, was made possible only by the long continuance of war itself. Before and during that war I urged greater American effort to rescue Jews and far more generous asylum for all victims of Hitler's persecution. War ended Hitler's monstrous power; it did not save millions of his victims or end the horrible use of slave camps. It added its own innumerable victims to the tragic total.

We cannot prove what might have been. We cannot live over again the years that are gone. We can learn from them. Hitler and the Japanese warlords are no more. There is a United Nations. It is for us, if possible, even now, to realize the hopes that made World War II endurable. But—and on this all men of good will must agree—our fairest chance of success lies in avoiding the method of war which, in two titanic conflicts fought before the atomic age and won by the better side, brought mankind so close to ruin.

So far I had written before June 25, 1950. Then came communist military aggression in Korea and for me the whole problem of the method of war was raised again. My depression at the news was greater because I had hoped that in that very week we would be able to make a real beginning of building a general committee to back the McMahon resolution in Congress. The Post War World Council, of which I was chairman, could honestly feel that we had had a part in persuading Senator McMahon to put in definite form his tie-up of universal and enforceable disarmament with large American economic aid in a common war against poverty. Necessarily, action in support of this resolution had to be postponed and eventually put in a somewhat different form.

As the days wore on, it became evident that, while there was moral and political validity in President Truman's claim that military action in Korea was really police action, it had all the quality of a peculiarly miserable war. American boys were killing and dying in a war which was not their choice in defense of a Korean people who in majority would probably have preferred the end of devastating war and the unification of their country even at the price of communism. Victory would be dearly bought and with no certainty that it would avert World War III.

Nevertheless, in the kind of world in which we live, I saw no alternative to the course taken by the U.N. with American support that would not in result have been worse. Any other course would virtually have destroyed the U.N. It would have encouraged Stalin to go on believing that men indefinitely would yield to communist aggression. That meant death or long generations of sleep for all those values which for me gave meaning to life. Even so, we should not escape new world wars.

Nothing in the pacifist or near-pacifist statements which I heard or read could alter this conviction. Again, there were the completely unrealistic appeals to precedents presumably set by Gandhi; again, a strong tendency to refuse to recognize Stalin's communism for what it is. Practically there were proposals for "mediation," necessarily on terms which would sanctify the crime of aggression by supinely granting it a large measure of success. More than ever I became convinced that the necessary basis for extreme pacifism is a kind of religious faith to which the fate of organized society on this planet is of comparatively little concern, or which offers the believer strong trust in God's intervention in behalf of a nation which will choose the way of suffering rather than any sort of violence. This faith I do not have.

As I look back on history and all our logical surmises about the conduct of men in prehistoric times, it seemed to me that always the great choices were relative; that never were men in social action able to seek the absolute good by means completely appropriate to it. Human tragedy throughout millenniums of time has been inherent in the imperfection of the means of social action available to men in times of crisis. Yet there would have been no progress if men had despised the importance of relative choices of good or evil or had refused to act at all or to try to judge what tactics would be most likely to give their children and their children's children better choices in the continuing struggle for a decent world. War has been only the most obvious and flagrant illustration of the imperfection of the tools men in society have found themselves compelled to use. Nevertheless, in social action I think it right to pursue that course than which on any clear evaluation of possibilities any alternative would be worse.

In this spirit have I supported the U.N. in the Korean crisis. Once more the bitter necessity to which I have submitted has sharpened my zeal that conflict may be transferred from the terrible method of war which at best can serve righteousness only by blocking the physical triumph of a supreme evil. He who rejects an absolute pacifism is under especial obligation to urge alternatives to war wherever they may be found and above all to seek those long-range policies which may deliver mankind from war's madness before it brings the race to destruction.

Index

323